Temporary Buildings

Temporary Buildings

The trade-fair stand as
a conceptional challenge

Edited by Karin Schulte
Preface by Frank Werner

GINGKO Press
Corte Madera 2000

Published by Gingko Press Inc.
5768 Paradise Drive, Suite J
Corte Madera, California 94925
415 924-9615 Tel
415 924-9608 Fax
gingko@linex.com

ISBN 1-58423-031-2

Published by arrangement with
avedition GmbH, Ludwigsburg

Editor	Karin Schulte
Editorial	Petra Kiedaisch
Design	Detlev Riller, Michael Götte, Birgit Binner, München
Translation	Sean McLaughlin
Lithographs	Pixelzoo GmbH, Stuttgart
Printing	Druckhaus Waiblingen
Paper	Euroart 150 g/qm
Cover illustration	H. G. Esch: Trade-fair stand Ansorg GmbH

Inhalt

Contents

Fliegende Bauten – eine Erzählung von Raum und Zeit

Frank Werner, Prof.
holder of the chair and
head of the Institut für
Architekturgeschichte
und -theorie (institute of
the history and theory
of architecture) at the
Bergische Universität in
Wuppertal

Messestände sind zweifelsfrei jener Gruppe ephemerer Architekturen zuzurechnen, die unter die gleichermaßen antiquierte wie treffende Gattung der fliegenden Bauten fallen. In der Geschichte der modernen Architektur nehmen solche Gebilde gleichwohl einen bedeutenden Platz ein. Natürlich hat es spätestens seit dem Mittelalter fliegende Bauten in Gestalt von Jahrmarktsbuden, Thespiskarren, Wanderzirkussen etc. gegeben. Und sogenannte Festarchitekturen sollten das Alltagsleben von Renaissance und Barock weniger für minderbemittelte denn für privilegierte Zeitgenossen bereichern, bis die Weltausstellungsarchitekturen des 19. Jahrhunderts die schier unersättliche „Seh-Lust" des stetig wachsenden Massenpublikums kaum noch zu befriedigen vermochten.

Gleichwohl sollte es der Moderne vorbehalten sein, die Ausstellungsarchitektur und mit ihr natürlich auch die Messestände als approbates Mittel nicht nur zur Erprobung neuer Konstruktionen und Materialien, sondern auch zur allmählichen Gewöhnung an radikal veränderte Vermittlungs- und Wahrnehmungsvorgänge zu entdecken. So sind die fliegenden Bauten der russischen Revolutionsarchitektur nicht etwa Kompensation für mangelndes baukonstruktives „Know-How" oder fehlende Baumaterialien gewesen; sie fühlten sich vielmehr einer geradezu emblematischen, d.h. spontanen Agitations-Rhetorik mit starkem Gesellschaftsbezug verpflichtet. Und auch die legendären Messebau-Installationen der Kölner „Pressa" von 1928 oder der Dresdener Hygiene-Ausstellung von 1930 verstanden sich, wie uns berichtet wird, als temporäre Experimentierfelder einer Neuen Sachlichkeit.

Vorwort
Preface

Frank Werner

Temporary Buildings – a Story of Space and Time

Trade-fair stands are, without doubt, to be counted among those ephemeral architectural phenomena which come under the antiquated but appropriate heading of temporary buildings. In the history of modern architecture, such structures nonetheless occupy an important position. Temporary buildings have, of course, existed at least since the Middle Ages in the form of fun-fair stalls, stages for travelling actors, circuses and so on. So-called festival-architecture was intended to enrich the everyday lives of the renaissance and baroque periods, not so much for the poor but for the privileged, until the world exhibition architecture of the 19th century was hardly able to still satisfy the sheer insatiable "craving for visual novelty" of a continually growing mass public.

Nevertheless, it was left to the modern age to discover exhibition architecture and of course the trade-fair stand as a suitable means not only for trying out new constructions and materials but also for gradually acclimatising people to radically changing processes of communication and perception. The temporary buildings of Russian revolutionary architecture, for example, were not intended to make up for a lack of building know-how or construction materials; on the contrary, they were regarded as an emblematic, i.e. spontaneous, rhetoric of agitation with a strong social element. The legendary exhibition installations of the Cologne "Pressa" of 1928 or the Dresden hygiene exhibition of 1930, as we are told, were also seen as temporary experimental fields for the new functionalism.

If one considers the historical events more critically, however, it soon becomes clear how cleverly someone like Lilly Reich, the brothers Heinz and Bodo Rasch and others were able to create trade-fair installations of great artistic expression even in the puritanical twenties and early

Betrachtet man die historischen Ereignisse indessen kritischer, dann wird bald deutlich, wie raffiniert – wenn auch unter dem Banner der Sachlichkeit – selbst in den puritanischen 20er- und frühen 30er Jahren eine Lilly Reich, die Gebrüder Heinz und Bodo Rasch oder andere es vermochten, Messe-Installationen von großer künstlerischer Aussagekraft zustandezubringen. Dabei dürfte Ludwig Mies van der Rohes und Lilly Reichs Arbeit für die Berliner Bauausstellung des Jahres 1931 in etwa die eine Seite und Alvar Aaltos Messestandensemble im Finnischen Pavillon der New Yorker Weltausstellung des Jahres 1938 die andere Seite der Skala innovativer Gestaltungsmöglichkeiten von fliegenden Bauten verkörpern.

Die Zeit nach dem Zweiten Weltkrieg ließe sich als höchst ambivalent bezeichnen, verlor doch das Thema fliegende Bauten allzu bald seine klammheimliche Vorreiterrolle, d.h. seinen Labor- und Experimentalcharakter. Zu groß wurde die subsidiäre Abhängigkeit nicht nur von einer allesbeherrschenden Architektur, sondern auch von einer stetig zunehmenden Beschleunigung des Werte- und Modewandels, als daß es zu einer neuerlichen Renaissance fliegender Bauten als „Denkmodelle" hätte kommen können. Mit wenigen Ausnahmen der 50er und 60er Jahre, vor allem auch aus der Phase des eo ipso ephemer gedachten „Metabolismus", reflektieren die Messestände jener Jahre kaum mehr als die solide Einfallslosigkeit der Architektur- und Innenarchitekturszene.

thirties, although doing so under the banner of functionalism. Ludwig Mies van der Rohe's and Lilly Reich's work for the Berlin architectural exhibition in 1931, on the one hand, and Alvar Aalto's trade-fair ensemble in the Finnish pavilion of the New York world's fair in 1938, on the other, demonstrated the range of innovative design possibilities inherent in temporary buildings.

The time after the Second World War can be described as highly ambivalent but temporary buildings all too soon ceased to act as the forerunners for other architectural work. In other words, they lost their laboratory and experimental character. Their subsidiary dependence not only on an all-ruling architecture but also on a constantly increasing acceleration of the change in values and fashions became too great to result in a further renaissance of temporary buildings as "working hypotheses". With a few exceptions from the fifties and sixties, especially from the phase of an eo ipso ephemerally conceived "metabolism", the trade-fair stands of those years hardly reflected more than the solid unimaginativeness of the architectural and interior-design scene.

It was primarily thanks to the post-modern or the overcoming of the post modern and the resulting acceptance of "stage-managed worlds" in all areas of life that temporary buildings were able to liberate themselves from the straight-jacket of architectural dominance and again become what they actually were in the first place: exciting and stimulating "think tanks" for a multitude of connotations in the tense interplay of space, time and object. In the meantime, other sensational fields of experimentation have arisen due to new design conceptions such as decomposition or

Frank Werner, Prof.
Lehrstuhlinhaber und Leiter des Instituts für Architekturgeschichte und -theorie an der Bergischen Universität Wuppertal

Erst der Postmoderne bzw. deren Überwindung und der hierdurch bedingten
Akzeptanz „inszenierter Welten" in allen
Lebensbereichen war es zu verdanken,
daß sich die fliegenden Bauten aus dem
Korsett architektonischer Dominanz
befreien konnten und wieder zu dem
wurden, was sie ursprünglich eigentlich
immer waren: auf- und anregende „Denk-
Räume" für eine Vielzahl von Kon-
notationen im Spannungsfeld von Raum,
Zeit und Objekt. Inzwischen haben
sich durch neue Entwurfskonzeptionen
wie Dekomposition oder Dekonstruktion,
durch Anwendung neuer Medien,
durch Einbeziehung von Simulation und
Virtualität weitere aufsehenerregende
Experimentierfelder aufgetan.

Messestände, auch im übertragenen
Sinne wieder als fliegende Bauten verstanden, sind der Architektur erneut um
einige Nasenlängen voraus, weil sie
ohne Fesseln des Schweren, Dauerhaften,
Tektonischen, ohne das Damoklesschwert
der Kosten-Nutzen-Analyse operieren können. Stattdessen sind sie selbst unter er-
schwerten Bedingungen, wie denen
der mageren Jahre von heute, noch
imstande, Raum und Zeit (von Materialien
ganz zu schweigen) zu verschwenden,
um dem ewigen Traum der idealen Inszenierung schlechthin auf der Spur zu
bleiben.

Die vielfältigen und verschlungenen Pfade
durch den Dschungel der „Bühnenbilder
von heute für Produkte von morgen"
zu entflechten, plausibel darzustellen und
zu bewerten ist dem vorliegenden Band
in trefflicher Weise gelungen. Anstatt
sie einfach aneinanderzureihen, werden
Messestände nämlich in eine groß an-
gelegte Erzählung eingebunden: in eine
Erzählung von Körper, Raum, Haus
und Stadt im ausgehenden Jahrhundert.
Dieser spannenden Erzählung wäre eine
große Leserschaft zu wünschen.

deconstruction, the application of new
media and the use of simulation and virtual reality.

Trade-fair stands, also understood in a
figurative sense as temporary buildings,
are again ahead of architecture because they can operate free from the
shackles of weight, permanence and the
tectonic, without the Damocles sword
of cost-benefit analyses. Instead, they are
able to waste space and time (not to
mention materials) even under today's
financially difficult conditions in order to
continue pursuing the dream of ideal
stage-management.

This volume succeeds outstandingly
in unravelling, portraying and evaluating
the multifarious and entangled paths
through the jungle of "stage sets of today
for products of tomorrow". Instead
of a list of trade-fair stands one after the
other, they are integrated in a pano-
ramic story of objects, spaces, houses and
cities in a century coming to an end.
It is a story which should be read by everyone.

„Fliegende Bauten sind bauliche
Anlagen, die geeignet und
bestimmt sind, an verschiedenen
Orten wiederholt aufgestellt
und zerlegt zu werden."[1]

Karin Schulte,
Dipl.-Ing. (FH)
artistic and scientific
associate at the
Weißenhof-Institut,
Stuttgart

Die Messearchitektur mit ihrer Gratwan-
derung zwischen fliegendem Bau und
dauerhaftem Gebäude ist ein Mittel der
Kommunikation. Sie bietet dem Entwerfer
die Möglichkeit, mit einem Bau von
temporärem Charakter, angemessenem
Materialeinsatz und finanziellen Mitteln
ein großes Publikum zu erreichen. Die
dokumentierten Stände, allesamt Gegen-
beispiele für die gestalterische Anspruchs-
losigkeit von Messeständen, bieten einen
Einblick in neue Ideen und Konzepte.
Die Auswahl zeigt Beispiele, bei denen
gestalterische Problemlösungen entwickelt wurden.

Die Architektur des Messestands als Plattform für die zu kommunizierenden
Inhalte muß optimale räumliche Voraussetzungen schaffen; sie muß deutlich und
aussagekräftig sein und beim Betreten
des Stands bereits die Botschaft des
Messeauftritts und das zu vermittelnde
Firmenimage unaufdringlich spürbar
machen. Ein überzeugender Messeauftritt
stellt nicht nur die Firmenphilosophie
dar und informiert individuell über Problemlösungen, sondern er kann in allen
Bereichen Kompetenz und Glaubhaftig-
keit vermitteln. Architektur und Idee,
Bild und Text müssen eine Strategie verfolgen, die mit dem Marketingkonzept
des Unternehmens übereinstimmt und
die Botschaft des Unternehmens präsentiert.

Neben der Erfüllung funktionaler und
technischer Anforderungen – der funktio-
nierenden Infrastruktur für einen rei-
bungslosen Standbetrieb – soll der Stand
sich deutlich von der üblichen Messestand-
Szenerie und der Konkurrenz absetzen.
Höherer Wettbewerbsdruck und Wirt-
schaftlichkeit erfordern Unverwechselbar-
keit im Standdesign mit individuellen
Lösungen von hoher technischer und
ästhetischer Qualität. Steiner Design wirbt
mit der Bemerkung: „Wir wollen, daß Ihre
Messe-Besucher Ihren Stand auch ohne
Logo erkennen."[2]

Namhafte Architekten und Designer
schaffen mit wenigen baulichen Mitteln
ein Höchstmaß an architektonischer
Aussage und räumlicher Qualität für individuelle Messestandarchitektur und
erzeugen dabei ganz verschiedenartige
Atmosphären, die auch aus den unterschiedlichen Gestaltansätzen resultieren:
das klare Erscheinungsbild der volume-
trischen Körper oder des rigiden konstruktiven Systems mit der Reduktion auf

Einleitung
Introduction

Karin Schulte

Trade-fair architecture with its tightrope
walk between the temporary and the
permanent is a means of communication.
It offers the designer the possibility of
reaching a large public with a building
of temporary character, a suitable use
of materials and the necessary financial
means. The documented works, all examples of the high standards of trade-
fair stands, provide an insight into new
ideas and concepts. The selection shows
examples of where design solutions to
problems have been developed.

The architecture of the trade-fair stand
as a platform for the signals and information which are to be communicated
has to entail optimum spatial conditions;
it has to be clear and expressive and, as
soon as the visitor enters the stand, must
unobtrusively transmit the company's
message and the image to be conveyed.
A convincing trade-fair appearance
not only represents the company philosophy and provides solutions to individual
problems but can also convey competence
and credibility in all areas. The architecture
and the idea, the picture and the text,
must pursue a strategy which matches
the marketing approach of the company
and also presents the message of the
company.

"Temporary buildings are
constructions which are suitable for
being and destined to be erected
and dismantled repeatedly at
different locations."[1]

In addition to the fulfilment of functional
and technical requirements – a functioning infrastructure for smooth opera-
tion of the stand – the stand should
also clearly distance itself from the usual
trade-fair scenery and the competition.
The greater pressure of the competition
and for economic efficiency requires
a uniqueness in the stand design which
should display characterising features of
a high technical and aesthetic quality.
Steiner Design advertises with the com-
ment: „We want trade-fair visitors to recognise your stand – even without a
logo."[2]

das Wesentliche, die Opulenz der Bühne des inszenierten Raumes für die Produkte, oder der Reiz der städtebaulichen Herangehensweise – immer entsteht mit bestimmten gestalterischen Elementen auch eine spezifische Raumatmosphäre.

Die Beschreibung der Entwurfsgedanken und Messestände der einzelnen Architekten und Designer steht im Vordergrund des Buches. Sie wird ergänzt durch eine Erläuterung betriebswirtschaftlicher Einflußfaktoren. Jörg Beier spricht in seinem Beitrag die hinreichend bekannte Konfliktsituation zwischen Kreativität des Standbauarchitekten und ökonomischen Zwängen an.

Da die Entwerfer ihre Gestaltansätze für die vorgestellten Messestandarchitekturen selbst ausführlich erläutern, sind im folgenden nur einige Beispiele ohne Gewichtung herausgegriffen, an denen exemplarisch einzelne Aspekte gezeigt werden können. Bei der Auswahl der Messebauten spielte weder die Art der Messe noch die Standlage, noch die Art der präsentierten Produkte eine Rolle. Die Zuordnung der Stände zu den vier Themengebieten „Konstruktion als formaler Schwerpunkt", „Komposition volumetrischer Körper", „Haus im Haus – Stadt im Kleinen", „Inszenierter Raum" ist keineswegs immer eindeutig und soll auch keinerlei Ausschließlichkeit beinhalten.

Konstruktion als formaler Schwerpunkt

Der Ausstellungsbau mit Systemen, basierend auf der Ausbildung von besonderen Verbindungsstücken, sei es für Raumfachwerke nach dem Stab-Knoten-Prinzip oder für selbsttragende Platten, erreicht hohe Flexibilität und Kombinationsmöglichkeit. So entstehen nicht nur modulare Standkonzepte mit viel-

Der temporäre Pavillon
Sobek & Rieger für BMW
The temporary pavilion
Sobek & Rieger for BMW

Well-known architects and designers generate a very high degree of architectural expression and spatial quality for individual trade-fair architecture and, in the process, create completely different atmospheres which result from their different approaches to designing. The clear image of volumetric bodies or of a rigid structural system reduced to the essentials, the opulence of the stage in the area stage-managed for the products, or the attraction of the urban-development approach – a specific atmosphere is always created by particular design elements.

Descriptions of design ideas and trade-fair stands presented by individual architects and designers are the main focus of this book. These descriptions are supplemented by an explanation of the commercial factors affecting their work. In his contribution, Jörg Beier addresses the well-known conflict between the creativity of the architects who build the stands on the one hand and economic constraints on the other.

The designers explain in great detail how they went about designing the architecture of their trade-fair stands. In the following, therefore, only a few examples are taken – though greater significance should not be attached to one more over others – in order to show individual features. In the selection of trade-fair constructions, neither the type of exhibition, the location of the stand nor the type of products presented played a role. The allocation of the stands to the four topics "Structural Design as a Main Formal Topic", "The Composition of Volumetric Bodies", "House within a House – a City in Miniature" and "The Stage Management of Space" is by no means clear cut and is not intended to be exclusive.

Structural Design as a Main Formal Topic

Exhibition construction using systems and based on the formation of special linking elements, whether for a framework effect with the rod-and-node principle or for self-supporting panels, has achieved a high degree of flexibility and allows a great variety of combinations. Not only modular stand designs which can be used in many different ways have resulted but low-cost intelligent designs with multiple applications as well. It is not only in systems that structural design is an important factor, it is also essential in draft designs which strive to translate a formal approach into reality. Structural design thus becomes an important, formal, architectonic element.

Karin Schulte,
Dipl.-Ing. (FH)
Künstlerisch-wissenschaftliche Mitarbeiterin am Weißenhof-Institut, Stuttgart

fältigen Einsatzmöglichkeiten, sondern auch kostenoptimierte intelligente Konzepte mit Mehrfachnutzen. Konstruktive Schwerpunkte finden sich jedoch nicht nur bei Systemen, sondern gerade auch bei Entwürfen, die einen formalen Ansatz gut übersetzen wollen: Konstruktion als wichtiges formales architektonisches Element.

Da der alte Messestand wegen Baumaßnahmen nicht genutzt werden konnte, ließ sich BMW von Sobek & Rieger einen modular aufgebauten Pavillon entwickeln, dessen Form an die großen Zeltkonstruktionen von Frei Otto erinnert.

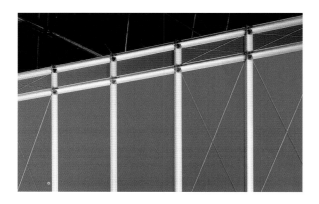

Reduzierte Konstruktion
Burkhardt Leitner
constructiv, Eigenstand
Reduced structural
design
Burkhardt Leitner
constructiv, own stand

Der Eigenstand von Burkhardt Leitner constructiv auf der EuroShop 1996 hat ähnliche Signalwirkung wie die Info Box auf dem Potsdamer Platz. Im Gegensatz zu Sobek & Riegers Zeltkonstruktion, die speziell für den Ort entwickelt wurde, ist Leitners roter Kubus eine sehr variable Systemlösung.

Komposition volumetrischer Körper

Die Tendenz zu typologischer Arbeit, bei welcher Raumformen, raumbildende Elemente und Gegenstände auf elementare Grundformen reduziert werden, führt häufig zu stark geometrisierten und stilisierten, oftmals auch monumentalisierten Ausformulierungen. In Stefan Zwickys strengen, aber durch den Einsatz roher Materialien nie kalten Entwürfen übernehmen einzelne Volumina, die wie Möbel im Raum geordnet werden, eine Funktion – im Falle des Stands für die Sonderschau CH-Kreativität handelte es sich um eine Art Regal, in welchem Produkte präsentiert wurden.

Schon in den 60er Jahren präsentierte sich Weishaupt mit reduziert modernen Messeständen von Hans Gugelot und Hans Sukopp; der neue Messestand von Richard Meier – der auch Firmengebäude für Weishaupt gebaut hat – ist auf das Wesentliche reduziert. Entsprechend den Gebäuden von Richard Meier wird der

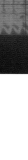

Langlebiges
Baukastensystem
Richard Meier für
Weishaupt
Long-life modular
system
Richard Meier for
Weishaupt

Hochregale als Rahmen
Stefan Zwicky für
CH-Kreativität
High shelves
as a framework
Stefan Zwicky for
CH-Kreativität

Stand durch seinen zurückhaltenden Gesamteindruck und durch präzise, abstrakte, schlichte Formen zum weißen Rahmen für die gezeigten Produkte.

Haus im Haus – Stadt im Kleinen

Rolf und Tim Heide demonstrierten mit ihrem architektonisch dramatisierten Messestand für Vebacom auf der CeBIT 1996, daß gestalterische Sparsamkeit durchaus ein Marketingkonzept sein kann: formal reduzierte planerische Ordnung, die nur das Wichtige mit architektonischer Formensprache zeigt. Das Produkt lag nicht offen und wurde dem Messebesucher aufgedrängt, sondern verborgen im Inneren. Produkt ist der Messestand selbst. Der Passant wurde in eine enge Kommunikation mit dem Unternehmen gezogen.

its essentials. Like his buildings, Richard Meier's stand is a kind of white framework for the products displayed due to its reserved overall impression and the precise, abstract and straightforward shapes.

Vernetzung + Verknüpfung – die digitale Stadt
Tim und Rolf Heide für Vebacom
Networking + Interlinking – the digital city
Tim and Rolf Heide for Vebacom

House within a House – a City in Miniature

With their architecturally dramatised trade-fair stand for Vebacom at CeBIT 1996, Rolf and Tim Heide demonstrated that economy of design is fully capable of being an approach to marketing: a formally reductionist arrangement which leaves out the unimportant, using the architectural language of shapes and forms. The product was not openly displayed for everyone to see or imposed on the visitors but was concealed within the stand: the product is the trade-fair stand itself. In this way, the passer-by was drawn into close communication with the company.

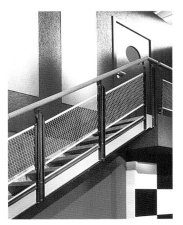

Der Erlebnistunnel
Arno Design für Sto
The adventure tunnel
Arno Design for Sto

Würfelspiele in Primärfarben
Dieter Thiel für Ansorg
Games of dice in primary colour
Dieter Thiel for Ansorg

Arno Designs Erlebnistunnel für Sto auf der Farbe 1996 arbeitete mit der Wegführung und den Raumverbindungen der Baukörper: nur durch die Bewegung des Betrachters innerhalb des Stands konnte ein Erlebnis stattfinden. Auch Dieter Thiels Messestand für Ansorg auf der EuroShop 1996 war ein sehr architektonisch aufgefaßter Messestand; wie Baukastenteile waren die verschiedenfarbigen Häuser entlang von Wegen und Plätzen angeordnet. Der anthrazitfarbene Vorhang, der das Ensemble verbarg, weckte Neugier. In Philippe Starcks und Dieter Thiels Entwurf für Thomson Multimedia prägte Ruhe und Klarheit die eindeutige Architektur der einzelnen

Arno Design's adventure tunnel for Sto at Farbe 1996 worked in conjunction with a guided route and the spatial links of the structures. An adventure was only created by the movement of the observer inside the stand. Dieter Thiel's stand for Ansorg at EuroShop 1996 was also a very "architectural" stand. The different coloured houses were arranged along the paths and squares like building blocks. The anthracite-coloured curtain which

Tempel und Nomadenzelt als Medienstars
Philippe Starck und Dieter Thiel für Thomson Multimedia
A temple and a nomad's tent as media stars
Philippe Starck and Dieter Thiel for Thomson Multimedia

Stände. Strukturen des Städtebaus werden transformiert, die einzelnen Marken verschiedenen Formensprachen zugeordnet. So zitierte beispielsweise ein auffallend farbiger, sich nach außen neigender Baukörper für Telefunken Haus-Formen. Stefan Zwickys Arbeit für das Forum kreativer Fabrikanten der Schweiz für die SMI 1989 schuf trotz der äußersten Reduktion und Abstraktion ein urbanes Ambiente. Der semitransparente Kubus, der orthogonal von Stegen auf der Mittelachse der Fläche durchschnitten wurde, beinhaltete im Inneren einen leicht angehobenen Platz.

Inszenierter Raum

Das geschickte Darstellen und Präsentieren von Produkten in einer architektonischen Inszenierung spricht den Besucher auf der emotionalen Ebene an. Phantastische, utopische oder bizarre Elemente entfalten eine suggestive Wirkung. Spezielle Arrangements ereignishafter Situationen von Ausstellungsarchitekturen führen zur Vergleichbarkeit mit einem Bühnenbild.

Adolf Krischanitz, der mit temporären Bauwerken sehr vertraut ist – man denke beispielsweise an seine temporäre Wiener Kunsthalle auf dem Karlsplatz –, arbeitete beim Österreich-Pavillon für den Themenschwerpunkt auf der Frankfurter Buchmesse 1995 mit der Schichtung mehrerer vertikaler Ebenen. Die transparente Haut mit Textfragmenten in weißer Schrift und die mit schwarzer Schrift bedruckten inneren Wände verschieben sich bei der Bewegung um den und im Raum gegeneinander.

Im Anfang war der (das) (W)Ort
Adolf Krischanitz für den österreichischen Buchhandel
The word as construction and the construction as word
Adolf Krischanitz for the Austrian association of book dealers

concealed the ensemble awoke people's curiosity. In Philippe Starck's and Dieter Thiel's design for Thomson Multimedia, quietness and clarity characterised the unique architecture of the individual stands. Structures of urban planning are transformed and the individual makes of product are presented using different languages of shape. A strikingly coloured tilting structure, for example, hinted at the typical shapes associated with the Telefunken company. Stefan Zwicky's work for the forum of creative manufacturers from Switzerland for SMI 1989 created an urban ambience in spite of its extreme reductionism and abstraction. The semi-transparent cube which was dissected orthogonally by bridges on the middle axis of the area contained a slightly elevated square on the inside.

The Stage-Management of Space

The ingenious display and presentation of products in an architectonic setting addresses the visitor on an emotional level. Fantastic, utopian or even bizarre elements create a highly suggestive effect. The special arrangements of eventful situations using the exhibition structures can be compared with stage sets.

Adolf Krischanitz who is very familiar with temporary constructions – think of his temporary hall of art in the Karlsplatz in Vienna – contributed to the Austrian pavilion at the Frankfurt book fair in 1995 with layers of several vertical levels. The transparent skin with fragments of text in white, and interior walls printed with black writing are moved past each

Laufstege zur Piazza
Stefan Zwicky für das Forum kreativer Fabrikanten
Catwalks to the Piazza
Stefan Zwicky for the Forum of Creative Manufactures

**Die gebirgige Ausstel-
lungs-Landschaft**
Kauffmann Theilig &
Partner für Mercedes
Benz
An exhibition landscape
of mountains
Kauffmann Theilig &
Partner for Mercedes
Benz

Kauffmann/Theiligs Mercedes-Benz-
Messestände haben bereits Hochbau-Aus-
maße. Auf der IAA 1995 besuchten täglich
über 10.000 Besucher den 12.000 qm
großen Ausstellungsbau in der alten Festhalle der Messe Frankfurt. Vergleichbar
mit der Wegführung im Guggenheim-
Musem New York, durchlief der Besucher
die verschiedenen Ebenen von oben:
erst mußte er mit der Rolltreppe unter
das Dach fahren; der Besucher wurde Teil
der Choreographie der Inszenierung.
Gegen die High-Tech-Welt der Automobile
setzten die Entwerfer den Reiz des Un-
fertigen. Einzelne Teile, z.B. die Light-Pipe
als weithin sichtbares Element auf dem
Dach, bekamen den Charakter eines
Zeichens. Auch auf der IAA Nutzfahrzeuge
in Hannover 1996 konnte sich kaum ein
Besucher der Wirkung der Erlebnisland-
schaft aus Sisalgewebe entziehen.

Arno Design präsentierte Produkt und
Firmenphilosophie für Loewe Opta
auf der IFA 1995 sehr konzentriert: der
Fernseher wurde Darsteller in einer Geschichte auf einer ausgestalteten Bühne.

other around and inside the area.
Kaufmann/Theilig's trade-fair stand
for Mercedes-Benz has the dimensions of
high-rise building. At IAA 1995 over
10 000 visitors visited the 12 000 sq. metres
exhibition building every day in the old
festival hall of the Frankfurt trade fair.
Similar to the route taken by the visitor
through the Guggenheim museum in
New York, the visitor here walked through
the different levels starting from the
top and travelling on an escalator to the
level beneath the roof. The visitor becomes a part of the choreography. In
order to achieve a contrast with the high-
tech world of the automobile, the designers exploit the stimulating effect
which unfinished materials can achieve.
Individual sections, for example the light-
pipe as a visible element on the roof, were
made to act as symbols. At the IAA for
utility vehicles in Hanover 1996, hardly
any visitor can escape the effect of an
adventure landscape made of sisal fabric.

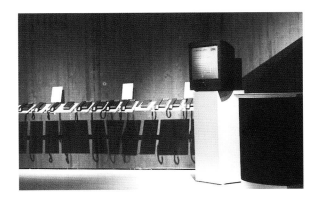

Film und Raum
Arno Design für Loewe
Opta
Film and room
Arno Design for Loewe
Opta

Arno Design presented the products and
the company philosophy of Loewe Opta
at IFA 1995 using a very concentrated
approach: the television became an actor
in a story on a carefully designed stage.
Using four "walls of the senses", Dietrich
Display's self-communicating stand at
EuroShop 1996 investigates the effect of
sounds, smells, materials, colours and light
on the senses. For a similar but considerably larger project in the context of
a special exhibition at Eurodomus 1972,
a complete "house of the five senses"
was created. Claude Maurel constructed
rooms in which vision, taste, touch, smell
and hearing were addressed synaesthe-
tically.

Die Sinneswände
Dietrich Display
Eigenstand
Walls of the senses
Dietrich Display
own stand

Dietrich Displays sich selbst kommunizierender Eigenstand auf der EuroShop 1996 untersuchte an vier Sinneswänden die Wirkung von Tönen, Gerüchen, Materialien, Farben und Licht auf die eigenen Sinne. Bei einem ähnlichen, allerdings wesentlich größer angelegten Projekt im Rahmen einer Sonderausstellung der Eurodomus 1972 entstand ein ganzes Haus der 5 Sinne. Claude Maurel baute Räume, in welchen synästhetisch das Sehen, der Geschmack, die Haptik, das Riechen und das Hören angesprochen wurden.

Gute Bilder lassen Phantasien zu, lösen Assoziationen aus, wecken Emotionen und bleiben so in Erinnerung, sind also wirksam.[3] Die räumlichen Ausformulierungen können vom Besucher und Betrachter unterschiedlich interpretiert werden: „Eins ist die Stadt für den, der vorbeikommt und nicht in sie hineingeht, ein anderes für den, der von ihr ergriffen wird und nicht aus ihr hinausgeht; eins ist die Stadt in die man zum erstenmal kommt, ein anderes ist die, die man verläßt, um nicht zurückzukehren; jeder gebührt ein anderer Name; vielleicht habe ich von Irene schon unter verschiedenen Namen gesprochen; vielleicht habe ich überhaupt nur von Irene gesprochen."[4]

Alle in diesem Buch in Bild und Wort vorgestellten Stände leben von der räumlich gestalteten Gesamtkonzeption mit ihrer einheitlichen, konsequenten und übergreifenden Gestaltung vieler Einzelaspekte. Die hohe ästhetische Prägnanz resultiert aus dem wohlausgewogenen Gestaltungskonzept, in das Material, Farbe, Beleuchtung, Werbung, Infrastruktur und Exponate integriert sind.

Anmerkungen

[1] LBO NRW § 74; Köln 1991 (1962).
[2] Werbung von Dietrich Display; in:
Design Report 3/1995.
[3] Dieter Krüger: Kommunikative Vermittlung.
Diskussion zum Thema Kommunikation und
Ladenbau auf dem EuroShop-Forum im Juni 1993,
u.a. mit Prof. Dr. Norbert Bolz, Eva Maria Herling
(Vitra), Carl Holste; in: AIT 11/1993; Leinfelden-
Echterdingen 1993.
[4] Italo Calvino: Die unsichtbaren Städte; München
1996 (1972); S.145.

Good images liberate the imagination, trigger associations, evoke emotions and thus remain in the memory. They are therefore effective.[3] Arrangements of space can be differently interpreted by the visitor and observer:"A city is one thing for someone who chances by but does not enter; it is another for someone who is moved by it and does not leave. It is yet again different for someone who arrives for the very first time but also different is the city you leave to never return again. Each one merits another name. Perhaps I have spoken about Irene under different names; perhaps I have only spoken of Irene."[4]

All the stands presented in this book in word and image are the offspring of a spatially designed, overall conception with a unified, consistent and interactive design of all their individual aspects. Their highly aesthetic succinctness is a result of the well-balanced approach adopted in which materials, colours, lighting, advertising, infrastructure and exhibits are integrated.

Notes

[1] LBO NRW § 74, Cologne 1991 (1962).
[2] Advertisement by Dietrich Display in:
Design Report 3/1995.
[3] Dieter Krüger: Kommunikative Vermittlung.
Diskussion zum Thema Kommunikation und
Ladenbau auf dem EuroShop-Forum im Juni 1993,
u.a. mit Prof. Dr. Norbert Bolz, Eva Maria Herling
(Vitra), Carl Holste; in: AIT 11/1993; Leinfelden-
Echterdingen 1993.
[4] Italo Calvino: Die unsichtbaren Städte
(The Invisible Cities), Munich 1996 (1972), p.145.

Vom Nomadenzelt zur Multimedia-Vision
Eine kleine Geschichte der fliegenden Bauten

Karin Schulte

From Nomad's Tent to Multimedia Vision
A short history of temporary buildings

Beginnend bei den prähistorischen Bauten, finden wir das Zelt als ersten fliegenden Bau. Die Möglichkeit, sich von Ort zu Ort fortzubewegen auf der Suche nach Nahrung war damals ein essentieller Faktor, um das Überleben der ersten Menschen zu sichern; das Zelt als Schutz bietende, transportable und demontierbare Behausung existiert bis heute im traditionellen Bauen einiger Völker weiter.[1] Nur wenige der transportablen Behausungen dagegen sind unzerlegt als Gesamtes zu bewegen: Hausboote und mit Rädern versehene Vehikel sind fast die einzigen Beispiele.[2]

Beginning with prehistoric buildings, we find the tent as the first temporary building. The possibility of moving from place to place looking for food was then an essential factor for ensuring the survival of the first human beings. The tent as a dwelling which provides protection, can be taken down and transported, continues to exist as a traditional accommodation for some peoples.[1] Only a few transportable dwellings, however, can be moved in one piece: houseboats and vehicles with wheels attached are almost the only examples.[2]

Indianer-Tipi
Indian tipi

Zirkuszelt
Cirkus tent

A temporary building implies a construction. It has spatial structures and can adapt itself to varying requirements. It is actually a form of transportable architecture which can either be moved in one piece or dismantled into individual sections and also assembled with little effort.

As early as the Middle Ages, there were mystery plays on transportable stages and, around 1500, there were temporary banqueting buildings for diplomatic relations. In the 17th century, floating pavilions were built and, at the end of the 18th century, the first circus tents

Ein fliegender Bau impliziert ein Gebäude, er hat räumliche Strukturen und kann sich den jeweiligen Anforderungen anpassen. Er ist eigentlich eine transportable Architektur, die entweder als Ganzes bewegt oder in Einzelteile zerlegt und ohne großen Montageaufwand zusammengesetzt werden kann.

Comedia dell'Arte in der Arena di Verona
Marco Marcola, 1772
Comedia dell'Arte in the Arena di Verona
Marco Marcola, 1772

Hausboote auf einem Wasserlauf in Shanghai
House-boats on a water-course in Shanghai

Bereits im Mittelalter gab es Mysterienspiele auf transportablen Bühnen, um 1500 temporäre Bankettgebäude für diplomatische Beziehungen, im 17. Jahrhundert entstanden schwimmende Pavillons, Ende des 18. Jahrhunderts tauchten erste Zirkuszelte auf, die mit unwahrscheinlicher Bequemlichkeit errichtet und wieder gefaltet werden konnten. Das größte dieser Zelte nahm bis zu 10.000 Menschen auf.

Die Entwicklung von Gußeisen und Stahl als Innovation für das Bauen machte Konzepte für leichte Gebäude möglich. Ende des 18. Jahrhunderts wurden die ersten vorfabrizierten Gebäude entwickelt, Mitte des 19. Jahrhunderts entstand das portable Kolonialhaus: leicht verschiffbar, leicht aufbaubar, modular. Doch nicht nur Wohngebäude, auch Kirchen, Banken, und andere Funktionsgebäude wurden geplant; bereits im Krim-Krieg 1854 kam noch die Nutzung als Unterkunftsgebäude im militärischen Bereich dazu.

Die großen Ausstellungen

Als ein Ergebnis des Industriezeitalters entstanden am Ende des 18. Jahrhunderts die großen Ausstellungen, die Vergleichsmöglichkeiten verschiedener Industrieprodukte bieten sollten. Bis in die erste Hälfte des 19. Jahrhunderts waren es meist nationale, danach avancierten sie zu internationalen Veranstaltungen. Großbritannien gab den Anstoß für die Weltausstellungen, durch welche der Entwurf und die Erstellung von Weltausstellungshallen – leicht, rasch zu erstellen, demontierbar – zwischen 1851 und 1889 zu einer gewichtigen Bauaufgabe wurde (London und Paris als Anfang und Ende).1851 in London, zur ersten wichtigen internationalen Ausstellung, der „Great Exhibition of the Works of Industry of all Nations", entstand eine der Ikonen der Architektur: der Crystal Palace von Sir Joseph Paxton und den Ingenieuren Fox & Henderson. Eine Ausstellungshalle – nach wie vor das größte präfabrizierte Gebäude der Welt –, die durch industrielle Vorfertigung und Montage, Standardisierung und Typisierung so konzipiert war, daß sie nach der Ausstellung demontiert werden konnte.[3]

Crystal Palace
Mittelalterlicher Hof
Pugin/Hardman
Crystal Palace
Medieval court
Pugin/Hardman

Crystal Palace
Westeingang
London, 1851
Crystal Palace
West entrance
London, 1851

Ausstellungsarchitekturen, beispielsweise von Pugin und Semper, strukturierten das Innere. In A. W. Pugins mittelalterlichem Hof öffnete sich das neugotische Gehäuse durch seine implizierte aber nicht vorhandene Decke zur genialen Glas-Eisen-Konstruktion.

„Das Eisenskelett hat seine Gestaltung gefunden … . Konstruktion wird Ausdruck."

Auch die im 19. Jahrhundert noch folgenden Weltausstellungen, von denen hier nur zwei genannt seien, boten Felder für Experimente von Konstrukteuren, die Eisen als Baustoff entdeckt hatten: die „Exposition Universelle" 1867 in Paris mit der Maschinengalerie als temporärem Bau, die bei einer Raumhöhe von fast 25 m eine Stützenweite von 35 m hatte; und 1889 die „Exposition Universelle" in Paris mit der 46.500 qm überdeckenden Maschinenhalle von Dutert und Contamin, zu der Giedion schreibt: „Das Eisenskelett hat seine Gestaltung gefunden ... Konstruktion wird Ausdruck."[4] Unterstützt durch die nationalen Regierungen basierten diese Ausstellungen in erster Linie auf der Präsentation von Gebrauchsgegenständen aus Handwerk und Gewerbe sowie nationalen Identitäten durch wissenschaftliche, technologische oder industrielle Produkte. In allen diesen Veranstaltungen war die ökonomische, gesellschaftliche und politische Entwicklung ablesbar. Daneben waren sie aber zunehmend auch Unterhaltung für das Volk; es entstanden Illusionskabinette und -architekturen in aufwendigen temporären Hüllen.

Monument des Eisens
IBA Leipzig, 1913
Bruno Taut
Monument of iron
IBA Leipzig, 1913
Bruno Taut

Maschinenhalle
Paris, 1889
Contamin/Dutert
Machinery hall
Paris, 1889
Contamin/Dutert

The exhibition hall – still the largest prefabricated building in the world – was designed so that it could be dismantled after the exhibition.[3] This was achieved by industrial prefabrication and assembly, standardisation and typification. Architectural trade-fair constructions, for example those of Pugin and Semper, gave structure to the interior. In A. W. Pugin's medieval court, the neo-gothic building is laid open to the eye by the implied, but not actually existing, ceiling for the brilliantly conceived glass and iron construction.

Subsequent world's fairs in the 19th century, of which only two are named here, provided opportunities for experimentation by structural designers who had discovered iron as a construction material. There was the "Exposition Universelle" of 1867 in Paris with a machinery gallery as a temporary building. It had a supported width of 35 m and a height of almost 25 m. 1889 saw the "Exposition Universelle" in Paris with

"The iron skeleton has found its form… . Structural design becomes the expression of an idea."

a covered machinery hall of 46 500 square metres by Dutert and Contamin about which Giedion writes: "The iron skeleton has found its form… . Structural design becomes the expression of an idea."[4] With support from the national governments, these exhibitions were primarily intended for the presentation of consumer goods produced by the trades and industry and portrayed national identities by means of scientific, technological or industrial products. At all these events, the economic, social and political development of the different countries could be detected. In addition, however, they increasingly became a form of entertainment for the public. Illusionist galleries and architectural structures were created in costly temporary shells.

Between 1890 and the First World War, interior structures became an important component of exhibitions. Henry van de Velde (Brussels 1897), Hoffmann, Olbrich and Behrens (Brussels 1910) created important contemporary interiors.

Formal Innovations: Confrontation and Clarification

At the beginning of this century, trade fairs where industry was able to address an interested specialist public were also established. The construction exhibition in Leipzig in 1913 displayed a

Zwischen 1890 und dem Ersten Weltkrieg wurden Innenausbauten zu wichtigen Ausstellungsbestandteilen: Henry van de Velde (Brüssel 1897), Hoffmann, Olbrich, Behrens (Brüssel 1910), schufen wichtige zeitgenössische Interieurs.

Formale Neuerungen: Konfrontation und Klärung

Mit Beginn dieses Jahrhunderts etablierten sich neben den großen Weltausstellungen verstärkt auch Messen, auf denen die Industrie die interessierte Fachwelt ansprechen konnte. Die Baufachausstellung in Leipzig 1913 demonstrierte mit dem Pavillon des „Stahlwerksverbands" und des „Vereins Deutscher Brücken- und Eisenbaufabriken" einen temporären Eisenbau von Bruno Taut, der stereometrische Körper stufenförmig auf einem Achteckgrundriß stapelte.

Auf der Kölner Werkbundausstellung 1914 entstand neben Bauten der älteren Architektengeneration[5] auch die Musterfabrik von Walter Gropius und das dem Dichter Paul Scheerbart gewidmete Glashaus von Bruno Taut: ein Ausstellungspavillon, bei welchem nicht nur das Innere den Auftraggeber – die Glasindustrie – repräsentieren sollte, sondern das Gebäude selbst.[6] Der Dichter Paul Scheerbart, Mentor Bruno Tauts, faßte in seinem 1914 veröffentlichten Buch „Glasarchitektur" zu Beginn des Ersten Weltkriegs die expressionistische Vision einer neuen, besseren Welt durch Glasarchitektur in folgende Worte: „Wollen wir unsere Kultur auf ein höheres Niveau bringen, so sind wir wohl oder übel gezwungen, unsre Architektur umzuwandeln. Und dieses wird uns nur dann möglich sein, wenn wir den Räumen, in denen wir leben, das Geschlossene nehmen. Das aber können wir nur durch Einführung der Glasarchitektur, die das Sonnenlicht und das Licht des Mondes und der Sterne noch nur durch ein paar Fenster in die Räume läßt – sondern gleich durch möglichst viele Wände, die ganz aus Glas sind – aus farbigen Gläsern. Das neue Milieu, das wir uns dadurch schaffen, muß uns eine neue Kultur bringen."[7] Zum oberen Glassaal des Glashauses, ausformuliert als Kuppelsaal mit rhombenförmigen Eisenbetongefachen und farbiger Haut, einem Fußboden aus Glas, Wänden aus Glas, der Treppe aus Glas, ein Wechselspiel der Lichterscheinungen zeigend, bemerkt Sigfried Giedion: „eine Netz-Geflecht Konstruktion ohne Zugstangen, die tatsächlich ... ein Vorläufer der räumlichen Tragwerke war, deren volle architektonische Auswirkung erst nach der Jahrhundertmitte einsetzte."[8]

temporary iron structure by Bruno Taut which stacked stereometric bodies in the form of steps in an octagonal area. This was the pavilion of the "Stahlwerkverband" (association of steel works) and the "Verein Deutscher Brücken- und Eisenbaufabriken" (union of bridge and structural-engineering factories).

At the Werkbund exhibition in 1914, there were constructions of the older generation[5] of architects but also the model factory of Walter Gropius and the glass house by Bruno Taut dedicated to the poet Paul Scheerbart. With this exhibition pavilion, not only the interior but also the building itself was intended to represent

Glashaus
Werkbund-Ausstellung
Köln, 1914
Bruno Taut
Glasshouse
Werkbund exhibition
Köln, 1914
Bruno Taut

the client, namely the glass industry.[6] At the beginning of the First World War, the poet Paul Scheerbart, Bruno Taut's mentor, wrote the following words in his book "Glass Architecture" published in 1914 to describe the expressionistic vision of a new and better world by means of glass architecture: "If we want to raise our culture to a higher level, we have to transform our architecture whether we like it or not. And we will only be able to do so if we remove the feeling of enclosure from the rooms in which we live. But we can only achieve this by introducing an architecture of glass which allows sunlight and the light of the moon and the stars not just through a few windows made of coloured glass but also through as many all-glass walls as possible. The new milieu which we thus create must generate a new culture."[7] The upper glass hall of the glass house was formed as a domed room with rhombus-shaped ferroconcrete sections and a coloured skin, glass floor, glass walls and a glass staircase showing an interplay of light phenomena.

In Rußland formulierte sich nach dem Sturm auf das Winterpalais 1917 – in der Epoche der russischen Revolutionsarchitektur – eine neue Architektursprache; es gab die Entwicklung einer neuen Syntax der gestalterischen Form. Viele, gerade entstehende avantgardistische Gruppen gingen zum Teil von der Literatur, hauptsächlich aber von der Malerei aus und tendierten insgesamt zur Verfremdung und Auflösung der konventionellen Formen und Darstellungsweisen bis zur völligen Abstraktion. Bald bezogen sie auch die Architektur in den allgemeinen Prozeß der Konfrontation und Klärung ein. „Fliegende Architekturen" entstanden, Gebäude die nur noch auf einer kleinen Fläche standen oder sich bewegten: El Lissitzkys Wolkenbügel, vom Erdboden abgehoben; Vladimir Tatlins Gedenkturm der III. Internationale, ein Projekt von 1919/20 bei welchem in einem 400 m hohen turmartigen Gerüst die innenhängenden stereometrischen Formen je nach Größe einmal im Jahr,

Wolkenbügel
1924-1925
El Lissitzky

Arch of clouds
1924-1925
El Lissitzky

In Russia, after the storming of the Winter Palace in 1917, the époque of Russian revolutionary architecture resulted in the formulation of a new language of architecture: a new syntax of design was developed. Some of the many avant-garde groups which were just being formed at the time were involved in literature but most of them in painting and, on the whole, tended towards the alienation and dissolution of conventional structures and methods of presentation and even complete abstraction. It was not long before they also included architecture in the general process of confrontation and clarification. Temporary buildings were created, constructions which only stood on a small area or could be moved about: El Lissitzky's arch of clouds, raised above the ground; Vladimir Tatlin's commemorative tower of the III. Internationale, a project of 1919/20 where a 400 m high tower-like frame in which the stereometric shapes suspended inside were intended to rotate once a year, month or day, depending on their size; Tatlin's speaker's platform for Lenin in 1924, a transportable frame with mobile platforms – all these were symbols of the new order, monuments to the movement and the dynamics of the time.

Café Kugelhaus
Jahresschau Deutscher
Arbeit, Dresden, 1937

Café Kugelhaus
Annual show of german
work, Dresden, 1937

Gedenkturm der
III. Internationale
Vladimir Tatlin

Commemorative tower
of the III. Internationale
Vladimir Tatlin

Pavillon der U.S.S.R.
Exposition Internat. des
Arts Décoratifs
Paris, 1925
Konstantin Melnikov

Pavillon der U.S.S.R.
Exposition Internat. des
Arts Décoratifs
Paris, 1925
Konstantin Melnikov

Monat oder Tag rotieren sol!ten; Tatlins Rednertribüne für Lenin von 1924, ein fahrbares Gestell mit beweglichen Plattformen – all dies waren Symbole der neuen Ordnung, Monumente der Bewegung und der Dynamik der Zeit. Mit diesen Utopien bekam auch der Kugelbau wieder eine wichtige Stellung: das Bodenlose der Form der Kugel verdeutlichte die Überwindung der Schwerkraft.[9]

Die 1917 gegründete holländische Künstlergruppe De Stijl bildete einen von ihr als Neoplastizismus bezeichneten Stil aus. In der Architektur sollten die Flächen vom Zwang der von außen festgelegten Form gelöst werden und

„Die Architekten leben in der Enge ihres Schulwissens, in der Unkenntnis neuer Regeln des Bauens, und ihre Einfälle bleiben gern bei den sich schnäbelnden Tauben. Aber die Konstrukteure der Ozeandampfer machen kühn und wissend Paläste, neben denen die Kathedralen ganz klein werden: und sie werfen sie ins Wasser. ...“

in ein freies Spiel eintreten. Die gegenseitige Durchdringung der Decken und Wände sowie ihre verschiedenen Farben machten ihre Funktion als konstituierende Elemente und das Ineinandergreifen von Innenräumen und Außenraum deutlich: Architektur als Prozeß. Fast zeitgleich nannte Le Corbusier in „1922 – Ausblick auf eine Architektur" den Ozeandampfer, das Flugzeug und das Auto als Vorbilder: „Die Architekten leben in der Enge ihres Schulwissens, in der Unkenntnis neuer Regeln des Bauens, und ihre Einfälle bleiben gern bei den sich schnäbelnden Tauben. Aber die Konstrukteure der Ozeandampfer machen kühn und wissend Paläste, neben denen die Kathedralen ganz klein werden: und sie werfen sie ins Wasser. ... Die Lehre des Flugzeuges liegt nicht so sehr in den gestalteten Formen, und zuerst muß man lernen, in einem Flugzeug nicht einen Vogel oder eine Libelle zu sehen; es ist eine Maschine zum Fliegen. ... Das Flugzeug beweist uns, daß ein richtig gestelltes Problem auch seine Lösung findet."[10]

With these utopias, the spherical building acquired an important status again; the "floorlessness" of the sphere underlines the defeat of gravity.[9]

The Dutch group of artists, De Stijl, founded in 1917 developed a style which they designated as neoplasticism. In architecture, areas were to be freed from the compulsions of an externally determined form and engage in a kind of free play. The mutual penetration of ceilings and walls and their different colours illustrated their function as a constituent element of the building and clearly showed how interior rooms and external space interlocked with each other. This was architecture as process.

Almost at the same time, Le Corbusier cited the ocean steamer, the aeroplane and the car as exemplary models in his book, "1922 – Towards an Architecture": "Architects live within the narrowness of the knowledge they have acquired during their training and in the

"Architects live within the narrowness of the knowledge they have acquired during their training and in the ignorance of new rules of building; their ideas prefer to huddle closely together. But the designers of ocean steamers boldly and knowingly create palaces which dwarf our cathedrals and launch them into the water. ..."

ignorance of new rules of building; their ideas prefer to huddle closely together. But the designers of ocean steamers boldly and knowingly create palaces which dwarf our cathedrals and launch them into the water. ...The study of the aeroplane is not so much concerned with the design of appearance. The first thing you learn is that a plane is not a bird or a dragonfly; it is a machine for flying. ...The aeroplane proves that a problem which is correctly formulated can also be solved."[10]

Pavillon de l'Esprit
Nouveau, Exposition
Internat. des Arts
Décoratifs, Paris,1925
Le Corbusier

Pavillon de l'Esprit
Nouveau, Exposition
Internat. des Arts
Décoratifs, Paris,1925
Le Corbusier

Stahlhaus Dessau, 1926
Georg Muche / Richard
Paulick

Steelhouse Dessau, 1926
Georg Muche / Richard
Paulick

Accordingly, the futuristic architects in Italy also developed their new language by completely breaking with historical architecture. This new architecture was characterised by the technical.

The "Exposition Internationale des art décoratifs et industriels modernes" in Paris in 1925 can be seen as the climax of pavilion construction. In addition to the greenhouse of Peter Behrens, the most important constructions are Melnikov's pavilion, a brightly coloured wood construction with glass,[11] Le Corbusier's "Pavillion de l'Esprit Nouveau" where a standardised residential block rejecting all that is related to arts and crafts is fitted with standardised series-production units and Friedrich Kiesler's Austrian theatre exhibition with its skeleton-like spatial conception.

Dementsprechend entwickelten auch die futuristischen Architekten in Italien ihre neue Sprache aus einem völligen Bruch mit den historischen Architekturen; die neue Architektur war geprägt von der Technik. Als Höhepunkt des Pavillonbaus kann die „Exposition Internationale des arts décoratifs et industriels modernes" 1925 in Paris angesehen werden. Neben einem Gewächshaus von Peter Behrens sind Melnikovs Pavillon, eine stark farbige Holzkonstruktion mit Glas,[11] Le Corbusiers „Pavillon de l'Esprit Nouveau", bei welchem in Ablehnung alles Kunstgewerblichen eine standardisierte Wohn-Zelle, eingerichtet mit Serienfabrikaten entstand und Friedrich Kieslers Österreichische Theaterausstellung mit ihrer skelettartigen Raumkonzeption die wichtigsten Bauten.

Das Stahl-Typenhaus von Georg Muche und Richard Paulick, das zur Eröffnungsausstellung des Dessauer Bauhauses 1926 erstellt worden war, zeigte mit industrieller Herstellung von Normelementen und schneller Montage der Häuser vor Ort, daß die Ideen der englischen Metallfertighäuser weiterentwickelbar waren.

Österreichische Theaterausstellung, Exposition Internat. des Arts Décoratifs, Paris,1925 Friedrich Kiesler

Austrian theatre exhibition, Exposition Internat. des Arts Décoratifs, Paris,1925 Friedrich Kiesler

The steel standardised house of Georg Muche and Richard Paulick which had been created for the opening exhibition of the Dessau Bauhaus in 1926, with industrial manufacture of standardised elements and rapid assembly of the houses on site, showed that the ideas of the English prefabricated metal dwellings were capable of being developed.

Lilly Reich, designer and architect (1885 to 1947) and for a time assistant to Mies van der Rohe, played an important role in the development of modern exhibition design. Her ideas were based on modernistic principles which were formulated by the Deutsche Werkbund.

Lilly Reich, Designerin und Architektin (1885 - 1947), zeitweilig Assistentin von Mies van der Rohe, nahm bis 1937 eine wichtige Stellung für die Entwicklung des modernen Ausstellungsdesigns ein. Ihre Ideen basierten auf modernistischen Prinzipien, die besonders durch den Deutschen Werkbund formuliert wurden. Für die Ausstellung „Die Mode der Dame" 1927 in Berlin entwarf sie das „Café Samt und Seide". Draperien aus schwarzem, orangenem und rotem Samt sowie goldene, silberne, schwarze und zitronengelbe Seide an gekurvten Metallstangen bildeten die vertikalen Abgrenzungen des Raumes.

„Die Wohnung", die Stuttgarter Werkbund-Ausstellung von 1927 im Auftrag von und in Kooperation mit Mies van der Rohe, präsentierte die Produkte aufgegliedert in Sachgruppen mit einheitlicher Gestaltung und Beschriftung in den verschiedenen Hallen. Statt simpler Abtrennungen, wurden diverse Codes zur Unterteilung eingesetzt: in der Spiegelglashalle unterschiedliche Glastypen; im Raum der DLW[12] verschiedenfarbige Linoleumböden. In diesem Raum, in dem Linoleum-Muster auf Plattformen gezeigt wurden oder an die Wände gehängt waren, erläuterte fette Grafik die Vorteile des Gebrauchs von Linoleum. Willi Baumeister (mit Karl Straub) war dafür verantwortlich. Es entstand ein einprägsames Gesamtbild von Grafik, Material und Farbe.

Eine kleinere Ausstellung diente als Versuchsfeld für neue Methoden: 1928 gab die GAGFAH/AHAG-Ausstellung[13] „Wohnen im Grünen" in Berlin-Zehlendorf einen Überblick über alte und neue Wohnkultur sowie moderne Bauweisen. In Zusammenarbeit von Walter Gropius und Laszlo Moholy-Nagy entstand eine demontable halboffene Holzhalle, bestückt mit modernen Ausstellungsmethoden.

For the exhibition "Die Mode der Dame" (The Fashion of the Lady) in Berlin in 1927, she designed the "Café Samt und Seide" (Café Satin and Silk). Drapes made of black, orange and red satin together with golden, silver, black and lemon-yellow silk on curved metal rods formed the vertical walls of the space.

"Die Wohnung" (The Apartment), the Stuttgart Werkbund exhibition of 1927 commissioned and cooperated in by Mies van der Rohe, presented the products divided up into groups with a uniform design and inscription in the different halls. Instead of simple partitions, diverse codes were used for dividing up the area: the hall of mirrors, for example, with different types of glass and the room of the DLW[12] with different coloured linoleum floors.

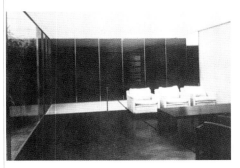

In a space where linoleum patterns were shown on platforms or hung on the walls, bold graphics explained the advantages of linoleum. This was the work of Willi Baumeister (with Karl Straub) and the result was an impressive overall pictorial combination of graphics, materials and colour.

A smaller exhibition served as a field of experimentation for new methods. In 1928, the GAGFAH/AHAG exhibition[13] "Wohnen im Grünen" (Living in the Green) in Berlin-Zehlendorf provided a survey of old and new décor as well as modern building methods. Walter Gropius and Laszlo Moholy-Nagy worked

GAGFAH / AHAG-Aus-
stellung, Wohnen im
Grünen, 1928
Walter Gropius/Laszlo
Moholy-Nagy
GAGFAH/AHAG-
exhibition, Living in the
Green, 1928
Walter Gropius/Laszlo
Moholy-Nagy

together to produce a half-open wooden hall which could be dismantled and was fitted out according to modern exhibition methods.

El Lissitzky's Russian pavilion "Pressa" for the 1928 International Art Exhibition in Cologne which was fitted with large photographic murals on the inside and the stand of the Rasch brothers for a propaganda company at the Werbeschau (advertising show) in Stuttgart in 1927 where drums larger than a man and with glued-on posters rotated at different speeds in opposite directions demonstrated the new application of media and motion.

„Bewegliche, mit neuen Forderungen beschriftete Wände, rotierende Farbenscheiben, Lichtapparate, Signaldemonstrationen und Reflektoren: Durchsichtigkeit, Licht und Bewegung sorgen für die Unterhaltung des Publikums. Alles so aufgestellt, daß es vom einfachen Menschen aufgenommen und verdaut werden kann. Dazu kommt der Reiz der Verwendung von neuen Materialien: große Zelluloidtafeln, Gittersysteme, Vergrößerungen, kleine und große Maschendrahtflächen, transparente Plakate, Losungen in luftgespannten Sätzen, überall helle, leuchtende Farben." [14]

GAGFAH / AHAG-Aus-
stellung Wohnen im
Grünen, 1928
Walter Gropius / Laszlo
Moholy-Nagy
GAGFAH/AHAG-
exhibition Living in the
Green, 1928
Walter Gropius / Laszlo
Moholy-Nagy

Auch El Lissitzkys Russischer Pavillon „Pressa" für die Internationale Kunstausstellung in Köln 1928, der im Inneren mit Großfotowänden ausgestattet war, sowie der Stand der Gebrüder Rasch für eine Propaganda-Firma auf der Werbeschau Stuttgart 1927, bei welchem sich übermannshohe, mit Plakaten beklebte Trommeln gegeneinander in unterschiedlichen Geschwindigkeiten drehten, zeigten den neuen Einsatz von Medien und Bewegung.

Einer der Marksteine der modernen Architektur, der Mitte der 80er Jahre wiedererrichtet wurde, entstand 1929 in Barcelona auf der „Exposición Internacio-

"Mobile walls inscribed with new demands, rotating coloured discs, lighting devices, signalling elements and reflectors; transparency, light and movement provide entertainment for the public. Everything is arranged so that it can be understood and digested by ordinary people. There is also the pleasure in using new materials: large celluloid boards, grid systems, enlargements, small and large areas of netting wire, transparent posters, watchwords in sentences suspended in the air, everywhere bright, glowing colours." [14]

One of the milestones of modern architecture which was re-erected in the middle of the 80's was originally created in Barcelona for the "Exposición Internacional de Barcelona". The Barcelona pavilion by Mies van der Rohe, an uncompromising expression of the new architecture, consisted of three basic elements: supports, plates and panels. The architecture of this pavilion is itself the exhibit. Due to fact that the wall panels are in front of or behind the supports and not between and that the roof plate is borne by supports, the wall does not have a load-bearing function. This allows a great deal of freedom in the layout of the ground plan and the inner and outer limits of the room continuously change. The equilibrium in the dimensioning of the spatial references is supported by a fine selection of materials: the terrace is made of travertine, the walls of onyx and marble (a kind of "stone

nal de Barcelona". Der Barcelona-Pavillon von Mies van der Rohe, ein kompromißloser Ausdruck der neuen Architektur, bestand aus drei Grundelementen: Stütze, Platte und Scheibe. Bei diesem Pavillon, der nur sich selbst ausstellt, ist die Architektur das Exponat. Dadurch, daß die Wandscheiben vor oder hinter den Stützen – nicht dazwischen – stehen, und die Dachplatte von den Stützen getragen wird, ist die Wand aus der Tragfunktion herausgelöst, eine freie Grundrißgestaltung ist möglich, die inneren und äußeren Raumgrenzen sind fließend. Die Ausgewogenheit bei der Proportionierung der räumlichen Bezüge wird unterstützt durch die feine Materialwahl: eine Terrasse aus Travertin, Wände aus Onyx und Marmor (eine Art „Stein-Furnier" auf einem konstruktiven inneren System), verschiedene opake und durchsichtige Spiegelglas-Paneele in verchromten Rahmen, Kreuzstützen aus Winkeleisen mit verchromten Winkelblechen.

Ein weiterer bemerkenswerter Bau auf dieser Ausstellung war der AEG-Pavillon der Deutschen Elektroindustrie, ebenfalls aus dem Büro Mies van der Rohe: ein fensterloser Kubus mit stützenlosem Innenraum, auf dessen Innenwände flächendeckend und um die Ecken herumlaufend, Photographien projiziert

veneer" on a structural inner system), different opaque and transparent mirror panels in chromed frames, and intersecting supports made of angled steel with chromed, angled metal sheets.

A further noteworthy construction at this exhibition was the AEG pavilion of the German electrical industry, also by Mies van de Rohe. This was a windowless cube with an interior lacking supports. Photographs were projected all over its interior walls and round the corners thus providing a view into imaginary rooms.

Hackerbräu-Bier-
Ausstellung
Barcelona, 1929
Lilly Reich/Ludwig Mies
van der Rohe
Hackerbräu-Bier-
exhibition
Barcelona, 1929
Lilly Reich/Ludwig Mies
van der Rohe

wurden, die Ausblicke in imaginäre Räume freigaben. Für die Deutsche Ausstellung kreierte Lilly Reich ein Ensemble aus freistehenden Glaswänden. In einem Ausstellungsentwurf in Kooperation mit Mies van der Rohe für Hackerbräu Bier standen in einem dreiseitig begrenzten Raum Bierflaschen auf einem Regal, das über zwei Wände lief.

Zur „20e exposition des artistes decorateurs français" im Grand Palais in Paris 1930 entwickelte Walter Gropius für den Deutschen Werkbund mit Marcel Breuer, Herbert Bayer und Laszlo Moholy-Nagy die unterschiedlichen Räume für Präsentationen von Leistungen der Architektur, Innenraumgestaltung, industriellen Formgebung von Gebrauchsgeräten sowie kunstgewerblicher Gegenstände.

Hauptthema war der Gemeinschaftsraum im Wohnhochhaus, dazu wurden in einer Mischung von Inszenierungen und Realsituationen weitere unterschiedliche Themen behandelt: Gesellschaftsraum, Appartement, Lichtgestaltung, serienmäßig hergestellte Gegenstände, ... Herbert Bayer beispielsweise hängte Großfotos in verschiedenen Winkeln und erweiterte dadurch das Blickfeld des Betrachters.

Ausstellung des Dt.
Werkbunds
Ausstellungsgestaltung
Paris 1930,
Herbert Bayer
Exhibition of the Dt.
Werkbund
Exhibitiondesign
Paris 1930,
Herbert Bayer

Lilly Reich created an ensemble composed of free-standing glass walls for the German exhibition. In a draft design prepared for Hackerbräu Bier in cooperation with Mies van der Rohe, bottles of beer stood on a shelf along two walls of a three-sided area.

For the "20e exposition des artistes decorateurs francais" in the Grand Palais in Paris in 1920, Walter Gropius together with Marcel Breuer, Herbert Bayer and Laszlo Moholy-Nagy developed different areas for presenting works of architecture, interior design, the industrial design of consumer items as well as arts-and-crafts objects. This was for the Deutscher Werkbund.

The main topic was the community room in the residential high-rise building. In a mixture of stage-settings and real

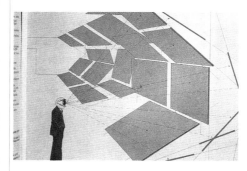

Ausstellung des Dt.
Werkbunds, Paris, 1930
Walter Gropius / Herbert
Bayer / Marcel Breuer /
Laszlo Moholy-Nagy
Exhibition of the Dt.
Werkbund, Paris, 1930
Walter Gropius / Herbert
Bayer / Marcel Breuer /
Laszlo Moholy-Nagy

Lesegalerie,
Deutsche Bauausstellung
Berlin, 1931
Walter Gropius
Reading gallery,
German building fair
Berlin, 1931
Walter Gropius

situations, other different topics were addressed: a community room, an apartment, light design, series-produced articles. Herbert Bayer, for example, hung blow-ups of photos in different corners, thus extending the observer's field of view.

The climax in the career of Lilly Reich was the exhibition "Die Wohnung unserer Zeit" (An Apartment of our Time) at the Berlin building fair in 1931, a purist presentation of materials which almost anticipated the installations of Minimal Art:

Höhepunkt der Laufbahn Lilly Reichs
war die Ausstellung „Die Wohnung unserer Zeit" der Berliner Bauausstellung 1931,
eine puristische Materialpräsentation,
die schon fast Installationen der Minimal
Art vorwegnahm: in der Glas-Ausstellung
Glasflächen in vertikaler Formation,
in der Holz-Ausstellung ein geometrisch-
grafisches Ensemble, das mit der Typografie harmonisierte, Holzplanken, rohes
Material – die Materie sollte für sich
wirken.

Die Ausstellung des 10. Jahrestags der
Faschistischen Revolution in Rom mit der
Ausstellungsarchitektur von Adalberto
Libera[15], kann als der Beginn der Liaison
des Regimes mit der rationalistischen
Architektur gesehen werden. Fast
alle futuristischen Architekten, so bei-
spielsweise Giuseppe Terragni und Mario
Sironi, entwarfen einzelne Räume. Die
Architekturen der Weltausstellung in Chi-
cago 1933/34 waren noch geprägt von
Bauformen der 20er Jahre, die Brüsseler
Weltausstellung 1935[16] stand dagegen
schon stark im Zeichen der politischen
Entwicklung: der italienische Pavillon
„Italia Padiglione del Littorio Italia" von
Adalberto Libera, war ein gigantisches
Gebäude, durchlöchert von unzähligen
Lichtöffnungen, so daß im Inneren eine
eigenartige Aura entstand.

Immer wieder sind die Einflüsse der
Kunst auf die Ausstellungsgestaltung zu
spüren. Bei der „Triennale di Milano",
1936 entwarf Max Bill die Schweizer Section. Ausgestellt waren Arbeiten der
angewandten Kunst und der industriellen
Produktion. Die räumliche Gliederung
entstand durch leichte Einbauten aus
fertigen, leicht transportablen Elementen
für das Ausstellungsgut. Der Besucher
mußte zwangsweise am gesamten Ausgestellten vorbei: „Die Schweizer Ausstellung an der 'Triennale di Milano' ist
ein Beispiel für die Nutzanwendung

Die Wohnung unserer
Zeit, Berlin, 1931
Lilly Reich / Ludwig Mies
van der Rohe
An apartment of our time
Berlin, 1931
Lilly Reich / Ludwig Mies
van der Rohe

The glass exhibition contained glass
surfaces which were vertically arranged;
in the wood exhibition, there was a
geometrical-graphical ensemble which
harmonised with the typography, and
wooden planks and untreated materials
– matter was intended to provide its
own effect.

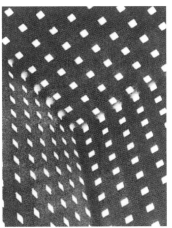

Italienischer Pavillon
Weltausstellung Brüssel,
1935
Adalberto Libera
Italian Pavilion
World's fair Brussels,
1935
Adalberto Libera

10. Jahrestag der
Faschistischen Revolution
Rom, 1932
Adalberto Libera
10th anniversary of the
Fascist Revolution
Rom, 1932
Adalberto Libera

The exhibition of the 10th anniversary of
the Fascist revolution in Rome with
the exhibition architecture of Adalberto
Libera[15] can be seen as the beginning
of the liaison of the regime with the
rationalistic architecture. Almost all futuristic architects, for example Giuseppe
Terragni and Mario Sironi, designed single
rooms. The architects of the world's
fair in Chicago in 1933/34 were still being
influenced by the shapes of the 20's.
The 1935[16] Brussels world's fair, in contrast,
was very much in line with political
developments: the Italian pavilion "Italia
Padiglione del Littoria Italia" by Adalberto Libera was a gigantic structure, with
innumerable holes for letting in light,
thus creating a strange aura inside it.

Schweizer Ausstellung
Triennale di Milano, 1936
Max Bill
Swiss exhibition
Triennale di Milano, 1936
Max Bill

The influences of art on exhibition design can be found again and again. At the "Triennale di Milano" in 1936, Max Bill designed the Swiss section. Works of applied art and industrial products were exhibited. The spatial layout was produced by lightweight built-in units made of ready-made, easily transportable elements for the exhibits and the visitor was almost forced to walk past every one of these exhibits. "The Swiss exhibition at the 'Triennale di Milano' is an example of how knowledge gained in the field of constructivist painting and sculpture could be applied in the new architecture. This firstly involves free integration of the different elements, based on a thematic program in a given space, secondly, a superior design of the shapes and, thirdly, excellent colouring. Point 1: the different elements, the display cases etc. are fixed suspended in the air with suspension fittings and lightweight supporting devices. The movement of air in the room causes individual elements (photomural 'Infinite Loop') to oscillate and rotate slightly. The arrangement of the components allows spatial restrictions and extensions in a horizontal and vertical direction. Point 2: the shapes of the elements are freely and individually designed and are developed in dependence on the functional and constructional conditions. The

der Erkenntnisse auf dem Gebiet der konstruktiven Malerei und Plastik im Zusammenhang mit der neuen Architektur. Diese sind 1. freie Einordnung verschiedener Elemente, gestützt auf ein thematisches Programm, in einen gegebenen Raum; 2. souveräne Formgebung; 3. souveräne Farbgebung. Punkt 1: Die verschiedenen Raumelemente, Vitrinen usw. sind mit Hänge- und leichten Stützvorrichtungen schwebend im Raum fixiert. Die Luftbewegung im Raume bringt einzelne Elemente (Photowand 'Unendliche Schleife') in leichte Schwingung und Drehung. Die Anordnung der Bauteile lässt räumliche Einengungen und Weitungen in horizontaler und vertikaler Ausdehnung entstehen. Punkt 2: Die Elemente erfahren eine aus den funktionellen und konstruktiven

Schweizer Ausstellung
Triennale di Milano, 1936
Max Bill
Swiss exhibition
Triennale di Milano, 1936
Max Bill

totality of shapes results in an unmistakable unity. Point 3: strong colours contrast with the white of the area which stretches over the built-in units, ..."[17]

The 1937 world's fair in Paris on the eve of the Second World War was a trade fair which represented national projections with an increasingly ideological message.[18] The trend moved away from large halls to pavilions. In addition to massive structures (for Germany, Albert

Finnischer Pavillon
Expo Paris, 1937
Alvar Aalto
Finnish pavilion
Expo Paris, 1937
Alvar Aalto

Bedingungen entwickelte freie und individuelle Formgebung. Die Gesamtheit der Formen bildet eine unverkennbare Einheit. Punkt 3: Zum Weiss des Raumes, das sich auch über die Einbauten erstreckt, kontrastieren starke Farben, … ."[17]

Die Weltausstellung in Paris 1937, am Vorabend des Zweiten Weltkriegs, war eine Messe, die in zunehmender Ideologisierung nationale Projektionen darstellte.[18] Die Tendenz bewegte sich weg von den großen Hallen hin zu Pavillons. Neben massiven Bauten (für Deutschland entwarf Albert Speer das „Deutsche Haus", eine in schwere Pfeiler gegliederte kubische Masse) gab es auch leichte Konstruktionen aus den Ländern, wo der Gedanke des modernen Bauens noch nicht verfemt und vertrieben war (die skandinavischen Länder, Belgien, Holland und die Schweiz). Alvar Aaltos finnischer Pavillon hatte über einem konstruktiven Gerüst eine Außenhautverkleidung aus Holz. Nur an wenigen Stellen waren die vorgefertigten Teile, die fast nur noch montiert werden mußten, von einem Stahlskelett ergänzt. Im Inneren befanden sich Holzgitter-, Holzstab- oder Birkenfurnierwände und Presszellulosekarton für die Produktpräsentation.[19] Le Corbusiers „Pavillon des Temps Nouveaux" erinnert an das Zelt als

Speer designed the "Deutsche Haus", German house, a cubic mass arranged in heavy pillars), there were also light-weight constructions from countries where the idea of modern architecture had still not been condemned and repulsed (the Scandinavian countries, Belgium, Holland and Switzerland). Alvar Aalto's Finnish pavilion had a wooden outer skin over a frame. The prefabricated parts which almost required nothing more than fitting into place were supplement by a steel skeleton only at a few points. On the inside, the walls were made

Le Pavillon des Temps Nouveaux
Expo Paris, 1937
Le Corbusier
Le Pavillon des Temps Nouveaux
Expo Paris, 1937
Le Corbusier

Finnischer Pavillon
Expo Paris, 1937
Alvar Aalto
Finnish pavilion
Expo Paris, 1937
Alvar Aalto

Le Pavillon des Temps
Nouveaux
Expo Paris, 1937
Le Corbusier
Le Pavillon des Temps
Nouveaux
Expo Paris, 1937
Le Corbusier

ursprüngliche Form: ein von Spannkabeln gehaltenes, 1.600 qm großes Zelt mit Fachwerkträger-Stützen außerhalb. Große Wandbilder, Fotos und eindrucksvolle grafische Darstellungen bildeten die Ausstellung in dem sehr farbigen Inneren.

1939 in New York, zur „New York World's Fair", erregte Alvar Aalto wiederum mit dem finnischen Pavillon Aufmerksamkeit: geschwungene Wandflächen mit vertikalen Rippen, geneigt und leicht versetzt, versehen mit Großfotos.

Während des Zweiten Weltkriegs beherrschten temporäre Militärgebäude die architektur der fliegenden Bauten: sind es im Ersten Weltkrieg noch die großen, beweglichen Luftschiffhallen gewesen, so waren es im Zweiten Weltkrieg mobile Hangars, später auch Army-Forts im Wasser und Pontonbrücken sowie Unterkunftsgebäude (Nissen-Hütten), die auch in den 50er Jahren eine große Rolle spielen sollten.

Weblee Portable Hut
1918
Weblee Portable Hut
1918

of wooden grids, wooden rods or birch veneer and compressed cellulose cardboard for presenting the products.[19] Le Corbusier's "Pavillon de Temps Nouveaux" is reminiscent of the original shape of the tent: a 1600 sq. metres tent held by tension cables with a lattice of supporting elements on the outside. Large murals, photos and impressive graphic illustrations were used for the exhibition in the very colourful interior.

In New York in 1939, Alvar Aalto's Finnish pavilion for the New York World's Fair attracted attention; flowing wall surfaces with vertical ribs, inclined and slightly offset, and covered with photomurals.

Finnischer Pavillon
Weltausstellung New
York, 1939
Alvar Aalto
Finnish pavilion
New York World's fair
1939
Alvar Aalto

During the Second World War, temporary military buildings dominated the architecture of temporary buildings. In the First World War, it had been the large mobile halls for airships and, in the Second World War, it was mobile hangars and, later, army forts in the water and pontoon bridges as well as barracks (Nissen huts) which were also to play an important role in the 50's.

Experimente und Utopien

Vor dem Krieg hatte das Messewesen aus wenigen übergroßen, die gesamte Wirtschaft umfassenden Veranstaltungen bestanden, etwa in der Art der Leipziger Messe. In den 50er Jahren dagegen entwickelte sich eine große Zahl kleiner Fachausstellungen, bei welchen die Gestaltung der Stände häufig noch wie auf einem Basar erschien: „Wie ist es sonst möglich, daß eine wirklich schön gestaltete, perfekt funktionierende Maschine immer noch auf einem Chippendalepodest ausgestellt wird? Die Möglichkeit und die Mittel hätten wir, diese unsere Maschine mit den straffen Requisiten unserer heutigen Ausstellungstechnik sachlich dem Betrachter zu präsentieren, ganz im Dienste der Maschine."[20] Rühmliche Ausnahmen waren beispielsweise Arbeiten von Herbert Hirche, einem ehemaligen Mitarbeiter von Mies van der Rohe und Lilly Reich: übersichtlich disponierte Ausstellungen mit feingliedrigen und zurückhaltenden Trägern sowie einer Beschriftung in gutem Rhythmus – nicht nur bei der Gestaltung von Themenausstellungen sondern auch bei zahlreichen Firmenmessesständen: „Wie Wohnen" 1949 in Stuttgart; „Gute Industrieform" 1952 in Mannheim; „Schönheit der Technik" 1953 in Stuttgart; die „Abteilung Bauen + Wohnen" der Landesausstellung 1955 in Stuttgart; der Stand der Stuttgarter Gardinenfabrik GmbH 1958 auf der Frankfurter Messe.

Ende der 50er Jahre gewann eine neue Architektengeneration zunehmend an Einfluß, beispielsweise auf die bedeutenden CIAM (Congrès Internationaux d'Architecture Moderne), wo sie als Team X (Bakema, Aldo van Eyck, Alison und Peter Smithson u.a.) die Auflösung der CIAM bewirkten. Für diese Generation war das Ausstellungswesen mit den großen Industriemessen und Weltausstellungen wieder zu einem bedeutenden Forum für Experimente geworden. Viele Architekturutopien der 60er Jahre konnten auf diesem Forum für kurze Zeit und mit hohem technischen Aufwand vorgeführt werden. Dabei sah man

Before the war, trade-fair activity had consisted of a few outsized events which each accommodated the whole range of industry, something like the Leipzig fair. In the 50's, however, a large number of small specialist exhibitions were developed where the design of the stands still had the feeling of a bazaar. "How is it otherwise possible that a very attractively designed and perfectly functioning machine is still exhibited on a Chippendale pedestal? We have the facilities and means for presenting our machine to the observer in an objective manner, using the robust apparatus of our present-day exhibition techniques in order to underline the advantages of the machine itself."[20] Notable exceptions were the works of Herbert Hirche, for example, a former associate of Mies van der Rohe and Lilly Reich. These were clearly arranged exhibitions with finely structured and discreet beams and pleasingly rhythmic inscriptions. They could be found not only in exhibitions with particular themes but also at many company trade-fairs such as "Wie Wohnen" ("A Manner of Living") in Stuttgart in 1949, "Gute Industrieform" (Good Industrial Design) in Mannheim in 1952, "Schönheit der Technik"

Wie Wohnen
LGA Stuttgart, 1949
Herbert Hirche
A Manner of Living
LGA Stuttgart, 1949
Herbert Hirche

Abteilung
Bauen + Wohnen
Landesausstellung
Stuttgart, 1955
Herbert Hirche
Department of Construction and Housing
State exhibition
Stuttgart, 1955
Herbert Hirche

Stand der Stuttgarter
Gardinenfabrik GmbH
Frankfurter Messe, 1958
Herbert Hirche
Stand of the Stuttgart
Gardinenfabrik GmbH
Frankfurt trade-fair, 1958
Herbert Hirche

(The Beauty of Engineering) in Stuttgart in 1953, "Abteilung Bauen + Wohnen" ("Department of Construction and Housing") at the state exhibition in Stuttgart in 1955 and the stand of the Stuttgart Gardinenfabrik GmbH in 1958 at the Frankfurt trade fair.

Breda-Pavillon
Internt. Messe Mailand,
1952
Luciano Baldessari
Breda-pavillon
International trade fair
Milan, 1952
Luciano Baldessari

At the end of the 50's, a new generation
of architects was beginning to exert
an increasing influence on the trade-fair
scene, for example at the important
CIAM (Congrès Internationaux d'Architecture Moderne) where – calling themselves Team X – Bakema, Aldo van
Eyck, Alison and Peter Smithson etc. were
responsible for 'loosening up' the CIAM.

variable Gestaltungsmöglichkeiten für verschiedene Situationen häufiger als einen
mehr zeichnerischen und freien Umgang
mit dem Material. Dies gab es nur bei
einzelnen Bauwerken, so z.B. bei Luciano
Baldessaris Breda-Pavillon auf der Internationalen Messe 1952 in Mailand:
die Mauer löste sich von der Erde und
durchzog die Luft. „Ich dachte an ein

"I thought of a structure which was
on the borderline between
architecture and sculpture and I
abandoned the classical orthogonal axes in favour of a mobile
dynamism which overcomes
the gravity of matter in parabolas,
hyperbolas and conchoids."

For this generation, exhibiting at the great
industrial trade-fairs and world's fairs had
again become an important forum for
experimentation. Many architectural
utopias of the 60's were presented at this
forum for a short time and involved a
great deal of technical work. Variable

„Ich dachte an ein Gebilde, das auf
der Grenze zwischen Architektur und Skulptur steht, und
ich verließ die orthogonalen klassischen Achsen zugunsten einer
bewegten Dynamik, die in
Parabeln, Hyperbeln und Konchoiden die Schwere der Materie
überwindet."

Philips-Pavillon
Weltausstellung Brüssel,
1958 Le Corbusier
Philips-pavilion,
Bruxelles World's fair,
1958 Le Corbusier

Gebilde, das auf der Grenze zwischen
Architektur und Skulptur steht, und ich
verließ die orthogonalen klassischen
Achsen zugunsten einer bewegten Dynamik, die in Parabeln, Hyperbeln und
Konchoiden die Schwere der Materie
überwindet."[21]

designs for different situations were to
be seen more often than the graphical
and free use of materials. This was the
case only for individual constructions, for
example Luciano Baldessari's Breda
pavilion at the 1952 international trade
fair in Milan: the walls were released from
the earth and soared through
the air. "I thought of a structure which
was on the borderline between architecture and sculpture and I abandoned
the classical orthogonal axes in favour
of a mobile dynamism which overcomes
the gravity of matter in parabolas, hyperbolas and conchoids."[21]

Philips-Pavillon
Weltausstellung Brüssel,
1958 Le Corbusier
Philips-pavilion
Bruxelles World's fair,
1958 Le Corbusier

The first world's fair after the Second
World War was the "Exposition Universelle
et Internationale de Bruxelles" in 1958.
The most sensational pavilion was
the one by Corbusier for Philips. For the
very first time, Philips did not want
to appear under the flag of a particular

Die erste Weltausstellung nach dem Zweiten Weltkrieg war die „Exposition Universelle et Internationale de Bruxelles" 1958. Den aufsehenerregendsten Pavillon bildete Le Corbusiers Arbeit für Philips. Philips wollte hier erstmals nicht unter der Flagge eines Landes, sondern multinational auftreten. „Ich werde Ihnen nicht eine Pavillon-Fassade machen, sondern ein elektronisches Gedicht, das im Inneren einer 'Flasche' enthalten sein wird. Diese Flasche, für einen symphonischen Ausdruck der bisher unverwendeten Möglichkeiten der Elektronik bestimmt, wird ihr Pavillon sein. Das Gedicht wird aus Bildern, farbigen Rhythmen, Musik bestehen. Das elektronische Gedicht wird in einem zusammenhängenden Ganzen vereinen, was Film, Musik auf Platte und Tonband, Farbe, Wort, Geräusch und Schweigen uns bisher getrennt gebracht haben. Das Gedicht wird zehn Minuten dauern; es wird sich jedesmal vor 500 Zuschauern entfalten. Der Pavillon wird also ein Magen sein, der 500 Zuhörer und Zuschauer aufnimmt und sie nach Beendigung des Schauspiels automatisch wieder ausstößt, um den 500 folgenden Platz zu machen"[22], so Le Corbusier zu L.C. Kalff, einem der Direktoren von Philips. Über einer Grundform wie ein Magen mit je einem Ein- und Ausgang, waren hyperbole und parabole Formen durch Drahtseile befestigt, Wände aus rohen Platten, die am Boden in Sand gegossen wurden. Für die Synthese von Farbe, Bild, Musik, Wort und Rhythmus waren Leinwände panoramisch angebracht; 400 Lautsprecher verteilten den Ton, einen dreidimensionalen Klang von Edgar Varèse und Iannis Xénakis, entlang der inneren Flächen an Seilen, die die „routes du son" formten, um zusammen mit den Bildprojektionen eine intensive räumliche Bewegung zu schaffen. Die Bilder folgten in unterschiedlicher Geschwindigkeit aufeinander und wurden um die Besucher herum projiziert. Dies waren die Medienwelten, die Marshal McLuhan analysierte, die Form wurde Inhalt: from medium to message.

Die Architektur der Variabilität und Flexibilität in der Nutzung innerhalb des Raumes führte zu Beginn der 60er Jahre einerseits zu Entwürfen mit Austauschbarkeit von Sekundärelementen innerhalb einer Primär-Tragstruktur. Plug-Ins und Clip-Ins wurden von Archigram, Yona Friedman, Konrad Wachsmann und den japanischen Metabolisten entwickelt. Archigrams „Plug-In-City" von 1964 schiebt Wohneinheiten in ein Tragwerk mit Technik und Verkehrssystem, die „Walking Cities" tragen humanoide, tierische und roboterhafte Züge.

country but to be seen as an international company. "I will not make you a pavilion facade but an electronic poem which will be enclosed inside a 'bottle'. This bottle, intended to give a symphonic expression of the previously unexploited possibilities of electronics, will be its pavilion. The poem will be made up of images, coloured rhythms and music. The electronic poem will unify in an integral whole everything that film, recorded music, colours, words, noises and silence, seen individually, have given us. The poem will last ten minutes; it will unfold each time before an audience of 500. The pavilion will thus be a stomach which accommodates 500 listeners and watchers and automatically thrusts them out after the play has ended in order to make room for the next 500."[22] These were the words of Le Corbusier to L.C. Kalff, one of the directors of Philips. Above a basic shape like a stomach with an entrance and exit, hyperbolic and parabolic shapes where fastened to each other by wire; the walls were made of red panels which were cast in sand on the floor. Screens were arranged panoramically for a synthesis of colour, image, music, word and rhythm; 400 loudspeakers distributed the sound – a three-dimensional arrangement of Edgar Varèse and Iannis Xénakis – along the interior surfaces on cables which formed "routes du son" with the aim of generating a feeling of intensive spatial movement together with the projected pictures. The pictures followed each other at different speeds and were projected around the visitors. These were the media worlds which Marshal McLuhan analysed. Form became content, the medium became the message.

At the beginning of the sixties, the architecture of variability and flexibility of use led to designs, on the one hand, where secondary elements could be interchanged

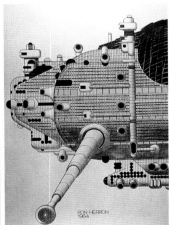

Walking Cities, 1964
Ron Herron / Archigram
Walking Cities, 1964
Ron Herron / Archigram

Andererseits entstanden mit dem Vorbild von Wohnwagen und neuen Entwicklungen auf dem Gebiet der Raumfahrt Projekte, die autarke Versorgung und hohe Beweglichkeit auszeichnete: Archigrams „Living Pod", „Mobile Village" (Fahrzeug und Haus) und „Drive In Housing" (Mike Webb, David Greene), 1964-66, nutzten neue Entwicklungen. „Um in der Lage zu sein, sich die architektonischen Moden von morgen auszuspinnen, muß man wissen, was die nächste Zeit an neuen Materialien zu bieten haben wird (zum Beispiel Plastikhüllen, die in der Sonne schmelzen und sich am Abend, wenn es kalt wird, wieder materialisieren; oder Gebäude, die durch eine Röhre auf den Baugrund geblasen werden und dort keimen und gedeihen dürfen); ..."[23] Mike Webbs „Cushicle" von 1966/67 ist eine ausklappbare Wohnzelle, die auf dem Rücken herumgetragen werden kann, und die sich von selbst entfaltet, sein Suitaloon von 1968/69 ein Haus-Anzug als Mini-Behausung.

Gegen Ende der 60er Jahre kehrte sich die Gestaltausbildung von der Kompaktheit ab und entwickelte sich in Richtung von Leichtem, Flexiblem, Transportablem, Provisorischem, Transitorischem als neuem Konzept; das adäquate technologische Medium für diese Ansätze waren pneumatische, aufblasbare Gebilde. Traglufthallen, Forschungszelte, Ausstellungspavillons – sie demonstrieren Offenheit, Leichtigkeit und Transparenz. Pneumatische Konstruktionen, entweder mit Luftdruckunterschieden zwischen Innen und Außen, oder als luftgefülltes konstruktives System, entstanden in den 60er Jahren als Projekte von Hans Hollein und Walter Pichler, Haus-Rucker-Co., Coop Himmelblau und Archigram, um nur einige zu nennen. „Entwurfsidee einer Architektur, die sich wie Wolken verändert. Pneumatische Konstruktionen erlauben Volumenveränderungen durch den neuen 'Baustoff' Luft. Und die neuen Formen beeinflussen – unterstützt durch Farbprojektionen, Ton und Gerüche – die Erlebnisqualität der Räume."[24] Die 1968 entstandene pneumatische Raumkapsel „Gelbes Herz" von Haus-Rucker Co., und die „Wolke 1968", 1968-72 von Coop Himmelb(l)au sollen

within a primary load-bearing structure. Plug-ins and clip-ins were developed by Archigram, Yona Friedman, Konrad Wachsmann and the Japanese Metabolists. Archigram's "plug-in city" of 1964 pushes residential units into a load-bearing structure with engineering and a traffic system; the "Walking Cities" carry humanoid, animal and robot-like trains.

On the other hand, based on the model of the caravan and new developments in the field of space travel, projects were conducted which praised autonomy and high mobility: Archigram's "Living Pod", "Mobile Village" (vehicle and house

Living Pod, 1966
David Greene / Archigram
Living Pod, 1966
David Greene / Archigram

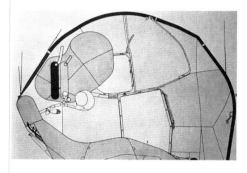

Cushicle, Traggestell und Wohnzelt, 1966/67
Mike Webb/Archigram
Cushicle, Living-cell,
1966/1967
Mike Webb/Archigram

at the same time) and "Drive In Housing" (Mike Webb, David Greene), 1964 to 1966, made use of new developments. "In order to be able to think up the architectural fashions of tomorrow, one has to know what new materials the future will have to offer (for example, plastic envelopes which melt in the sun and, when it gets colder in the evening, materialise again; or buildings which can be blown up by a pipe on the ground and can germinate there and flourish.)... ."[23] Mike Webb's "Cushicle" of 1966/67 is an unfoldable living-cell which can be carried around on the back and unfolds itself; his Suitaloon of 1968/69 is a house-cum-suit as a mini dwelling.

Towards the end of the sixties, design training turned away from compactness and developed in the direction of the lightweight, the flexible, the transportable, the provisional and the transitory as a new way of looking at things. The appropriate technological medium

Gelbes Herz
Haus-Rucker-Co
1968
Yellow Heart
Haus-Rucker-Co
1968

Wolke 1968
Coop Himmelblau
Cloud 1968
Coop Himmelblau

als Beispiele dienen. „Die Wolke ist ein Organismus zum leben. Die Struktur ist mobil, der Raum kann modifiziert werden. Die Baumaterialien sind Luft und Dynamik."[25]

Übrigens hatte Bodo Rasch bereits 1938 ein „Transportables Haus aus luftgefüllten Zellen" zum Reichspatent

> „Die Wolke ist ein Organismus zum leben. Die Struktur ist mobil, der Raum kann modifiziert werden. Die Baumaterialien sind Luft und Dynamik."

angemeldet. Auf diesen Ideen basierend, entstand beispielsweise das sehr humorvolle Projekt für eine Wurstbraterei-Halle in Form eines Schweins. Johannes Canis schreibt in einem Brief an Bodo Rasch: „... Tatsächlich werden Sie der erste Mensch sein, der Luftschlösser so zu bauen vermag, daß man darin wohnen kann! ... Häuser aus Luft, Städte aus Luft – wie wär's, wenn Sie dem Staatsbaumeister Speer vorschlügen, das neue Berlin zunächst einmal – so versuchsweise aus Luft zu bauen, ...? Dann wäre Berlin transportabel, könnte verrückt und verschoben werden ... vielleicht kommen dann die Menschen zu einer neuen Art des Nomadisierens; ... ."[26]

Auf der „Universal and International Exhibition" „Der Mensch und seine Welt" in Montreal 1967 zeigten vielfältige Architekturen die Tendenz zu Raumtragwerken: räumliche Fachwerkkonstruktionen aus den zwei Grundelementen Knoten und Stab, überdachten große Spannweiten. Richard Buckminster-Fullers US-Pavillon, eine spektakuläre geodätische Kuppel, ein klimatisch kontrolliertes Environment bei geringstem

for these approaches were pneumatic structures which could be blown up. As self-supporting air halls, research tents, exhibition pavilions, they featured openness, lightness and transparency. Pneumatic constructions, either with differences in air pressure between the inside and outside or as an air-filled constructed system, were created in the sixties as projects of Hans Hollein and Walter Pichler, Haus-Rucker-Co., Coop

> "The cloud is an organism for living in. The structure is mobile, the room can be modified. The building materials are air and movement."

Himmelblau and Archigram, to name but a few. "Design ideas of an architecture which changes like clouds. Pneumatic constructions allow alterations in volume by means of air – the 'new building material'. And the new shapes – supported by colour projection, sound and smells – influence the way in which rooms are experienced."[24] The pneumatic room capsule "Gelbes Herz" (Yellow Heart) produced in 1968 by Haus-Rucker-Co. and the "Wolke 1968" (Cloud 1968) of 1968-72 by Coop Himmelblau can serve as examples. "The cloud is an organism for living in. The structure is mobile, the room can be modified. The building materials are air and movement."[25]

Bodo Rasch, by the way, had already registered a "transportable house made of air-filled cells" at the patent office in 1938. Based on this idea, a very humorous project for a sausage-frying factory, for example, was created in the shape of a pig. Johannes Canis writes, in a letter to Bodo Rasch; "...You will indeed be the first man to build castles in the air which you can live in! ... houses made of air, cities made of air – how would it be if you proposed to Speer, the state's master builder, that the new Berlin should be made of air, at least just to try it out

Pneumatische Konstruktionen Wurstbraterei, 1938 Bodo Rasch Pneumatic Structures Sausage-frying factory, 1938 Bodo Rasch

Energieaufwand, war das Ergebnis seiner intensiven Studien von Konstruktionen, die bei geringem Gewicht Schutz vor äußeren Einwirkungen bieten sowie schnell und billig aufbaubar sein sollten. Die zur Expo errichtete Kuppel, eine Dreiviertelkugel, hatte eine Höhe von 61 m, das konstruktive Gerüst war ein sphärisches Raumtragwerk aus Stahl (Drei- und Sechsecke), die Abdeckung bestand aus Acrylkunstharzelementen mit Sonnenschutzmarkisen.

Neben den räumlichen Tragwerken war die Zeltkonstruktion eine weitere bemerkenswerte Konstruktion. Frei Otto und Rolf Gutbrod erstellten für den Pavillon der BRD eine Hülle für die darunter liegende Sekundärarchitektur. Das Zeltdach, eine zugbeanspruchte Konstruktion aus einem vorgespannten Seilnetz, erstellt nach zahlreichen Modellversuchen, ausprobiert schon 1957 auf der Internationalen Garten Ausstellung in Köln und auf der Interbau in Berlin, konnte durch wissenschaftlich-technische Arbeit und den Einsatz neuer Baustoffe realisiert werden: „... ein dünnes Stahlseilnetz ist die Konstruktion (Kabelnetzstruktur), darunter teils eine durchscheinende, teils eine durchsichtige Haut. Der Innenraum wird bestimmt durch das Dach; er ist insbesondere durch die acht hohen und durch die drei niedrigen Punkte gegliedert, und damit ergeben sich verschiedene Raumbezirke oder verschiedene Bezirke, die aber untereinander zusammenhängen. Die Großhülle erstreckt sich nicht über eine Ebene, sondern die Ausstellungslandschaft ist reich gegliedert durch Mulden und durch ein- bzw. zweigeschossige Terrassen."[27]

at the beginning ...? Then Berlin would be portable, could be slid about and moved... perhaps people will then arrive at a new form of nomad living; ... ."[26]

At the "Universal and International Exhibition, The Man and His World" in 1967 in Montreal, versatile architectural structures indicated the tendency toward rooms inside load-bearing structures; spatial framework-like constructions, made of two basic elements, the node and the rod, covered enormous spans. Richard Buckminster-Fuller's US Pavilion, a spectacular geodesic dome, an air-conditioned environment with the minimum use of energy, was the result of his intensive studies of constructions which offered protection against the outside while being lightweight and easy to set up. The dome erected for the Expo, a three-quarter sphere, was 61 m high. The structural framework was a spherical load-bearing structure made of steel (triangle and hexagon). The cover was made of acrylic-resin elements with sunblinds.

In addition to supporting structures containing rooms, the tent construction was another notable creation. For the GDR's pavilion, Frei Otto and Rolf Gutbrod devised a shell for the secondary architecture beneath. The roof of the tent, a tensioned construction made of a pre-tensed network of cables, and built after many attempts at finding the right model, was tried out in 1957 at the "Internationale Garten Ausstellung" (International Garden Show) in Cologne and at the "Interbau" in Berlin. Thanks to scientific work and the use of new building materials, it was then actually possible to create: "... a thin network of steel cables as the construction (cable-network structure) with partly a diaphanous, partly a transparent skin, underneath. The inside is determined by the roof; its structure is especially determined by the eight high and three low points, thus resulting in different areas which nevertheless are related to each other. The large shell not only covers one level but the exhibition landscape is richly structured by hollows and by one or two-levelled terraces."[27]

Takara Beautilion
Weltausstellung
Osaka 1970
Kisho Noriaki Kurokawa
Takara Beautilion
Japan World Exhibition
Osaka 1970
Kisho Noriaki Kurokawa

Landmark-Turm
Weltausstellung
Osaka 1970
Kiyonori Kiyutake
Landmark-Tower
Japan World Exhibition
Osaka 1970
Kiyonori Kiyutake

The Japan World Exhibition in Osaka in 1970 was dominated by metabolistic large-scale structures with flexible building systems. In Osaka, there were experiments for the first time in large buildings which could be dismantled. Under the overall supervision of Kenzo Tange and as a result of the pleasure being taken in experimental design, open structures were developed, which, architectonically, were one-off works with pioneering innovations: Kisho Kurokawa's pavilion for the cosmetics industry, for example,

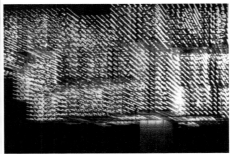

Schweizer Pavillon
Weltausstellung
Osaka 1970
Walter/Schmid/Leber
Swiss pavilion
Japan World Exhibition
Osaka 1970
Walter/Schmid/Leber

Telekommunikations-
Pavillon der Nippon
Telegraf & Telefon Public
Corp., Weltausstellung
Osaka 1970
Telecommunications-
pavilion of the Nippon
Telegraf & Telefon Public
Corp., Japan World
Exhibition
Osaka 1970

Die „Japan World Exhibition" in Osaka 1970 wurde dominiert von metabolistischen Großstrukturen mit flexiblen Bausystemen. Es gab in Osaka erstmals ernsthafte Experimente zu großen demontierbaren Gebäuden. Unter der Gesamtkonzeption von Kenzo Tange entstanden dank der gestalterischen Experimentierlust offene Baustrukturen, architektonisch gesehen einmalige Leistungen mit zukunftsweisenden Neuerungen: Kisho Kurokawas Pavillon der Kosmetikindustrie, ein gerüstartiges Stahlrohrtragwerk, darin Ausstellungsraumzellen aus Stahlblech; Kenzo Tanges Riesen-Raumtragwerk, nach oben mit transparenten Pneumatik-Polyesterkissen abgedeckt; Kiyonori Kiyutakes 120 m hoher Expo-Turm, ein räumliches Gitterkonstruktions-Fachwerk mit Raumkapseln; der Deutsche Pavillon von Fritz Bornemann aus Mero-Elementen, ein kugelförmiger Kuppelbau mit 30 m Durchmesser; der Schweizer Pavillon von Walter, Schmid und Leber, ein fachwerkartiges Stahltragewerk, verkleidet mit Aluminiumplatten, daran angeschlossen Äste mit Glühbirnen, sodaß eine schwerelos erscheinende filigrane Struktur entstand; der Telekommunikationspavillon der Nippon Telegraf & Telefon Public Corp., eine Kunststoffhaut, gespannt über eine Strahlkonstruktion.

Im Feld der pneumatischen Konstruktionen fanden sich zwei Vertreter unterschiedlicher Systeme. Im Pavillon der Japanischen Fuji Group von Yutaka Murata, einem Vertreter des geschlossenen Systems, wurden auf einer schräg im Raum hängenden Leinwand Filme gezeigt und auf den Innenseiten aus 16 aufgeblasenen Vinyl-Schläuchen von 4 m Durchmesser und 80 m Länge liefen Multivisionen

a scaffolding-like structure of steel pipes containing exhibition cells made of sheet steel; Kenzo Tange's huge room structure, covered on top with transparent pneumatic polyester cushions; Kiyonori Kiyutake's 120 m-high exhibition tower, a gridwork construction with room capsules; the German pavilion by Fritz Bornemann made of mero elements, a spherical dome structure with a diameter of 30 m; the Swiss pavilion by Walter, Schmid and Leber, a grid-like load-bearing structure made of steel, panelled with aluminium plates with branches holding glow lamps attached to them so that an apparently weightless filigree structure was created; the telecommunications pavilion of Nippon Telegraf & Telefon Public Corp., a plastic skin tightened over a steel construction.

In the field of pneumatic constructions, there were two representatives of different systems. In the pavilion of the Japanese Fuji Group from Yutaka Murata, a representative of the closed system, films were shown on a screen suspended at a slant in the room and, on the insides made of 16 blow-up vinyl hoses with

für die Zuschauer, die sich auf einer im Inneren befindlichen, sich drehenden Plattform aufhielten. Die andere Form, der US-Pavillon von Louis Davis und Samuel Brody, war eine einwandige Konstruktion in der Größe fast zweier Fußballfelder: eine Membran, gestützt durch den Überdruck des Raumvolumens. Bereits auf dieser Ausstellung war eine verstärkte Tendenz zu Film, Projektion, Ton und Geräuschkulisse ablesbar.

a diameter of 4 m and 80 m long, multivisions were shown for the audience who were on a rotating platform on the inside. The other form, the US pavilion by Louis Davis and Samuel Brody, was a one-wall construction, almost the size of two football fields: a membrane, supported by the excess pressure inside the enclosed space. There was already an increased tendency at this exhibition towards backgrounds composed of film, projection, sound and noise.

Hyperraum-Truppen-
transporter 16.5. 2526
Angus McKie
Hyperroom-Troup-
transporter 16.5. 2526
Angus McKie

Szene aus:
2001 – Odyssee im
Weltraum
Stanley Kubrick
Scene from:
2001 – A space Odyssey
Stanley Kubrick

Schwimmende Städte, transportable, bewegbare Kunststoffhäuser, wie sie etwa in Lüdenscheid auf der „ika '72" entstanden, zeigen Ergebnisse der Experimente mit neuen Materialien.

Swimming cities, transportable, mobile plastic houses, for example those created in Lüdenscheid at the "ika '72" showed some results of experimentation with new materials.

Das Dynamische und Bewegliche wurden neue Architekturkonzeptionen. Das Bauwerk fährt, wandert, klappt, fliegt, die Architektur selbst beginnt, sich zu bewegen, Hüllen beginnen, sich durch Einsatz von Elektronik zu verändern. Beim Projekt „Generator" von Cedric Price von 1976 wird ein Gebäude (ein Vorrat an Gebäudeelementen sowie bewegliche Kräne) über ein Computerprogramm in verschiedenen Stufen erstellt. Wenn der Nutzer das Gebäude nicht mehr ändert, nimmt der Computer eigenständig Änderungen vor.

The dynamic and the mobile were new architectural conceptions. The building can drive, wander about, be folded up and even fly; architecture itself begins to move, exterior shells begin to change through the use of electronics. In the "Generator" project of Cedric Price in 1976, a building (a stock of building elements as well as mobile cranes) is erected in different stages by using a computer program. When the user no longer alters the building, the computer makes modifications to it autonomously.

In den Arbeiten der Gruppe Future Systems werden Technologien aus anderen Bereichen in die Projekte eingearbeitet. Das Projekt 124 von 1984, „Peanut", nutzt Maschinen aus dem Brückenbau und der Wartung, um dynamische Archi-

In the work of the Future Systems group, technologies from other fields are worked into the projects. The 124 project of 1984, "Peanut", uses machines from bridge construction and maintenance in order to create dynamic architecture with different building heights and locations. The group also prepared extraterrestrial design projects for NASA. Plans for NASA or the Russian space authority were often based on science-fiction architecture with their flying buildings, building transporters and cities.[28]

Micromegas
Time Sections
Daniel Libeskind
Micromegas
Time Sections
Daniel Libeskind

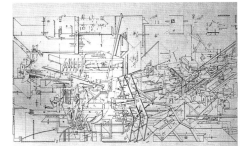

Folly 9
Osaka Follies, 1990
Daniel Libeskind
Folly 9
Osaka Follies, 1990
Daniel Libeskind

The Peak
Hong Kong, 1982-83
Zaha Hadid
The Peak
Hong Kong, 1982-83
Zaha Hadid

tektur mit verschiedenen Gebäudehöhen und -standorten möglich zu machen. Die Gruppe erarbeitete auch für die NASA extraterrestrische Design-Projekte. Planungen für die NASA oder die russische Weltraumbehörde fanden häufig ihre Vorbilder in Science Fiction-Architekturen mit ihren fliegenden Architekturen, Gebäude-Transportern und Städten.[28]

Fliegende Bauten, die sich noch mehr bewegen, die in ihre Einzelteile auseinanderzufliegen scheinen, finden wir in Daniel Libeskinds Micromegas oder Zaha Hadids Zeichnungen; ihr Dekonstruktivismus lebt von der Idee des Zerschneidens, Zerstörens, Abhebens und Fliegens, der auseinanderberstenden Details. In Bernard Tschumis Masterplanung und Bau von La Vilette, einem Vergnügungs-, Wissenschafts-, Technik- und Medienpark in Paris, überziehen 35 Follies den Park

Temporary buildings which become even more temporary and which appear to fall apart into their individual components, can be found in Daniel Libeskind's Micromegas or Zaha Hadid's drawings. Their deconstructivism is nourished by concepts of cutting, destroying, lifting off and flying, the elements almost exploding away from each other. In Bernard Tschumi's master plans for and construction of La Vilette, a pleasure park, scientific park, technology park and media park all in one in Paris, 35 follies are suspended above the park on a structured

"In the Manhattan transcripts, the materialisation of movement in space ... is very clear, a kind of manifesto. ..."

grid. "In the Manhattan Transcripts, the materialisation of movement in space ... is very clear, a kind of manifesto. But in architectural work, it assumes other aspects. An example of this is the cinematic promenade in the Parc de la Vilette. This is merely composed of a

„In den Manhattan transcripts ist die Materialisierung der Bewegung im Raum ... sehr deutlich, geradezu eine Art Manifest. ..."

auf einem Strukturraster: „In den Manhattan transcripts ist die Materialisierung der Bewegung im Raum ... sehr deutlich, geradezu eine Art Manifest. Aber in der architektonischen Arbeit nimmt sie noch andere Aspekte an. Ein Beispiel dafür ist die Kinematische Promenade im Parc de la Vilette – letzten Endes eine Bewegung, die sich im Raum des Parks materialisiert, sich hebt, sich senkt und sich durch das Territorium des Parks gräbt. Die Organisationssysteme der Follies bestehen ebenfalls immer aus einer Hülle und einer Bewegung: einer Rampe, einer Treppe oder einem Aufzug. Das sind Mittel, die Bewegung fortzuführen, nur diesmal auf der Basis konkreter Erfordernisse."[29]

Folly
La Vilette, Paris, 1991
Bernard Tschumi
Folly
La Vilette, Paris, 1991
Bernard Tschumi

Folly 2
Osaka Follies, 1990
Bolles-Wilson
Folly 2
Osaka Follies, 1990
Bolles-Wilson

In den Osaka Follies, zur „International Garden and Greenery Exposition" 1990, konnten einige der Architekten ihre bisher nur in Zeichnungen vorhandenen, fliegenden Bauten erstmals realisieren. Architekten sollten das Design eines Gebäudes, das traditionellerweise keine Funktion hat, interpretieren. Die temporären Follies sollten keine Architektur und keine Skulptur sein; sie hatten keine spezielle Funktion und keine 'Message' zu kommunizieren.[30]

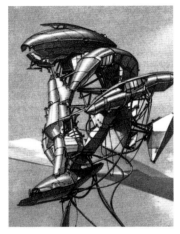

Videopavillon
Groningen, 1990
Bernard Tschumi

Videopavilion
Groningen, 1990
Bernard Tschumi

Aerial Paris, 1989
Lebbeus Woods

Aerial Paris, 1989
Lebbeus Woods

Lebbeus Woods ging in seinen visionären Architekturen noch weiter. Alle Architektur soll für das Individuum entwickelt sein, free-zones, free-spaces mit in der Atmosphäre befindlichen extraterrestrischen Architekturkörpern und Raketen.

Die Ausstellungen der 80er Jahre waren geprägt von großen postmodernen Ausstellungsinszenierungen. Hans Holleins Gestaltung der Ausstellung „Traum und Wirklichkeit. Wien 1870-1930" im Künstlerhaus Wien 1985 oder Hans Dieter Schaals Ausstellung „Berlin, Berlin" im Martin Gropius Bau Berlin 1987, mit ihren inszenierten Räumen, sind nur zwei von zahlreichen Beispielen.

1992 in Sevilla entstand die erste Expo – seit Brüssel 1958 – auf europäischem Boden. Bei den Pavillons und ihren Interieurs gab es keine großen Innovationen: es waren große, teure Gebäude mit unvergleichbaren Material- und Baukosten: „But if future Expos are to fend off increasingly unflattering comparisons

movement which materialises in the area of the park, rises, falls and digs its way through the territory of the park. The organisational systems of the follies always consist of a shell and a movement: a ramp, a stairway or a lift. These are the methods of continuous movement, only this time on the basis of concrete requirements."[29]

In the Osaka follies for the International Garden and Greenery Exposition in Osaka in 1990, some of the architects were able to actually build temporary buildings which had only existed in drawings up to then. Architects were to interpret the design of a building which traditionally has no function. The temporary follies were not to be architecture or sculpture; they had no special function and no message to communicate.[30]

Lebbeus Woods goes even further in his visionary architecture. All architecture is to be developed freely for the individual; free zones, free spaces with extraterrestrial architectural objects and even rockets in the atmosphere.

The exhibitions of the eighties were characterised by large, post-modern exhibition stage settings. Hans Holleins design of the exhibition "Traum und Wirklichkeit. Wien 1870-1930" (Dream and Reality. Vienna 1870-1930) in the Künstlerhaus Vienna in 1985 or Hans Dieter Schaal's exhibition "Berlin, Berlin" in the Martin Gropius building in Berlin in 1987 with its stage-set rooms, are only two examples out of many.

Momi-Zelt
Projekt 189, 1991
Future Systems

Momi-Zelt
Projekt 189, 1991
Future Systems

with Uncle Walt and have any greater relevance to humanity than being just colourful marketing binges, there must be some reassessment of their values and agendas. Anything else is simply rearranging the deckchairs in the Titanic."[31]

Nur selten wurden seither neue transportable Konstruktionen entwickelt. Einige der Ausnahmen sind Entwicklungen für „post-disaster-situations", in denen große Menschenmengen temporäre Unterkunft benötigen;[32] das Buckingham Palace Besucher-Kartenhäuschen von Michael Hopkins; das Projekt 189, mobiles Zelt für Sonderveranstaltungen des „Museums for the Moving Image" in London von Future Systems; die Wanderbühne der „Neuen Metropol" in Hamburg von Klaus Latuske; die „Airtecture"-Präsentationshalle von Festo in Esslingen, deren statische Konstruktion aktiv auf das Steuerungselement, das mit einer Wetterstation in Verbindung steht, reagiert oder auch die Info Box am Potsdamer Platz. Die Info-Box am Potsdamer Platz von Schneider/Schumacher ist ein leuchtend roter, aufgeständerter, demontierbarer, 62,50 m langer, 15 m breiter, 13 m hoher Ausstellungspavillon, der in seiner unverwechselbaren Signalhaftigkeit Besucher anlockt, „temporäre Kontinuität".[33]

Festo-Ausstellungshalle
Esslingen
Festo-presentation hall
Esslingen

Info Box
Potsdamer Platz Berlin
Schneider/Schumacher
Info Box
Potsdamer Platz Berlin
Schneider/Schumacher

In Seville in 1992, the first Expo since Brussels in 1958 took place on European soil. There were no great innovations in the pavilions and their interiors. They were large, expensive buildings with unrivalled costs for materials and construction: "But if future Expos are to fend

Buckingham Palace
Kartenhäuschen
Michael Hopkins &
Partner
Buckingham-Palace
Ticket box for visitors
Michael Hopkins &
Partner

Musical-Zelt
Neue Metropol
Hamburg
Musical traveling stage
Neue Metropol
Hamburg

off increasingly unflattering comparisons with Uncle Walt and have any greater relevance to humanity than being just colourful marketing binges, there must be some reassessment of their values and agendas. Anything else is simply rearranging the deckchairs in the Titanic."[31]

It is rare that architects are asked to develop a new transportable construction. Some of the exceptions are developments for "post-disaster situations" where large numbers of people require temporary accommodation.[32] Others, for example are the ticket box for visitors to Buckingham Palace by Michael Hopkins; Project 189, a mobile tent for special events of the Museum for the Moving Image in London by Future Systems; the travelling stage of the "Neue Metropol" in Hamburg by Klaus Latuske; the "Airtecture" presentation hall of Festo in Esslingen whose structural composition actively reacts to a control element which is linked to a weather station or the Info Box in Potsdamer Platz. The Info Box in Potsdamer Platz by Schneider/Schumacher is a glowing red construction. It can be erected and dismantled and is 62.5 m long, 15 m wide and 13 m high, an exhibition pavilion which attracts visitors with its unmistakable appearance. This is what one might refer to as "temporary continuity".[33]

In a time of cyberspace and virtual reality, the next step will be an imaginary and immaterial architecture whose forerunners are to be found in the gothic cathedrals and the glass palace as well as Speer's light dome, Le Corbusier's pavilion for Philips and laser installations of the 70's (Friedrich St. Florian, Laser Space, an architecture beyond solid material with electronically simulated space).

In the exhibition installations, "Aleph 1" and "Aleph 2", as well as "Fractal Cube" by Serge Salat and Francoise Labbe, reflections, lights and transparent elements produce an apparent infinity of space. The Netherlands pavilion for the Triennale 1996 in Milan by Ben van Berkel and Caroline Bos was designed with the computer. As a result, the building is not just conceived as an object but has other features: an acoustic and tactile program, climate and light, movements outside and inside. With the help of the computer, these aspects were combined and correlated. Changes in the information which were made during the design process alter the output, the consequence of which is that the input alters. An amorphous structure made of plywood on cement segments manufactured by computer according to a computer wire model – similar to a Moebius strip and also to the Breda-pavilion by Baldessari – supports the exhibition and is a projection surface at the same time. Video films, acoustics and interactive light installations as well as VR simulations form a virtual room. The reality thus conveyed is a projection of the viewer's own perception.[34] In an interview, Ben van Berkel was put

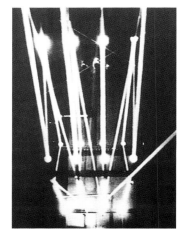

Laser Space
1970
Friedrich St. Florian
Laser Space
1970
Friedrich St. Florian

Aleph 2
Serge Salat /
Françoise Labbe
Aleph 2
Serge Salat /
Françoise Labbe

Projektion und Simulation

In der Zeit von Cyberspace und Virtual Reality wird der nächste Schritt eine imaginäre und immaterielle Architektur sein, als deren Vorläufer sowohl die gotische Kathedrale und der Glaspalast als auch der Speersche Lichtdom, Le Corbusiers Philips-Pavillon und Laser-Installationen der 70er Jahre (Friedrich St. Florian, Laser Space) zu finden sind; Architektur jenseits der festen Materie, als elektronisch simulierter Raum.

In den Ausstellungsinstallationen „Aleph 1" und „Aleph 2", sowie „Fractal Cube" von Serge Salat und Françoise Labbe wurde durch Spiegelungen, Lichter und transparente Elemente eine Schein-Unendlichkeit erzeugt. Der niederländische Pavillon für die Triennale 1996 in Mailand von Ben van Berkel und Caroline Bos wurde mit dem Computer entworfen. Das Gebäude ist dadurch nicht ausschließlich objekthaft gedacht, sondern mit anderen Aspekten: akustisches und taktiles Programm, Klima und Licht, Bewegungen außerhalb und innerhalb. Mit Hilfe des Rechners wurden diese Aspekte kombiniert und korreliert: Änderungen an der Information, die im Entwurfsprozeß vorgenommen wurden, ändern den output, was zur Folge hat, daß der input sich ändert. Eine amorphe Struktur aus Sperrholzplatten auf Betonsegmenten, die computerunterstützt nach einem Computerdrahtmodell gefertigt wurde – ähnlich einem Möbiusband und auch dem Breda-Pavillon von Baldessari –, trägt die Ausstellung und

Niederländischer Pavillon
Triennale di Milano, 1996
Ben van Berkel /
Caroline Bos
Netherlands pavilion
Triennale in Milan, 1996
Ben van Berkel /
Caroline Bos

„ ... Videofilme, Akustik und interaktive Lichtinstallationen sowie VR-Simulationen formen einen virtuellen Raum."

ist Projektionsfläche. Videofilme, Akustik und interaktive Lichtinstallationen sowie VR-Simulationen formen einen virtuellen Raum: die vermittelte Wirklichkeit als Projektion der eigenen Wahrnehmung.[34] In einem Interview wurde Ben van Berkel die Frage gestellt: „It seems to me that for you a building is not defined as an object, but an assemblage of scenarios. Is this a consequence of the influence of media within daily life?" Er antwortete: „You are referring to what I have myself termed the 'tactile programme'; the difference with an assemblage of scenarios is that I allow a far greater penetration and interactivity of haptic and programmatic data in the development of the architecture of a building. The assemblage of scenarios suggests a linguistic, critical approach, which is less interesting to us."[35]

Fliegende Bauten: ob Science-Fiction-Projekte, Zelte, Jahrmarkt- und Zirkusbauten, ob Pavillon als temporäre Bauform oder Ausstellungsarchitektur bis hin zu den Sprengkünsten und -künstlern – das Fliegende faszinierte den Entwerfer durch alle Epochen.

Demontage XV
Flatz
Demontage XV
Flatz

the following question: "It seems to me that for you a building is not defined as an object, but an assemblage of scenarios. Is this a consequence of the influence of media within daily life?" He answerered: "You are referring to what I have myself termed the 'tactile programme'; the difference with an assemblage of scenarios is that I allow

" ... Video films, acoustics and interactive light installations as well as VR simulations form a virtual room. ..."

a far greater penetration and interactivity of haptic and programmatic data in the development of the architecture of a building. The assemblage of scenarios suggests a linguistic, critical approach, which is less interesting to us."[35]

Temporary buildings can be science-fiction projects, tents, fairgrounds and circus buildings. They can be pavilions as temporary structures, exhibition architecture or even works by artists of the explosion. Whatever their form, the temporary has fascinated designers throughout the ages.

Anmerkungen

1 s.a. Bernard Rudofsky; Architektur ohne Architekten, Eine Einführung in die anonyme Architektur; Salzburg und Wien 1989 (1964).

2 Richtige Caravans als Unterkünfte für Schausteller findet man ab dem Beginn des 19. Jhds., die Zigeuner oder Roma adaptierten den Caravan erst 1860.

3 Wiederaufbau 1852-1854 als Crystal Palace II in Sydenham bei London.

4 Sigfried Giedion; Bauen in Frankreich, Eisen, Eisenbeton; Leipzig / Berlin 1928; S. 58.

5 so z. B. Henry van de Veldes Theater, Joseph Hoffmanns Österreichisches Haus und Peter Behrens' Festhalle

6 wie schon auf der Leipziger Bauausstellung 1914 der Eisenbau

7 Paul Scheerbart; Glasarchitektur; München 1971 (1914); S. 25.

8 Sigfried Giedion; Walter Gropius, Mensch und Werk; Stuttgart 1954; S. 47.

9 s.a.: Hans Sedlmayer; Die Kugel als Gebäude, oder: Das Bodenlose; in: Klaus Jan Philipp (Hrsg.); Revolutionsarchitektur; Braunschweig 1990; original in: Das Werk des Künstlers 1; 1939/40; S. 279-310. Gebaute Kugelhäuser finden sich z.B. auf der Dresdner Hygieneausstellung von 1928 oder auf der „Jahresschau deutscher Arbeit", 1937, ebenfalls in Dresden (das sechsgeschossige „Café Kugelhaus").

10 Le Corbusier; 1922 – Ausblick auf eine Architektur; Braunschweig 1982; S. 78f., S. 89, S. 92.

11 zurückgehend auf Ideen der Landwirtschaftsausstellung 1923 in Moskau

12 Deutsche Linoleum Werke

13 GAGFAH: Gemeinnützige Aktiengesellschaft für Angestelltenheimstätten AHAG: Sommerfeldscher Baubetrieb (ausführender und beauftragter Betrieb)

14 Laszlo Moholy-Nagy; zit. nach: Sigfried Giedion; Walter Gropius, Mensch und Werk; Stuttgart 1954; S. 49.

15 mit M. De Renzi und A. Valente

16 z. B. Adalberto Libera mit dem Italienischen Pavillion

17 zit. nach: Schweizer Ausstellung an der „Triennale di Milano" 1936; in: Alfred Roth; Die neue Architektur; Erlenbach-Zürich 1948; S. 176.

18 s.a. Henry Russel-Hitchcock; Die Architektur des 19. und 20. Jahrhunderts; München 1994.

19 Bereits 1929 hatte Alvar Aalto einen interessanten provisorischen Bau, eine Orchesterbühne der Ausstellung für die 700 Jahr Feier der Gründung von Finnlands erster Hauptstadt Turku entwickelt: eine licht gekurvte hölzerne akustische Wand mit plastischer Qualität.

1 See also: Bernard Rudofsky: Architektur ohne Architekten. Eine Einführung in die anonyme Architektur, Salzburg und Wien 1964.

2 Real caravans as homes for fairground and circus performers can be found from the beginning of the 19th century. The gypsies adapted the caravan in 1860 for the first time.

3 Rebuilt in 1852 - 1854 as Crystal Palace II in Sydenham near London.

4 Sigfried Giedion: Bauen in Frankreich, Eisen, Eisenbeton, Leipzig / Berlin 1928, p.58.

5 For example, Henry van de Velde's Theater, Joseph Hoffmann's Österreichisches Haus (Austrian House) and Peter Behren's Festhalle (Festival Hall)

6 as already at the Leipzig building exhibition in 1914 for iron construction

7 Paul Scheerbart: Glasarchitektur, München 1971 (1914), p. 25.

8 Sigfried Giedion: Walter Gropius, Mensch und Werk, Stuttgart, 1954; p. 47.

9 See also: Hans Sedlmayer: Die Kugel als Gebäude, oder: Das Bodenlose, in: Klaus Jan Philipp (Ed.): Revolutionsarchitektur, Braunschweig 1990; original in: Das Werk des Künstlers 1, 1939 / 40, p. 279-310. Spherical houses were built, e.g. at the Dresden hygiene exhibition 1928 or at the "Jahresschau deutscher Arbeit" (annual show of German work), in 1937, also in Dresden (the Sixfloor "Café Kugelhaus").

10 Le Corbusier: 1922 – Ausblick auf eine Architektur, Braunschweig 1982, p. 78ff; p. 89; p. 92.

11 based on ideas from the agricultural exhibition in Moscow in 1923

12 Deutsche Linoleum Werke

13 GAGFAH: Gemeinnützige Aktiengesellschaft für Angestelltenheimstätten (non-profit company for homes for employees) AHAG: Sommerfeldscher Baubetrieb (Sommerfeld construction company – company acting as client and contractor)

14 Laszlo Moholy-Nagy; cit. from: Sigfried Giedion: Walter Gropius, Stuttgart 1954, p. 49.

15 with M. De Renzi and A. Valente

16 E.g. Adalberto Libera with the Italian pavilion.

17 cit. from: Swiss exhibition at the Triennale di Milano in 1936; in: Alfred Roth: Die neue Architektur, Erlenbach-Zürich 1948, p. 176.

18 cf. Henry Russel-Hitchcock: Die Architektur des 19. und 20. Jahrhunderts, Munich 1994

20 Paolo Nestler; Ausstellung und Messen, Situation 1956; in: Bauen + Wohnen 1956; München 1956; S. 435.

21 Luciano Baldessari; zit. nach: Ulrich Conrads / Hans G. Sperlich; Phantastische Architektur; Stuttgart 1983 (1960); S. 164.

22 Le Corbusier; Mein Werk; Stuttgart 1960; S. 186.

23 Drive-in Housing. Ein Vorschlag von Mike Webb; Archigram; Basel / Berlin / Boston 1991; S. 54.

24 Erläuterung zur pneumatischen Wohneinheit Villa Rosa von 1968; in: Coop Himmelblau; Architektur muß brennen; Graz 1980; S. 13.

25 "The cloud is an organism for living. The structure is mobile, the space can be modified. The building materials are air and dynamics." In: Coop Himmelb(l)au, Austria, Biennale di Venezia 1996; Klagenfurt 1996; S. 17.

26 aus einem Brief von Johannes Canis an Bodo Rasch 1938; in: Zirkel 9; Bodo Rasch, Ideen, Projekte, Bauten, Werkbericht 1924 bis 1984; Stuttgart 1984; S. 57.

27 zit. nach einem Interview mit Frei Otto von Roland Conrad; in: Baumeister Nr. 11 / 1966; S. 17.

28 Bereits 1838 in Jonathan Swifts „Gullivers Reisen" fliegt die Idealstadt Laputa und kann die Sonne verdunkeln, und auch Wenzel Habliks kristalline Luftkolonie von 1908 ist eine Architektur zwischen Luftschiff und Heiß-luftballon.

29 Bernard Tschumi im Gespräch mit ARCH+, Andreas Ruby; in: ARCH+ 119/120 Dezember 1993; Aachen 1993; S. 70.

30 Ein spezielles Thema, welches eine ausführlichere Betrachtung nötig machen würde und auf das auch im historischen Abriß nicht näher eingegangen wurde, sind die Follies in der Gartenarchitektur (vgl. Schinkels Zeltzimmer im Schloss Charlottenhof ca. 1829). Weitere kleine zeitgenössische temporäre Bauten ent-standen 1990 in Groningen: Videopavillions von Coop Himmelblau, Peter Eisenmann, Zaha Hadid, Rem Kool-haas und Bernard Tschumi.

31 Catherine Slessor; Seville and Expo; in: The Architectural Review No. 1144; London Juni 1992; S. 2.

32 Und wo nicht einfache Container-„Städte" aufgetürmt werden können, weil Sie nur unzerlegt zu transpor-tieren und dadurch zu sperrig sind – dieses Thema beschäftigte schon beispielsweise Buckminster Fuller, Alvar Aalto und Future Systems.

33 Ulrich Brinkmann; Ein Kessel Buntes; in: RISZ Dez. 1996; Dortmund 1996; S. 16.

34 siehe dazu: Ben van Berkel / Carolin Bos; RealSpace in Quick Times; in: ARCH+ 131, April 1996; Aachen 1996; S. 42f.

35 Ben van Berkel im Fax-Interview von Northon Flores Troche / Rajan Ritoe / Peter Trummer; in: Berlage Paper 18; Amsterdam 1996.

Konstruktion als formaler Schwerpunkt

Konstruktion und architektonischer Ausdruck – die Entwicklung der Gestalt

Werner Sobek

Structural Design and Architectonic Expression – Development of the Gestalt

Das Vorübergehende, vielleicht an unterschiedlichen Orten für jeweils beschränkte Zeitspannen neu Entstehende, das ist der Grundcharakter der fliegenden Bauten. Gleichzeitig wird diese Architektur präzise wie sonst kaum auf einen Bauherrn oder ein Produkt hin orientiert. Sie unterstützt Intention und Exposition in extremer Weise, indem sie sich einerseits bis zur Nichterkennbarkeit zurücknimmt oder andererseits, indem Architektur, Intention und Exposition zu einer Einheit verschmelzen.

Die Konstruktion als wesentlicher Bestandteil der Architektur besitzt bei den fliegenden (oder besser: temporären) Bauten einen besonderen Stellenwert. Die konstruktive Durchbildung des temporären Baus bestimmt beispielsweise ganz wesentlich dessen Funktionieren: Einfache Montage, Zerlegbarkeit, standardisierte Bauelemente, beschränkte Stückgrössen und Minimierung des Massenaufwandes sind eine Reihe von Schlagworten aus dem Bereich der Bautechnik. Größere Spannweiten und Gebäudehöhen, neue Werkstoffe und Konstruktionsweisen stehen für das Bemühen, den gestalterischen und technischen Anspruch eines Produktes, eines Exponates, durch die Konstruktion des Gebäudes selbst zu bestätigen oder gar zu überhöhen.

Konstruktion ist bei den temporären Bauten auch deshalb wesentlicher Bestandteil der Architektur, weil andere, den Entwurf wesentlich beeinflussende Parameter und Anforderungen bei fliegenden Bauten entweder nicht oder nur in reduzierter Form zur Anwendung kommen. Hierzu gehören beispielsweise Aspekte des Wärme- und Schallschutzes. Brandschutzanforderungen können wegen der zumeist sehr spezifischen Benutzungsmuster dieser Gebäude häufig genauso reduziert werden, wie die durch temporäre Bauten aufzunehmenden Belastungen aus Schnee und Wind. Darüber hinaus erlaubt man beim Benutzungskomfort häufig gewisse Einschränkungen.

The basic character of temporary buildings is that they are impermanent or that they are only created at different locations for limited periods of time. At the same time, this kind of architecture like hardly any other is precisely oriented to a specific client or product. It is an extreme method of supporting intention and exposition and it does so by withdrawing almost to the limits of visibility, on the one hand, and, on the other, by fusing itself with intention and exposition to form a unified whole, the gestalt.

Structural design as an essential component of architecture is of special importance where temporary buildings are concerned. The constructional aspects of temporary buildings have a basic determining influence, for example, on their function: ease of assembly and dismantling, standardised components, a limited number of parts and minimisation of mass are a series of key concepts in the field of structural engineering. Larger spans and higher buildings, new materials and methods of construction are all signs of an effort to underline or even exaggerate the design-related and technical claims made by a product, an exhibit, through the construction of the building itself.

Durch die reduzierte Zahl von Auflagen und Restriktionen wird das Entwerfen zunächst einfacher. Die architektonische Intention läßt sich rigoroser formulieren, die Demonstration einer technischen und ingenieurkünstlerischen Position kann hierin, wenn immer angemessen, einfacher eingewoben werden. Es ist deshalb nicht verwunderlich, daß beispielsweise Ausstellungsbauten immer wieder zu Avantgardeprojekten der Ingenieurkunst, der Baukunst wurden. Gerade Ihnen kommt eine grundlegende Bedeutung als Innovationsquelle, als Experimentierfeld der Architektur, zu.

Diese Innovationsquelle muß aber auch gepflegt werden. Der teilweise absurde Wildwuchs architektonischer Beliebigkeiten, der insbesondere in den vergangenen beiden Jahrzehnten viele wichtige Ausstellungen durchzog, hat zu einer kritischen, teilweise a priori distanzierten Benutzerhaltung geführt. Dies gilt zunehmend auch für das restliche Gros der fliegenden Bauten. Es bedarf deshalb einer gemeinsamen Anstrengung aller Bauschaffenden, die fliegenden Bauten zur Baukunst zurückzuführen. Die stetige und enge Zusammenarbeit von Architekten und Ingenieuren ist Grundvoraussetzung hierfür.

Wie aber entwickelt man innerhalb eines Planungsteams die architektonische Gestalt von Gebäuden, die diesem sehr spezifischen Anforderungsprofil der fliegenden Bauten unterliegen? Diese Frage ist nicht generell und pauschal beantwortbar, da man zumindest diejenigen beiden Gruppen von Bauten unterscheiden muß, bei denen entweder die Konstruktion von vollkommen untergeordneter Bedeutung und von rein dienender Funktion ist oder derjenigen Gruppe, bei der das Tragwerk und die konstruktive Durchbildung die architektonische Erscheinung ganz wesentlich prägen (sollen). Nur diese zuletzt beschriebene Gruppe soll nun Gegenstand weiterer Überlegungen sein.

For temporary buildings, structural design is also an essential component of architecture because other parameters and requirements which normally have an important influence on the design are either not applied at all or only to a limited extent. These include, for example, heat insulation and soundproofing. Due to the usually very specific use to which these structures are put, fire-protection requirements can often be reduced to the same extent as measures for withstanding snow and wind. In addition, certain limitations are acceptable as regards comfort of use.

Due to the reduced number of regulations and restrictions, preparing a conceptual design is, at the beginning, much easier. The architectonic intention can be formulated more rigorously and the demonstration of a technical, engineering or artistic standpoint can, wherever appropriate, be woven into this intention more easily. It is therefore no wonder, for example, that exhibition buildings are always among the avant-garde projects of engineering and architecture. Exhibition buildings can be of fundamental importance as a source of innovation and as a field of experimentation in architecture.

This source of innovation, however, has to be nurtured. The sometimes absurd proliferation of architectural fancies which has permeated many important exhibitions during the past two decades has led to a critical, partly a priori, distanced stance on the part of the users. This is becoming more and more the case with other temporary buildings. A joint striving of all those concerned with building is therefore required to bring temporary buildings back into the domain of architecture. Continuous and close cooperation between architects and engineers is a basic prerequisite for this.

Insbesondere dort, wo die tragende Konstruktion die architektonische Erscheinung wesentlich beeinflußt, wo Tragwerk und Konstruktion Architektur werden, müssen die in einen Entwurfsprozeß eingebundenen Ingenieure ein hohes Maß an Verständnis architektonischer Zusammenhänge besitzen. Ansonsten können ihre Beiträge nie optimal zielorientiert sein. Dies wird evident angesichts der Tatsache, daß es für jedes konstruktive Problem üblicherweise eine ganze Reihe von „richtigen" Lösungen gibt. Entgegen der immer wieder genannten Hypothese der Existenz einer einzigen „klassischen" und „richtigen" Lösung wird die tatsächlich vorhandene Lösungsvielfalt durch die Vielzahl unterschiedlicher verwendbarer Baustoffe, durch die unterschiedlichen Bauweisen (Formen und Fügen der Komponenten) und durch die Vielzahl unterschiedlicher Strukturkonzepte (aufgelöste oder geschlossene Bauteile, biegebeanspruchte Konstruktionen versus ausschließlich normalkraftbeanspruchte Konstruktionen, etc.) beschrieben. Damit kann man aber als Ingenieur für jede Bauaufgabe eine ganze Palette von konstruktiven Lösungen entwickeln, die alle die vorgegebenen ökologischen und ökonomischen Randbedingungen erfüllen.

Die Frage, welche dieser vielen jeweils vorhandenen Lösungen in den Entwurfsprozeß, in die gemeinsame Arbeit von Architekt und Ingenieur eingebracht werden soll, führt direkt auf eines der großen und bis heute nicht erkannten Probleme der Ingenieurbaukunst, den Stilbegriff. Es mag Außenstehende überraschen, aber ein Stilbegriff, wie er z.B. in der Architektur, der Malerei oder der Musik vorhanden ist, ist in der Ingenieurbaukunst nicht existent. Es ist natürlich selbstverständlich, daß die Zuordnung einzelner Arbeiten zu unterschiedlichen Stilen stets mit gewissen Unvollkommenheiten verbunden ist. Dies soll hier nicht zur Diskussion stehen.

But how can a planning team develop an architectonic gestalt for buildings which are subject to the very specific range of requirements for temporary buildings? This question cannot be given a general and uniformly valid answer as a distinction has to be made between those two groups of structures where, in the one case, either structural design is of completely subordinate significance and has merely a supporting function or, in the other group, where the load-bearing structure and structural layout have (or are intended to have) a considerable influence on the architectonic appearance. Only the latter type of structures will be considered in the following.

Especially where the load-bearing structure has a strong influence on the architectonic appearance, where the load-bearing aspects and the structure itself become the architecture, the engineers involved in the design process have to have a great deal of understanding for architectonic interrelationships. Otherwise, their contributions can never quite live up to the stated goal. This is made evident by the fact that, for every structural problem, there is usually a whole series of "correct" solutions. Contrary to the repeatedly quoted hypothesis of the existence of a unique "classical" and "correct" solution, the variety of solutions which actually exist is prescribed by the variety of different construction materials which can be used, by the different methods of building (shapes and joints of the components) and by the many different structural approaches (dispersed or closed sections, constructions subjected to bending stress versus constructions which are only subjected to normal forces). But for any structural problem, an engineer can develop a whole range of solutions which fulfil all the ecological and economic boundary conditions which are stipulated.

The question as to which of the many possible solutions should be implemented in the initial design process, in the joint work of architect and engineer, leads directly to one of the great and, up to now, unrecognised problems of structural engineering: the concept of style.

Das Bemerkenswerte ist, daß ein Stilbegriff und damit die Bewußtwerdung, daß Ingenieurbaukunst, insbesondere hinsichtlich ihrer formalen und konstruktiven Erscheinung differenzierbar, in einzelne Stile unterscheidbar ist, vollkommen fehlt. Damit mangelt es noch schwerwiegender an der Fähigkeit zur Bewertung einer Ingenieurkonstruktion hinsichtlich formaler und konstruktiver Aspekte durch die Ingenieure selbst. Die Folge hieraus ist, daß es weltweit nur sehr wenige Ingenieure gibt, die innerhalb eines Entwurfsprozesses zusammen mit Architekten und anderen Planern in optimaler Weise Konstruktionen als dominanten, stimmigen und inhärenten Bestandteil von Architektur entwerfen können. Letzteres wiederum hat zur Konsequenz, daß die Architekten häufig selbst versuchen, Tragwerk und konstruktive Durchbildung eines Gebäudes zu entwickeln. Ingenieurmäßige Brillianz, wie sie gerade bei der hier diskutierten Gruppe der fliegenden Bauten gefragt ist, kann dabei nicht erreicht werden.

Die Entstehung der Gestalt als Symbiose aus den Beiträgen der einzelnen am Entwurfsprozeß Beteiligten, die Entstehung von baukünstlerischer Leistung bedarf dringend und zwingend einer grundlegend veränderten Ausbildung der Ingenieure und einer darauf aufbauenden, neuen Qualität in der Zusammenarbeit zwischen Architekten, Ingenieuren und allen anderen am Prozeß des Bauschaffens Beteiligten. Fliegende Bauten werden aufgrund ihrer eingeschränkten und sehr spezifischen Anforderungsprofile ein ideales Arbeitsfeld für diese Entwurfteams darstellen – mit grundlegenden und positiven Auswirkungen auf die ingenieurmäßige und architektonische Qualität der Baukunst der fliegenden Bauten selbst.

It may surprise outsiders but a concept of style such as there is in architecture, painting or music, is non-existent in structural engineering. It is, of course, self-evident that the allocation of individual pieces of work to different styles is always associated with a certain amount of uncertainty. This is not a question to be discussed here.

What is remarkable is that a concept of style and thus the awareness that structural engineering, especially with regard to its formal and design-related aspects, can be differentiated into individual styles is totally lacking. Even more seriously, engineers themselves lack the ability to evaluate an engineering structure with regard to its formal and design-related aspects. The consequence of this is that there are only a few engineers in the world who are fully capable of designing structures as a dominant, coherent and inherent component of the architecture when working together with architects and other planners within an overall process of design. The consequence of this is that the architects themselves often try to plan the load-bearing structure and the constructional layout of a building. Engineering brilliance – especially necessary for the kind of buildings designated as temporary – cannot be achieved in this way.

The creation of the gestalt as a symbiosis of the contributions from the individuals participating in the design process namely the performance of architectural art, requires urgently and necessarily a completely different education for engineers and, based on this education, a new level of quality in the work shared between architects, engineers and all the others involved in construction. Temporary buildings, due to the limited and very specific requirements placed on them, will be an ideal field of activity for this kind of design team – with fundamental and positive effects on the engineering and architectural quality of the temporary buildings themselves.

Der temporäre Pavillon

Sobek und Rieger für BMW
Sobek und Rieger for BMW

The Temporary Pavilion

Das Haus BMW verlegte auf der IAA 1995 in Frankfurt seinen Ausstellungsbereich erstmals aus den Messehallen hinaus, auf einen zentralen Platz innerhalb der Messe Frankfurt. Hierzu entstand ein eigenes, temporäres Gebäude: der BMW-Pavillon. Er besteht aus einer hochleistungsfähigen Membrane, die zeltartig über eine Reihe von bis zu 30 m hohen Stahlgittermasten gespannt wurde. Entlang ihres Randes wird die Membrane von seilabgespannten Stahlstützen gehalten, die Fassade selbst besteht aus pneumatisch stabilisierten Kissen und aus Glaslamellen. Letztere lassen sich öffnen und bilden so mit den ebenfalls durch Glaslamellen bedeckten, augenförmigen Öffnungen in der Membrane im Bereich der Mastspitzen ein natürliches Lüftungssystem für das Gebäude.

Der Pavillon überdeckt eine rechteckige Grundrißfläche von 100 m x 50 m Seitenlänge. An einer der schmalen Seiten ist der Grundriß zusätzlich halbkreisförmig ausgeschnitten. Dieser halbkreisförmige Ausschnitt umfaßt den auf dem Platz stehenden Obelisk sowie eine Reihe von Wasserbecken und Springbrunnen.

Entsprechend den erforderlichen kurzen Auf- und Abbauzeiten wurde das – temporäre – Gebäude in allen seinen konstruktiven Details standardisiert und auf eine extrem schnelle Montier- bzw. Demontierarbeit ausgelegt. Die erforderlichen Fundationsarbeiten wurden vorab so ausgeführt, daß sich die Oberkanten der einzelnen Fundamente unterhalb des zum Platz gehörenden Pflasterbelages und der Kiesbettung befinden.

At the IAA 1995 in Frankfurt, the BMW company, for the very first time, moved its exhibition area out of the trade-fair halls to a central square inside the Frankfurt trade-fair grounds. An independent temporary building was erected here: the BMW pavilion. It consists of a high-quality membrane which is stretched over a series of steel lattice masts up to 30 m in height. The membrane is held along its edges by cable-anchored steel supports. The facade itself consists of pneumatically stabilised cushions and glass lamellas. The latter can be opened and, together with the eye-shaped openings covered with glass lamellas in the membrane near the top of the masts, form a natural ventilation system for the building.

The pavilion covers a rectangular area whose sides are 100 m x 50 m in length. On one of the short sides, there is a semi-circular cut-out. This semi-circular area contains the obelisk in the square and a series of water basins and fountains.

Eine Randabspannung, bestehend aus einem druckbeanspruchten Pfosten und zwei Abspannseilen.
An anchor at the edge consisting of a tensioned post and two anchoring cables.

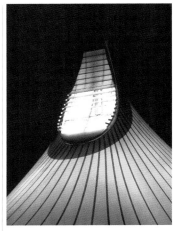

Eine Detailaufnahme des
Pavillons bei Nacht.
Die zur Durchlüftung
geöffneten Glaslamellen
sind sowohl im Bereich
der Fassade wie auch
an der Mastspitze gut
erkennbar.

A detailed photo of the
pavilion at night. The
glass lamellas opened for
ventilation purposes
are easily detectable in
the facade and at the
top of the masts.

In order to comply with the very short
assembly and dismantling times allowed,
the temporary building was standardised
in regard to all its structural details and
designed for extremely fast assembly
and dismantling. The required foundation
work was done in advance so that the
upper edges of the individual foundations
were below the paved surface and gravel
bedding of the square. For assembly,
only a few paving stones and some gravel
had to be removed. The steel masts or
their feet could then be fastened to the
foundations with a few bolts. The dismantling procedure was similar. After the
pavilion was taken down, the foundations
remain invisible under the square and
wait for the next assembly of the building.

Für die Montage waren dann jeweils nur
wenige Pflastersteine und etwas Kies
zu entfernen. Danach konnten die Stahl-
masten bzw. ihre Fußpunktkonstruktion
mit wenigen Schrauben an den Funda-
menten befestigt werden. Ähnlich einfach
verlief die Demontage. Nach dem Abbau
des Pavillons ruhen die Fundamente
unsichtbar unter dem Platz und warten
auf die nächste Montage.

Ein bemerkenswertes
Konstruktionsdetail: Seile
beranden die textile
Fläche und führen die
Kräfte auf einen voll-
kommen gelenkigen
Punkt, über den die Kräf-
te dann in die Randab-
spannung gelangen. Die
Gelenkigkeit der Lage-
rung ermöglicht zwän-
gungsfreie Verformung-
en der Membranhaut,
insbesondere während
der Montage.

A noteworthy detail of
the construction. Cables
are attached along the
edges of the textile sur-
face and conduct the
forces to a fully articulated point through which
the forces can then be
absorbed by the ancho-
ring. The articulated
retention system enables
deformation of the
membrane, especially
during assembly.

Der temporäre Pavillon

Aussteller
BMW AG, München
Messe
IAA – Internationale Automobilausstellung
Jahr
1995

The Temporary Pavilion

Exhibitor
BMW AG, Munich

Ort
Frankfurt
Größe
ca. 5.000 qm
Architektonische und ingenieurmäßige
Bearbeitung
Sobek und Rieger, Stuttgart
Werner Sobek, Stefan Schäfer, Peter Mutscher,
Thomas Müller
Formfindung und Zuschnittsberechnung
Tensys Limited, Bath, Dr. David Wakefield
Ausstellungskonzeption
Zinsmeyer & Lux, Zürich
Bauausführung
Koit High-Tex, Rimsting
Ausführung der Glaslamellenkonstruktion
Glastec, München
Fotos
Werner Sobek, Ralph Richter

Trade fair
IAA – international automobile exhibition
Year
1995
Location
Frankfurt
Size
approx. 5000 sq. metres
Architectural and engineering consultants
Sobek und Rieger, Stuttgart
Werner Sobek, Stefan Schäfer, Peter Mutscher
Thomas Müller
Form finding and cutting-pattern analysis
Tensys Limited, Bath, Dr. David Wakefield
Exhibition conception
Zinsmeyer & Lux, Zurich
Construction work
Koit High-Tex, Rimsting
Glass lamella construction
Glastec, Munich
Photos
Werner Sobek, Ralph Richter

Erinnerungswürdige Räume in modularer Bauweise

Burkhardt Leitner

Memorable Rooms in Modular Form

Das Einfache und das Komplexe

Am Anfang: hat der Paravent Pate gestanden? Jenes flexible und variable Element, welches schon seit Jahrhunderten und in den unterschiedlichsten Kulturen weltweit Räume gliedert, Diskretion schafft, Räume aber auch öffnen und definieren kann? Das erste Ausstellungssystem Leitner_1, vor 30 Jahren entwickelt, ist reduziert auf neutrale Flächen und einfachste Verbindungs-Elemente – genauso rasch und flexibel veränderbar wie jene Paravents. Der gestalterische Grundgedanke ist der, nicht in Erscheinung zu treten, sondern Hintergrund zu sein für die individuelle Präsentation. Die absolute Wandelbarkeit ist Programm, die einfachste Handhabung Gesetz.

Später steigen die Anforderungen und die Systeme wachsen mit diesen Ansprüchen. Komplexe Systemstrukturen schaffen unbegrenzt wandelbaren architektonischen Raum. Dennoch gilt die Forderung weiterhin: der gestalterische Grundgedanke ergibt sich aus der Konstruktion, kein „designtes" Element schiebt sich selbstsüchtig in den Vordergrund. Alles ordnet sich der Struktur unter, welche wiederum den Hintergrund bildet für die individuelle Inszenierung mit Inspiration. Montageprinzipien sind so optimiert, daß schnell, einfach und ökonomisch immer wieder neue Räume entstehen können. Einblicke werden verwehrt oder gewährt, Deckenstrukturen weiten sich nach oben oder bilden ein beruhigendes Dach und sind der Ort für Integration von Lichtinszenierung. Doppelgeschossigkeit erweitert die architektonischen Möglichkeiten und schafft mehr Raumökonomie.

The Simple and the Complex

The beginnings: has the screen produced any offspring? A flexible and variable element which has divided up rooms in the most varied of cultures all over the world for centuries, it ensures discretion but can also open up rooms and define them. The first exhibition system, Leitner_1, developed 30 years ago, is reduced to neutral surfaces and the simplest of linking elements – a system which can be altered just as quickly and flexibly as screens. The basic idea is for them not to be visible but to act as a background for the individual presentation. Absolute flexibility is the aim and simple handling is an absolute must.

Later, the requirements increase and the systems grow with these demands. Complex system structures create architectonic space which can be altered in unlimited ways. But one requirement continues to exist: the basic design concept should result from the structural combination of parts. There is no particular "designed" element which egoistically pushes itself into the foreground. Everything is subordinate to the overall structure which, in turn, forms the background to an individually inspired setting. The principles of assembly are improved so that new areas can be created quickly, simply and economically again and again. Views are blocked off or opened up, ceiling structures stretch upwards or form a comforting roof and accommodate the lighting for setting the scene. Double-levels extend the architectonic possibilities and ensure more economy of space.

The challenge

The central factor in the development of a trade-fair system is its function as a back-up element, i.e. its invisibly effective benefits. The challenge is to unify the demands placed on individual trade-fair construction – which is without limits – with the advantages of modular systems. The advantages of these systems are, without doubt, that they are ecological (parts can be recycled, waste is avoided) and economical (cost reduction due to recycling and avoidance of waste and due to the speed with which they can be assembled and dismantled).

Der Anspruch

Schwerpunkt bei der Entwicklung eines Messe-Systems ist die dienende Funktion, d.h. der unsichtbar wirksame Nutzen. Die Herausforderung ist die Vereinigung der Ansprüche an den individuellen Messebau „ohne Grenzen" mit den Vorteilen von modularen Systemen. Zweifellos liegen die Vorteile dieser Systeme in der Ökologie (Wiederverwendbarkeit, Abfallvermeidung) und in der Ökonomie (Kostenreduzierung durch Wiederverwendbarkeit und Abfallvermeidung, und durch schnellen Auf- und Abbau). Aber nicht allein diese beiden Kriterien sind wichtig. Genauso wichtig ist es, daß Systeme den hohen Anforderungen der Kreativen gerecht werden. Nur dann sind sie für Architekten, Planer und Designer geeignetes Instrumentarium, um unverwechselbare Firmenpräsentationen in Szene zu setzen. Da in Zukunft die platte Produktschau noch mehr als bisher durch professionell inszenierte Unternehmenspräsentation abgelöst werden wird, darf es nicht mehr heißen: Individualität kontra System, sondern Individualität als System. Das Messesystem muß geeignet sein, im kreativen Dialog mit dem Kunden unverwechselbare Lösungen zu erarbeiten, welche auf der Messe die Haltung des Unternehmens vermitteln. Ein- und dasselbe System wirkt je nach Verwendung völlig anders. Einfache Integrationsmöglichkeiten von Materialien aller Art ermöglichen dieses. Reduzierte und der Konstruktion folgende Gestaltung hat außerdem den Vorteil der optischen Langlebigkeit bei vielfacher und vielfältiger Verwendbarkeit. Einfachheit in Ästhetik und Funktion läßt das System als selbstverständliches Bau-Element in den Hintergrund treten und dominiert nicht die Wirkung des Messeauftritts. Daß saubere Detaillösungen Robustheit und damit Langlebigkeit des Produktes garantieren, versteht sich dabei genauso von selbst, wie die Durchschaubarkeit von Montageprinzipien.

Die Perspektive

Die Herausforderung bei zukünftigen System-Entwicklungen: noch mehr Reduktion bei noch mehr Individualisierung. Es wird viel geredet über „virtual reality", dennoch ermöglichen nur reale Räume und Orte den Handschlag und das persönliche Gespräch. Und nur reale Systeme schaffen die Struktur für diese Räume und Orte – aber ganz diskret und im Hintergrund, bitteschön.

But it is not only these two criteria which are relevant. It is just as important that systems can fulfil the high requirements that creative people place on them. Only then can they be a suitable instrument for the architects, planners and designers whose task it is to stage unmistakable company presentations.
Since, in future, the uninspired display of products will be replaced to an even greater extent by the professionally staged presentation of a company, the old idea of "individuality versus system" has to be changed to "individuality as system". The trade-fair system must be such that uniquely identifiable solutions can be worked out in a creative dialogue with the customer so as to illustrate the style of the company at the trade fair.
One and the same system can have a completely different effect, depending on how and what it is used for. Simple methods of integrating materials of all kinds can facilitate this. A "reductionist" design which complies with the pre-given structure also combines the advantage of optical longevity with multiple and variable usability. Simplicity in its aesthetic and functional aspects allows the system to act in the background as a taken-for-granted element of the construction and to avoid dominating the appearance of the stand. The fact that clean, detailed solutions guarantee robustness and therefore longevity is as self-evident as the comprehensibility of the principles of assembly.

Perspective

The challenge for future development of these systems is to achieve an even greater level of reduction with more individualisation. There is a lot of discussion about virtual reality but shaking hands and face-to-face discussions are only possible inside real rooms and at real locations. And only real systems create the structure for these rooms and locations but, of course, discreetly and in the background, if you don't mind.

Reduzierte Konstruktion

Klar gegliederte Architektur demonstriert
die konstruktiven Möglichkeiten des
Systems in der Doppelstock-Ausführung.
System: constructiv PILA

Clearly delineated architecture demonstrates
the constructional possibilities of the system
in a double-level version.
System: constructiv PILA

Reduzierte Konstruktion

Reduced Structural Design

Company
Burkhardt Leitner constructiv GmbH & Co,
Stuttgart
Trade fair
EuroShop
Year
1996
Location
Düsseldorf
Size
Basic area 115 sq. metres, total 165 sq. metres
Design
Burkhardt Leitner constructiv
Work done by
Burkhardt Leitner constructiv
Photos
Bernd Kammerer

Aussteller
Burkhardt Leitner constructiv GmbH & Co,
Stuttgart
Messe
EuroShop
Jahr
1996
Ort
Düsseldorf
Größe
Grundfläche 115 qm, gesamt 165 qm
Gestaltung
Burkhardt Leitner constructiv
Ausführende Firma
Burkhardt Leitner constructiv
Fotografie
Bernd Kammerer

Komplexe Systemstrukturen

Burkhardt Leitner constructiv
für Zeyko
Burkhardt Leitner constructiv
for Zeyko

Complex System Structures

In warmem, wohnlichem
Ambiente präsentiert Zeyko
sein neues Küchenkonzept
„Mobilo".
System: constructiv PILA

In a warm, cosy ambience,
Zeyko presents its new kitchen
design "Mobilo".
System: constructiv PILA

Aussteller
Zeyko Schwarzwälder
Küchenmöbelwerke GmbH, Althengstett
Messe
Internationale Möbelmesse
Jahr
1996
Ort
Köln
Größe
ca. 560 qm
Gestaltung
Burkhardt Leitner constructiv
Andreas Boll, Zeyko
Ausführende Firmen
Burkhardt Leitner constructiv, Messebausystem
Coenen, Systemaufbau
Zeyko, Inneneinrichtung und Aufbau
Fotografie
Bernd Kammerer

Complex System Structures

Company
Zeyko Schwarzwälder Küchenmöbelwerke
GmbH, Althengstett
Trade fair
Internationale Möbelmesse (international
furniture exhibition)
Year
1996
Location
Cologne
Size
approx. 560 sq. metres
Design
Burkhardt Leitner constructiv
Andreas Boll, Zeyko
Work done by
Burkhardt Leitner constructiv,
trade-fair construction system
Coenen, system construction
Zeyko, interior furnishings and installation
Photo
Bernd Kammerer

Innovative Lösungen für die
industrielle Reinigungstechnik
Innovative solutions for
industrial cleaning systems

Transluzente
Messestandarchitektur

Burkhardt Leitner constructiv
für Dürr Ecoclean
Burkhardt Leitner construktiv
for Dürr Ecoclean

Translucent Trade-Fair
Stand Architecture

Filigran, schwebend, fast immateriell –
In transluzenter Architektur präsentiert
Dürr die neue Generation seiner modular
aufgebauten Kompakt-Anlagen.
System: constructiv INSIDE

Filigree, floating, almost immaterial –
In translucent architecture, Dürr presents
the new generation of its modular compact systems. System: constructive INSIDE

Aussteller
Dürr Ecoclean GmbH, Filderstadt / Monschau
Messe
Hannover Messe
Jahr
1996
Ort
Hannover
Größe
72 qm
Gestaltung
Burkhardt Leitner constructiv
Ausführende Firmen
Burkhardt Leitner constructiv
Fotografie
Bernd Kammerer

Translucent Trade-Fair Stand Architecture

Company
Dürr Ecoclean GmbH, Filderstadt / Monschau
Trade fair
Hanover Trade Fair
Year
1996
Location
Hanover
Size
72 sq. metres
Design
Burkhardt Leitner constructiv
Work done by
Burkhardt Leitner constructiv
Photo
Bernd Kammerer

Messestände und Architektur – eine ganz persönliche Betrachtung

Carl Holste

Wenn man Aussteller befragen würde, ob ihr Messestand geplant wurde, würde wohl jeder „ja" sagen. Bei der Frage „Ist Ihr Messestand Architektur?" wird man dagegen wahrscheinlich verunsichert reagieren. Dabei ist jedoch alles, was im ursprünglichen Sinn gebaut wird, das was unsere Umwelt belästigt, belastet oder erfreut und bereichert, Architektur. Es findet also immer ein Prozeß statt, der zu einem Produkt führt, das irgendwie – gut oder schlecht – gestaltet ist.

Bei meiner Arbeit steht an erster Stelle das Konzept. Dies besteht aus einer umfassenden Analyse, aus der Sichtung von Möglichkeiten, Gegegebenheiten, Vorgaben und Anforderungen. Hier wird die Aufgabe ganz abstrakt bearbeitet – vielleicht wäre auch Treatment das richtige Wort. Es werden klare Anforderungen aufgestellt für die Funktion, die räumliche Gestaltung, die Information, die Präsentation und den Charakter. An zweiter Stelle steht der Entwurf mit der Konzeption im Hinterkopf. Es wird eine Gestaltungsidee, eine Umsetzung in architektonische Gebilde, erarbeitet.

Als drittes folgt die technische Umsetzung dazu. Hier gibt es eine durch den Entwurf bestimmte Grundkonzeption, die den Willen des Gestalters sichtbar macht. Machbarkeit und Bezahlbarkeit sind zu überprüfen – Einzeldetails sind bis zum letzten festzulegen und zu entwerfen.

Den wichtigen Abschluß des Gesamtprozesses bildet die gestalterische Überwachung. Kurze Planungs- und Bauzeiten führen oft dazu, daß Planen und Bauen gleichzeitig geschieht. Dies bringt mit sich, daß Planer und Ausführender viel miteinander reden müssen, um die Produktqualität zu erreichen, die man im Entwurf definiert hat. Technisch-organisatorische Kompetenz, Sachverstand und gegenseitige Akzeptanz haben hier einen hohen Stellenwert.

Trade-Fair Stands and Architecture – a very personal view

If exhibitors were to be asked if their trade-fair stand had been planned, each of them would probably say "Yes". But asked if their stand is architecture, they would probably react with uncertainty. Yet everything which has been built in the original sense, anything which contaminates and pollutes, or pleases and enriches our environment is architecture. There is always a process which leads to a product that is somehow designed – either well or badly.

In my work, the overall design concept comes first. This consists of a comprehensive analysis as regards the possibilities, the given situation, the stipulations and the requirements. Here, the task is dealt with completely abstractly – perhaps treatment would be the right word. Clear demands are made regarding function, spatial layout, information, presentation and character. The second stage is a draft of the design, with the basic conception of the stand always at the back of my mind. A design idea is then worked out, namely how to convert the abstract conception into an architectural structure.

The third stage is technical implementation. There initially exists a basic conception which is determined by the draft design and discloses the intention of the designer. An investigation has to be made to see if the approach is feasible and if it can be paid for, and individual aspects also have to be worked out and planned down to the smallest detail.

Monitoring of the design aspects is the final important activity within the whole process. Short planning and construction times often lead to planning and construction work taking place at the same time. This entails that the planner and those carrying out the construction work have to consult each other frequently in order to attain the product quality which has been defined in the draft design. Technical and organisational expertise, specialist understanding and mutual acceptance are extremely important here.

Stützen und Träger

atelier holste
für Bergmann + Langer
atelier holste
for Bergmann + Langer

Supports and Beams

Die Aufgabe: Das Unternehmen des Bauherrn ist ein mittelständischer Handwerksbetrieb, der sich mit außergewöhnlichen Lösungen im Stahl- und Metallbau befaßt. NE-Metalle wie Aluminium, Kupfer und Messing spielen ebenso eine wichtige Rolle wie Edelstahl. Besonderer Wert wird auf die handwerkliche Verarbeitung und die materialgerechte Lösung von Details gelegt. Der Messestand sollte in der eigenen Werkstatt gefertigt werden und er sollte mehrfach einsetzbar, also modular im Aufbau sein.

Zielgruppen: Architekten, Innenarchitekten, öffentliche Bauherren, Kaufhäuser, Banken und Messebauer.

Überlegungen zum Produkt: Es gibt keine auszustellende Produktpalette, das Produkt ist letztlich der Messestand selbst mit seinen vielfältigen Materialien und Details, die das Know-How des Unternehmens sichtbar machen.

Material: Für den Bau steht eine große Auswahl von Materialien zur Verfügung, dennoch soll der Stand keine Materialsammlung werden, die aussieht wie ein Baumarkt.

Konstruktion/Details: Bei der Konstruktion und den Detailausbildungen muß es darum gehen, metallgerecht und materialtypisch zu entwerfen.

Kommunikation: Der Messestand selbst muß diese Botschaft vermitteln und auch haptisch erlebbar machen.

The task: The client's company is a medium-sized business which provides services in the field of unusual steel and metal construction. Non-precious metals such as aluminium, copper and brass play just as important a role as stainless steel. Special value is placed on skilled metal working and detailed solutions which fit in with the specific materials being used.

Der Entwurf: Auf der quadratischen Grundfläche wird ein Raum gebildet, der durch eine gebogene Wand nach hinten abgeschlossen ist. Über die Diagonale verläuft ein ebenfalls gebogener und nach vorn hin ansteigender Hauptträger, der im hinteren Bereich durch drei Portale läuft und vorne in einem doppelten Stützenpaar aufliegt. Die bewußte Nutzung der Perspektive soll Größe und Dynamik erzeugen. Vor die runde Wand wird als Galerie eine erhöhte Besprechungsebene gesetzt, erschlossen durch einen zentralen Treppenaufgang. Die Decke wird aus verschiedenen konstruierten Einschichtgitterbindern gebildet, die zentral an der Hauptstütze zusammenlaufen.

Nach außen hin bilden konische, gewölbte Dachelemente den Standabschluß. Darunter stehen speziell entwickelte Leuchtvitrinen, in die Dias ausgeführter Objekte gespannt sind. Die konstruktiven Stahlteile sind sandgestrahlt und klar lackiert oder mit einer blauen Oberfläche versehen.

Die gebogene Rückwand ist rohes, gezundertes Blech. In den ausgebrannten Flächen werden verschiedene Metalle und Oberflächen als farbige Collagen präsentiert. Der Fußboden und alle anderen Holzteile sind aus Buche gefertigt, die Geländer aus Edelstahl mit Glasfüllungen.

The trade-fair stand was to be prepared in the company's own workshop, in other words it was to be given a modular structure.

Target groups: Architects, interior designers, public clients, department stores, banks and trade-fair builders.

Product information: There was no range of products to be exhibited. The product was the trade-fair stand itself with its variety of materials and details which demonstrate the know-how of the company.

Materials: A large selection of materials were available for construction but the stand was not to be a collection of materials which looks like a building market.

Structural design/details: During structural design and detailed preparation, the aims was to draw up plans which do justice to the materials used and which illustrated the typical uses of such materials.

Communication: The trade-fair stand itself had to pass on the message and also allow visitors to experience the products by handling them directly.

The draft plan: On the available square area, a space is formed which is closed off at the rear by a curved wall. A main beam which is also curved and rises towards the front is arranged diagonally. At the rear, this beam passes through three portals and, at the front, rests on a double pair of supports. The intentional use of perspective is meant to generate a feeling of size and dynamism. In front of the curved wall, there is an elevated discussion level in the form of a gallery which is reached by means of a central ascending staircase. The ceiling is made of variously constructed single-layer lattice trusses which converge centrally at the main support.

The stand is covered over by conical, domed roof elements. Under this, there are specially developed illuminated showcases in which slides of exhibited objects are hung. The steel cables are sand-blasted and coated with a clear lacquer paint or given a blue coating.

The curved rear wall is rough, scaled metal sheeting. In the burned out areas, different metals and surfaces are presented as coloured collages. The floor and other wooden parts are made of beech, the railings made of stainless steel with glass fillings.

Stützen und Träger

Aussteller
Bergmann + Langer GmbH, Lingen/Ems
Messe
Constructec
Jahr
1994
Ort
Hannover

Größe
10 m x 10 m = 100 qm,
zweiseitig offener Eckstand
Standkonzeption, Entwurf
atelier holste, Martin Kniesburges,
Isernhagen
Realisation
Bergmann + Langer GmbH
Projektleitung
Klaus Langer
Fotos
Heiko Wrensch

Supports and Beams

Exhibitor
Bergmann + Langer GmbH, Lingen/Ems
Trade fair
Constructec
Year
1994
Location
Hanover
Size
10 m x 10 m = 100 sq. metres,
corner stand open on two sides
Stand conception, design
atelier holste, Martin Kniesburges,
Isernhagen
Implementation
Bergmann + Langer GmbH
Project management
Klaus Langer
Photos
Heiko Wrensch

Eine Methode,
Lösungsansätze zu finden

Karlheinz Thurm

A Method for Finding Specific Approaches
to Specific Problems

Es gibt auch heute noch keine Zweifel daran, daß gestaltete Objekte Aufgaben zu erfüllen haben. Kunst- und Designobjekte können unterhalten oder ökonomische, ökologische, ergonomische und andere Funktionen erfüllen.

Die Aufgabe ist die Ausgangssituation, je genauer die Aufgabe gestellt ist oder das zu erreichende Ziel beschrieben wird, um so präziser und objektiver läßt sich das gestaltete Objekt im Rückblick auf die Aufgabe bewerten.

Je nach Kategorie der Aufgaben gibt es sehr präzise Briefings, Lastenhefte, Vorgaben usw. aber auch nebulöse Wunschvorstellungen. Dabei können genau beschriebene Wünsche durchaus als Aufgabe dienen, besonders im Bereich des Kommunikationsdesigns.

Denn anders als z.B. im Automobildesign, wo es meistens um Absatzzahlen in Zielgruppenbereichen geht, werden beim Kommunikationsdesign diese Absatzzahlen oder andere Geschäftsanbahnungen vorbereitet. Nicht nur Vorgaben wie Gebrauchsfeld, Ergonomie, Sicherheit, Kostenrahmen usw. liegen im Automobildesign sehr konkret vor, auch die Kataloge fast aller Scheinwerfer-, Türgriff-, Radausschnitt-, Dachsäulen-Lösungen usw. sind den Designern verfügbar (Das heißt nicht, daß es einfach wäre, neue Trends im Automobildesign zu kreieren, die die gewünschten Umsatzzahlen erreichen).

Im Kommunikationsdesign läuft dagegen die Fluktuation der Trends rasch, heterogen und relativ unbeobachtet ab, so daß andere Anforderungen an den Designer gestellt werden. Ein Teil dieses Gestaltungsbereichs ist Messestanddesign, ein Konglomerat von Konstruktion, Beleuchtung, Grafik, Typografie, AV-Medien, Literatur, Menschen.

Even today, there is no doubt that designed objects are expected to perform certain tasks. Objects of art and design can entertain or perform economical, ecological, ergonomic and other functions.

The initial situation is that there is a problem to be solved. The more accurately the problem is represented or the more exactly the goal to be achieved is described, the more precisely and more objectively can the designed object be evaluated with regard to the problem at hand.

Depending on the category of problem, there can be very precise briefings, specifications, stipulations etc. but also nebulous wishes and ideas. Exactly described wishes are the best way to illustrate the problem to be tackled, especially in the field of communications design.

The reason is that, in contrast to automobile design for example where sales figures in target-group areas are most important, these sales figures or other prospective business are prepared in communication design. Not only are stipulations such as the field of application, safety, costs and so on very concretely apparent in automobile design. A catalogue of nearly all the problems relating to headlamps, door handles, wheel sections, roof columns etc. is also available to the designer (This does not mean that it would be easy to create new trends in automobile design and achieve the desired sales figures).

In communications design, in contrast, fluctuations in trends are rapid, heterogeneous and relatively un-monitored so that other requirements are placed on the designer. One part of this field of design is trade-fair design, a conglomerate of structural planning, lighting, graphics, typography, media, literature and people.

In der Praxis stellt sich häufig heraus, daß die Aufgabenstellung oder das Briefing unpräzise, unvollständig, unpriorisiert sind und dadurch unterschiedliche Auslegungen des Ziels zugelassen werden. Rückfragen nach den Problemen, den Teilzielen, der Situation, nach den Mitbewerbern können helfen, das Zielfeld einzugrenzen. Besser ist es jedoch, in einer Art Interview, mit der verantwortlichen Person, das Ziel nach einer bestimmten Methode gemeinsam zu formulieren.

Nach der Aufgabe folgt das Finden des Lösungswegs, der Strategie oder des Konzepts. In einer ersten Teamrunde werden Umformulierungen vorgenommen; der Kunde wählt für ihn neuartige und interessante Umformulierungen aus.

In einer weiteren Teamrunde werden zu dieser Auswahl Ideen kreiert. Danach entscheidet erneut der Kunde, welche Ideen weiter zu verfolgen sind. Dies setzt sich so lange fort, bis ein Lösungsansatz gefunden wird.

Diese von Bernd Rohrbach entwickelte Methode bietet mehrere Vorteile: durch die Einbeziehung des Kunden oder Auftraggebers kann das Ziel nicht verfehlt werden. Durch die Umformulierungen und die spezielle Fragetechnik werden ungewöhnliche, neue Ideen gefunden. Durch die Teamrunden wird in kürzester Zeit ein größeres Ideenspektrum erschlossen, als dies von einer einzelnen Person geleistet werden kann. Und außerdem wird im Vorfeld nicht über Formales gesprochen, um keine Einengungen festzulegen.

Erst nach dieser inhaltlichen Findung und verbalen Formulierung der Lösung beginnt die formale Umsetzung. Auch dafür gibt es Methoden, im Team zu arbeiten, um eine größere Bandbreite von Teillösungen in kürzerer Zeit zu erhalten, aus denen letztlich die erfolgversprechenden Teile zum Entwurf ausgearbeitet werden.

In practice, it often happens that descriptions of work to be done or the briefing are imprecise, incomplete and lack priorities, the result being that different interpretations of the goal are permitted. Questions regarding the problems, the subordinate aims, the actual situation and competitors can help to delimit these goals. It is better, however, to jointly formulate the goals by conducting a kind of interview with the person responsible in accordance with a specific method.

After the problem has been defined, an attempt is made to find a solution, a strategy or a concept. In a first team meeting, reformulations are made after which the client selects those new formulations which he finds innovative and interesting.

In a further team meeting, ideas for this selection are created. Then, the client again decides which ideas should be pursued. This continues until a solution is found.

This method, as developed by Bernd Rohrbach, offers several advantages. By involving the client or contracting company, achievement of the goals is guaranteed. By means of reformulations and special questioning techniques, it is possible to come up with unusual and innovative ideas. In team meetings, a larger range of ideas is developed than can be thought up by a single person. And, last but not least, formal matters are not discussed in the foreground, the consequence being that no restrictions are laid down.

Only after a solution has been found and verbally formulated does formal implementation begin. There are also methods of teamwork for obtaining a wider range of partial solutions in a very short time. The most promising features of these partial solutions can then be expanded to create the design itself.

Innen- und Außentragwerk

Für den Messestand der Firma Dietrich auf der EuroShop 1993 wurde folgende Aufgabe formuliert: Wie kann man erreichen, daß alle Besucher der EuroShop (die Zielgruppe) mit uns sprechen wollen?

Das Kommunikationsziel lautete: Dietrich Display baut individuelle Messestände in hoher Qualität!

Die Vorgaben:
· Das Dietrich-System „cubus" muß eingesetzt werden!
· Der Stand soll sich laufend verändern!
· Das Gesamtbudget ist im Vergleich zur EuroShop 1990 um die Hälfte reduziert!

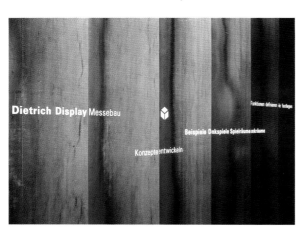

Das in Teamsitzungen gefundene Konzept – der Rahmen des Standes besteht aus dem System „cubus", und an wandhohen Charts, die verschiebbar sind, werden laufend Präsentationen gehalten – wurde folgendermaßen umgesetzt: In ein äußeres Tragwerk aus „cubus", das die Außenbeleuchtung trug, wurde ein inneres Tragwerk gestellt. In dieses innere Tragwerk wurden auf den vier Seiten, auf Rollen verschiebbar, 3 m hohe, 70 cm breite, 3 mm starke, roh gesinterte Stahlblechfahnen gehängt. Diese Fahnen trugen außen Firmenlogo, Firmenbezeichnung und den neuen Slogan „Denken, Planen, Bauen". Innen dienten diese Fahnen als Präsentationscharts. Sie waren bedruckt mit Darstellungen von realisierten Messeständen, Konstruktionsdetails, Dienstleistungsangeboten und anderen Texten für die Präsentationen.

So entstand ein großer Gesprächsraum, der sich fortwährend veränderte, denn die Charts wurden laufend, entsprechend der Gespräche, verschoben. Von allen Seiten konnte man in den Stand sehen und die Präsentationen verfolgen, das machte neugierig. Das Publikum betrat ungehindert den Stand und beteiligte sich an den Gesprächen.

Internal and External
Load-bearing Structures

For the trade-fair stand of the Dietrich company at the EuroShop 1993 the following question was put: "How can all the visitors to the EuroShop (the target group) be persuaded to talk to us?"

The message to be put across:
Dietrich Display builds individual trade-fair stands to a high level of quality!

The stipulations:
· The Dietrich System „cubus" must be used!
· The stand should continually alter!
· The overall budget is to be reduced by half in comparison to EuroShop 1990!

During the team meetings, an underlying concept was found. The general framework of the stand was to consist of the "cubus" system and wall-high charts which could be moved in order to allow continuous presentations. This concept was implemented as follows. An internal load-bearing structure was placed inside an external load-bearing structure consisting of "cubus" which carried the exterior lighting. Roughly sintered steel-sheet flags, 3 m high, 70 cm wide and 3 mm thick which could be moved on rollers were hung on four sides of the internal structure. The outside of the flags bore the company logo, the company name and the new slogan "Think, Plan, Build". On the inside, these flags acted as presentation charts. They were printed with illustrations of trade-fair stands which had already been built, details of construction, services offered and other texts for the presentations.

The result was a large discussion area which was continually being modified as the charts were repeatedly moved, depending on the particular subject being talked about. It was possible to see into the stand from all sides and follow the presentations, the result being that people became curious. The public had unobstructed access to the stand and took part in the discussions.

Innen- und Außentragwerk

Aussteller
Dietrich Display GmbH, Friolzheim
Messe
EuroShop

Internal and External
Load-bearing Structures

Exhibitor
Dietrich Display GmbH, Friolzheim
Trade fair
EuroShop
Year
1993
Location
Düsseldorf
Size
144 sq. metres
Design layout
Dietrich Team, 3 to 5 employees
Construction work
Dietrich Display GmbH
Photos
Ralf Baumgarten

Jahr
1993
Ort
Düsseldorf
Größe
144 qm
Gestaltung
Dietrich Team, 3 - 5 Mitarbeiter
Bauten
Dietrich Display GmbH
Fotos
Ralf Baumgarten

Internal and External
Load-bearing Structures

Komposition
volumetrischer Körper

Die Analyse des Produkts – der „genius loci" beim Messestand

Stefan Zwicky

The Analysis of the Products –
the "genius loci" in trade-fair construction

Ähnlich wie bei festen Bauten, bildet beim Messestand, respektive bei Ausstellungsarchitektur, die Analyse des Orts und der Produkte oder Dienstleistungen, die zur Ausstellung gelangen sollen, eine wichtige Grundlage. Mit dem Ort sind der Messeplatz, der Bauplatz, die Erschliessung, die Nachbarschaft und die spezifischen Baubedingungen gemeint.

Die Analyse der Produkte oder Dienstleistungen ist die Suche nach der eigentlichen Botschaft und sollte den Entwurf maßgeblich mitbeeinflussen, im besten Fall aus ihr herauswachsen. Dies ist die Gewähr für ein authentisches, auf das ausgestellte Produkt bezogenes Resultat, oder anders gesagt, der Entwurf sollte unmittelbar mit dem Produkt verknüpft sein. Die Analyse des Produkts bringt, wenn sie ernsthaft betrieben wird, automatisch eine Reihe von unterschiedlichen Lösungsansätzen, die so oft von Unternehmern gesucht werden, um eine Abgrenzung und Unterscheidung gegenüber der Konkurrenz zu erreichen. „... Denn alleine mit der konsequenten Durchführung eines Formgedankens wird nicht allein ein künstlerisches Ziel erreicht, im Gegenteil: Eine allzu leicht abzulesende Gesetzmäßigkeit hat das Verdächtige einer rein intellektuellen Konstruktion. Die Freude an der Geometrie zum Beispiel, sollten wir nicht mit der Architektur verwechseln. Wirklich schöpferische Architektur beginnt dort, wo ein vernunftmäßig erkennbares Gesetz unvermutet an einer Stelle gesprengt wird, wo also scheinbar etwas 'Falsches' gemacht wird, was sich in der Folge auf einer Ebene auswirkt, die sich dem rein vernunftmäßigen Ausdeuten entzieht." (Ernst Gisel) Ein allgemeingültiges Rezept für die Gestaltung von Messeständen gibt es somit nicht. Die Lösungen ergeben sich aus den spezifischen Aufgabenstellungen immer wieder neu.

Ein weiterer, wichtiger Punkt bei Messe- und Ausstellungsbauten ist die Kurzlebigkeit. Dies eröffnet in der Konstruktion und der Materialwahl immer wieder ungeahnte Möglichkeiten und macht dieses Genre, ähnlich wie die Installation in der Kunst, zum Experimentierfeld von neuen Gestaltungsmöglichkeiten. Der Messestand hat zudem, wie die Grafik, die große Chance, unmittelbar auf Zeitgeschmack, Tendenzen und Trends zu reagieren.

For trade-fair stands or exhibition architecture as well as for permanent constructions, an analysis of the location and the products or services to be exhibited is an important basic premise. The location means the trade-fair area, the construction area, access, the neighbourhood and the specific conditions of construction.

An analysis of the products or services is a search for the actual message to be conveyed and should have a determining influence on the design, should preferably develop naturally from the message. This guarantees an authentic result which is related to the exhibited product. In other words, the draft design should be directly linked to the product. An analysis of the product, if performed seriously, should automatically generate the series of different approaches which are so often sought after by company owners in order to delimit and differentiate themselves from the competition. "...Consistent implementation of a formal idea alone does not ensure attainment of an artistic goal. On the contrary, an all-too-visible regularity generates the suspicion that the construction is a purely intellectual creation. The joys of geometry, for example, should not be confused with architecture. Really creative architecture begins where a rationally detectable regularity is smuggled in unsuspectedly at a place where, to all appearances, something 'false' has been done, which has an effect on a level that withdraws from purely rational interpretation." (Ernst Gisel) A generally valid recipe for designing trade-fair stands does not therefore exist. The approaches taken are a result of the specific range of tasks which have to be confronted. The final solutions which are adopted are always in fact new ones.

An additional important factor with regard to trade-fair and exhibition structures is their short lifetime. This always opens up unsuspected possibilities regarding construction and materials and makes this genre, similar to installation in art, into a field of experimentation for new approaches to design work. The trade-fair stand, like graphics, also has the opportunity of directly reacting to contemporary taste, tendencies and trends.

Präsentations-Kästen

Presentation Boxes

„Schweizer Architekten entwerfen für Melchnau" lautete das Thema der Weberei Lantal Textiles Melchnau an einer Sonderschau der Messe Heimtextil 1993 in Frankfurt. Von Mario Botta, Ernst Gisel, Robert und Trix Haussmann, Jaques Herzog und Pierre de Meuron sowie Vincent Mangeat sollten sieben großformatige Bildteppiche verschiedener Techniken ausgestellt werden. Die Situation, die aus dem Konzept der Sonderschau Spectrum von Ulf Moritz entstand, war eine quadratische Fläche von 10 m x 10 m, einseitig offen.

"Swiss architects create designs for Melchnau" was the topic of the Lantal Textiles Melchnau weaving mill at a special exhibition during the Heimtextil trade fair in Frankfurt in 1993. Mario Botta, Ernst Gisel, Robert and Trix Haussmann, Jaques Herzog and Pierre de Meuron as well as Vincent Mangeat were to exhibit seven large-format tapestries produced with different techniques. The result, which arose out of a concept for the special exhibition range of Ulf Moritz, was a square area of 10 m x 10 m, open on one side.

Um dem individuellen Ausdruck der Teppiche gebührend gerecht zu werden, wurde jedem Ausstellungsstück ein kastenförmiges freistehendes Element zugewiesen. Diese Elemente, die vom Boden leicht abgehoben waren, bildeten mit einer geringen Raumtiefe einen Rahmen, der genügend Platz bot für Exponat und Umfeld, für Headline und Legende. Um die Teppiche zum Leuchten zu bringen, wurde, deren Farbgebung entsprechend, die Innenseite der Elemente mit neapelgelb, ziegelrot, anthrazit, hell- und dunkelblau unterlegt. Die frei in den Raum gestellten Elemente waren so angeordnet, daß ein fließender Galerieraum mit eigener Wegführung entstand. Die Teile waren, ohne sich zu berühren, so ineinander verschoben, daß keine toten Winkel entstanden und auch keine eigentliche Rückwand benötigt wurde.

Ein Element an der Frontseite des Stands trägt den Titel der Ausstellung und zeigt mit schwarz-weiß-Portraits die Autoren der Teppiche. Die Ausstellung steht auf einem neutralen, schieferfarbenen Sisalteppich und wird mit Bühnenscheinwerfern ausgeleuchtet.

Präsentations-Kästen

Presentation Boxes

Exhibitor
Lantal Textiles, Langenthal
Trade fair
Heimtextil (home textiles)
Year
1993
Location
Frankfurt
Size
100 sq. metres

Aussteller
Lantal Textiles, Langenthal
Messe
Heimtextil

Jahr
1993
Ort
Frankfurt
Größe
100 qm
Konzept und Gestaltung
Stefan Zwicky, Zürich
Ausführende Firmen
Strickler Reklame, Zürich
Fotos
Stefan Zwicky

Conception and design
Stefan Zwicky, Zurich
Work done by
Strickler Reklame, Zurich
Photos
Stefan Zwicky

CH-Kreativität

Sonderschau der Schweizer Möbelmesse International SMI Bern 95 vom 18.–22.5.1995

Christian Anderegg
Florin Baeriswyl
Christof Wuthrich
Eduard O. Baumann
Heinz Baumann
Catherine Bender
Carlo Parmigiani
Ueli Biesenkamp
Mario Botta
Peter Maria Brunner
Valentino Bruno
Lucas Buol
Marco Zünd
Andreas Bürkl
Matthias Buser
Daniel Buser
Andreas Christen
Christoph Dietlicher
Andreas Giupponi
Thomas Drack
Jean-Pierre Dovat
Hans Eichenberger
Kurt Erni
Gabi Faeh
Roland Fässer
Ueli Frauchiger
Jörg Grunder
Fritz Sieber
Frank Wirz
Susann Guempel
Urs Kamber
Kurt Greter
Alfredo W. Häberli
Christophe Marchand
Trix Haussmann
Robert Haussmann

Christoph Hindermann
Ubald Klug
Edith Meier
Franz Giger
Bruno Muff
Ruedi Müller
Werner Schmid
Peter Steinmann
Kurt Thut
Benjamin Thut
Gabriela Vetsch
André Riemens
Hanspeter Weidmann
Hannes Wettstein
Robert A. Wettstein
Martin Zbären
Martin Schäfer
Béatrice R. Zurlinden

Hochregale als Rahmen

Stefan Zwicky
für CH-Kreativität
Stefan Zwicky
for CH-Creativity

High Shelves as a Framework

„CH-Kreativität" war eine Sonderschau der Schweizer Möbelmesse, die mit zwei verschiedenen Themen 1994 und 1995 stattfand. Im ersten Jahr standen 21 ausgewählte Schweizer Hersteller im Zentrum. Diese wurden ergänzt durch eine Auswahl von Möbeln aus den 30er bis 60er Jahren, die immer noch oder wieder zu haben sind. Im zweiten Jahr wurden 20 Schweizer Designer vorgestellt und in der Mitte der Ausstellung mit aktuellen Prototypen, Editionenmöbeln oder Kleinserien ergänzt.

"CH-Creativity" was a special exhibition at the Swiss furniture fair which was held in both 1994 and 1995 with a different topic each year. In the first year, 21 selected Swiss manufacturers were focused on. These were complemented by a selection of furniture from the 30's to the 60's which are still obtainable or again on sale. In the second year, 20 Swiss designers were introduced and, in the middle of the exhibition, complemented with current prototypes, edition furniture or small series.

So that visitors could quickly recognise and distinguish items among the great variety of different products, a frame in the form of high shelves was assigned to each make of furniture and each designer. These shelves were intentionally constructed with simple roof battens and joiners plates, namely from poor materials, in contrast to the products. They did not therefore compete with the exhibited products but gave them a systematic framework. Each narrow side of the frame was covered with semitransparent material on which the relevant inscription was printed.

The shelves were placed in rows like a chess board on a rectangular surface of 460 sq. metres which was open on all sides. Two groups formed a centre, an open interior section. In this "patio", auxiliary products were exhibited on two low wooden platforms. Large suspended sheets of fabric curtained off these platforms and bore the headings and further information.

Um die Menge und die unterschiedlichen Produkte schnell erkennen und unterscheiden zu können, wurde jeweils jeder Marke und jedem Designer ein eigenes Gestell in Form eines Hochregals zugeteilt.

Diese Regale waren im Gegensatz zu den Produkten bewußt mit schlichten Dachlatten und Tischlerplatten, also aus armen Materialien konstruiert. Sie konkurrierten so mit den ausgestellten Produkten nicht und gaben ihnen einen ordnenden Rahmen. Jedes Gestell war auf einer Schmalseite mit einem halbtransparenten Stoff bespannt und mit der jeweiligen Beschriftung bedruckt.

Die Regale waren auf einer allseitig offenen rechteckigen Fläche von 460 qm schachbrettartig aufgereiht. Zwei Gruppen bildeten ein Zentrum, einen offenen Innenteil. In diesem „Patio" wurden ergänzende Produkte auf zwei niederen Holzpodesten ausgestellt. Große abgehängte Tücher, als Abschluß dieser Podeste, übernahmen die Funktion der Überschrift und weiteren Informationen.

Hochregale als Rahmen

Aussteller
SMI – Schweizer Möbelmesse International
Messe
Schweizer Möbelmesse International,
Sonderschau „CH-Kreativität"

Jahr
1994 und 1995
Ort
Bern
Größe
460 qm
Konzept und Gestaltung
Stefan Zwicky, Zürich
Ausführende Firmen
Strickler Reklame, Zürich
Fotos
Urs Siegenthaler, Stefan Zwicky

High Shelves as a Framework

Exhibitor
SMI – Schweizer Möbelmesse International
Trade fair
Schweizer Möbelmesse International
(Swiss furniture fair), special exhibition
"CH-Creativity"
Years
1994 and 1995
Location
Bern
Size
460 sq. metres
Conception and design
Stefan Zwicky, Zurich
Work done by
Strickler Reklame, Zurich
Photos
Urs Siegenthaler, Stefan Zwicky

Langlebiges Baukastensystem

Die Max Weishaupt GmbH war über die legendäre Ulmer Schule für Gestaltung seit den frühen 60er Jahren den formalen Ideen der Bauhaus-Schule verbunden. Als das Unternehmen ein neues Messestandkonzept wollte, sprach Siegfried Weishaupt auch mit Richard Meier.

Ein solches Standkonzept ist nicht für einen einzigen Messeauftritt gemacht. Das Baukastensystem von Meier ist für mindestens 10 Jahre gedacht. Die Primärkonstruktion besteht aus Aluminiumträgern, verkleidet mit weiß beschichteten Aluminiumblechen im Rastermaß 90 x 90 cm. Je nach Größe und Form des zur Verfügung stehenden Raums kann der Stand dem Platzangebot angepaßt werden.

Long-Life Modular System

The name of the Max Weishaupt company had been associated with the formal ideas of the Bauhaus school since the early sixties through the legendary Ulmer Hochschule für Gestaltung (Ulm School of Design). When the company was looking for a new trade-fair design, Siegfried Weishaupt also consulted Richard Meier.

Such a design for a stand is not created for just a single appearance at one trade fair. Meier's modular system is intended to last for at least 10 years. The primary construction consists of aluminium girders

Die pure Schlichtheit dieser Konzeption soll das Augenmerk des Betrachters auf den eigentlichen Ausstellungszweck, die Produkte, lenken und deren Qualität sichtbar machen.

panelled with white-coated aluminium sheet in a grid pattern of 90 x 90 cm. Depending on the size and shape of the area available, the stand can be adapted to the space available.

The pure simplicity of this conception is intended to attract the attention of the observer to the actual purpose of the exhibition, namely the products, and to illustrate their quality.

Langlebiges Baukastensystem

Aussteller
Max Weishaupt GmbH, Schwendi
Messe
ISH - Internationale Fachmesse
Sanitär Heizung Klima
Jahr
1995
Ort
Frankfurt
Größe
550 qm
Konzept
Richard Meier, New York
Umsetzung
MAV Studio, Hamburg
Godenrath, Preiswerk und Partner, Leonberg
Max Weishaupt GmbH, Schwendi
Fotos
Weishaupt-Werkfotos

Long-Life Modular System

Exhibitor
Max Weishaupt GmbH, Schwendi
Trade fair
ISH - Internationale Fachmesse
Sanitär Heizung Klima
(international fair for sanitary, heating
and air conditioning equipment)
Year
1995

Location
Frankfurt
Size
550 sq. metres
Design
Richard Meier, New York
Implementation
MAV Studio Hamburg
Godenrath, Preiswerk und Partner, Leonberg
Max Weishaupt GmbH, Schwendi
Photos
Weishaupt-Werkfotos

Die animierte Fassade

Der Anspruch des Fernsehprogramm-Anbieters Kabel 1 lag in der konsequenten Übersetzung einer neuen Corporate Identity und Programmstruktur in die Ausstellungsarchitektur. Sämtliche Inhalte der unternehmerischen Konzeption wurden dabei in ihrer Gesamtheit dargestellt und auf den Messeauftritt übertragen.

The Animated Facade

It was the wish of Kabel 1, a TV broadcasting company, that its new corporate identity and programme structure should be consistently reflected in the architecture of the exhibition. All aspects of the company's make-up were illustrated in their entirety and incorporated in the exhibition.

During the IFA 1995, a direct demonstration of the image the company claimed for itself was to be given on the exhibition platform. A "working area" was asked for which was to be simultaneously a showcase platform and an inviting meeting point for all media fans. An exclusive lounge was provided for business associates, giving them somewhere quiet to talk but letting them take part in the atmosphere of the trade-fair exhibition.

The stand was given its characteristic appearance by 6-metre-high, dynamically shaped CI-orange textile objects which translated the company's logo into the medium of the exhibition architecture. The themes of torsion, dynamics, aspiration and openness were interpreted very expressively but without competing with the logo itself.

The facade which was constantly reanimated in different ways by means of lighting effects drew the attention of the trade-fair visitor, attracted the eye into the interior of the stand and, in the stand itself, created a peaceful, relaxing atmosphere, just the right surroundings for being entertained. The imaginative sweeping layout of the actual stand area created information islands for each of the different programmes.

Dem Anspruch an das eigene Image sollte während der IFA 1995 dann der direkte Beweis auf der Bühne folgen. Gefordert war ein „Arbeitsplatz", der zugleich Showbühne und einladender Treffpunkt für alle Medienfans darstellte. Für Geschäftspartner war eine exklusive Lounge vorgesehen, die Ruhe zum Gespräch bot und gleichzeitig an der Atmosphäre des Messeauftritts teilhaben ließ.

Als standprägende Elemente entstanden 6 m hohe, dynamisch geformte CI-orangene Stoffvolumenkörper, die eine Übersetzung des Logos in das Medium der Ausstellungsarchitektur darstellen. Die Themen Torsion, Dynamik, Aufstreben und Öffnung werden ausdrucksstark interpretiert, ohne jedoch in Konkurrenz mit dem eigentlichen Logo zu treten.

Die mittels Licht ständig neu animierte Fassade zieht die Aufmerksamkeit des Messebesuchers auf sich, leitet die Blicke ins Innere des Stands und schafft im Stand selbst eine ruhige, entspannende Atmosphäre, den richtigen Rahmen, um sich unterhalten zu lassen. Durch die schwungvolle Grundrißgestaltung entstehen Informationsinseln für die unterschiedlichen Programme.

Die animierte Fassade

Aussteller
Kabel 1, Unterföhring
Messe
IFA – Internationale Funkausstellung
Jahr
1995
Ort
Berlin
Größe
ca. 440 qm
Entwurf
Steiner Design, München
Thomas Bauer, Frank Schaffrath
(Neu: messebauer GmbH)
Realisation
H. Steiner GmbH, Berg / Starnberger See
Fotos
Frank Böttner

The Animated Facade

Exhibitor
Kabel 1 TV, Unterföhring
Trade fair
IFA – Internationale Funkausstellung
(international broadcasting exhibition)
Year
1995
Location
Berlin
Size
approx. 440 sq. metres
Design
Steiner Design, Munich
Thomas Bauer, Frank Schaffrath
(New: messebauer GmbH)
Implementation
H. Steiner GmbH, Berg / Starnberger See
Photos
Frank Böttner

Haus im Haus –
Stadt im Kleinen

Emotionalität muß sein.
Stille kann sein.

Arno Design

Emotionality is Necessary. Silence can be.

Ein Aspekt steht bei jeder Lösung im Mittelpunkt: Emotionalität. Dem liegt die einfache Erkenntnis zugrunde, daß jeder Mensch sich emotional ansprechen läßt, aber durchaus nicht jeder auf Rationales reagiert. Stille kann – je nach Aufgabenstellung und Produkt – eine andere Maxime sein; in eine Oase der Ruhe zu kommen, ist für lärmerschöpfte Besucher eine Wohltat – selbst wenn es auf dem Stand durchaus nicht „ruhig" zugeht, was die Besucherfrequenz anbelangt.

Natürlich herrscht auf einem von Arno Design gestalteten „stillen" Stand kein Schweigen – wohl aber immer eine Atmosphäre der Ruhe. So war z.B. auf dem Stand der Sto AG bei der Farbe 1996 in München sehr wohl Musik zu hören – aber nicht als Berieselung, sondern als akustisches Gestaltungselement. In einem „Erlebnistunnel" durchschritten die Gäste verschiedenfarbige Räume. Und jeder Farbe war ein entsprechendes akustisches Element zugeordnet: Sphärenmusik im Eingangsbereich mit rotierenden Farbpaneelen, menschliches Herzklopfen im daran anschließenden roten Raum, der Gesang der Wale im blauen Raum und schließlich wieder Sphärenklänge in der Ausgangszone, wo die Symbolik der Farben auf einer Schriftwand erklärt wurde.

For every kind of trade-fair stand, there is one aspect of the design which is of central significance: emotionality. This assertion is based on the simple realisation that everyone responds when addressed in emotional terms but not all people react to the rational. But, depending on the specified aims and the product itself, silence can also be a maxim. Finding peace in an oasis of silence can be a great relief for visitors exhausted by the noise – even when a stand is not really a "peaceful" place as far as the frequency of visitors is concerned.

Of course, on a "silent" stand designed by Arno Design, silence does not exist – there is more an atmosphere of peace. At the company stand of Sto AG in Munich during Farbe 1996, for example, it was possible to hear music but it was not a constant stream; it was in fact an acoustic design element. In an "adventure tunnel", the guests walked through differently coloured areas. An acoustic element was allocated to each colour: the music of the spheres in the entrance area with rotating coloured panels, the human heartbeat in the red room adjacent, the singing of whales in the blue room and, finally, the sounds of the spheres again in the exit area where the symbolism of the colours was explained on a printed wall panel.

Der Erlebnistunnel

Die Aufgabe: Technologische Neuerungen und Produkt-Highlights aus dem Baubereich spektakulär erlebbar zu machen.

Die Lösung: Die Farben der neuartigen Baubeschichtungen werden zum ästhetischen Thema der Standarchitektur. Im Zentrum steht der „Erlebnistunnel" – eine Folge verschiedenfarbiger Räume, die das Farbangebot des Fassadenspezialisten Sto symbolisieren. Hinter einer Präsentationswand liegt der Besprechungsteil mit Bar und Küche.

The challenge encountered here was how to make the presentation of technological innovations and product highlights from the construction sector into a spectacular experience.

The answer was to arrange the colours used for the company's new kind of building coatings into an aesthetic theme of the stand architecture. At the centre of events was the "adventure tunnel" – a sequence of differently coloured areas which symbolised the range of colours supplied by Sto, a company specialising in facades. A discussion section with bar and kitchen was situated behind a presentation wall.

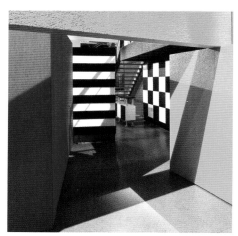

Der Erlebnistunnel

Aussteller
Sto AG, Stühlingen
Messe
Farbe 1996

The Adventure Tunnel

Exhibitor
Sto AG, Stühlingen
Trade fair
Farbe 1996
Location
Munich
Size
300 sq. metres

Ort
München
Größe
300 qm
Entwurf / Konzept
Claus Neuleib
Projektleitung
Karsten Reinhold
Technische Dekoration
Madeleine Wellern
Licht
Müller Music
Ausführung
Arno Design GmbH, München
Illustration
Margit Pawle
Fotos
Frank Kotzerke

Design / layout
Claus Neuleib
Project management
Karsten Reinhold
Technical decoration
Madeleine Wellern
Light
Müller Music
Work done by
Arno Design GmbH, Munich
Illustration
Margit Pawle
Photos
Frank Kotzerke

vebacom
>HIER IST DAS VEBACOM GEWINNSPIEL-TERMINAL :-?
>Return to...
>HIER IST DAS VEBACOM GEWINNSPIEL-TERMINAL :-?
>Return to...

Vernetzung und Verknüpfung
– die digitale Stadt

Tim und Rolf Heide
für Vebacom
Tim and Rolf Heide
for Vebacom

Networking and Interlinking
– the digital city

Der Entwurf basiert auf der Überlegung sich vernetzender Raum- und Weggebilde, die die Parallelität aktiver und passiver Wahrnehmung sowie die Möglichkeiten kommmunikativen Handelns auf verschiedenen Ebenen thematisiert. Grundsatz war, eine starke Symbolkraft auf der einen, als auch einen vielschichtigen sinnlichen Eindruck auf der anderen Seite zu erzeugen. Der strukturelle Ansatz soll auf eindringliche Weise die Möglichkeiten unhierarchischer Partizipation an den Telekommunikationsmedien dokumentieren.

The design is based on a conceptualisation of self-networking formations of space and pathways which thematise the parallelism of active and passive perception and the possibilities of communicative action on different levels. The basic intent was to create a powerful symbolism, on the one hand, and a many-layered sensorial impression, on the other. The structural approach taken is intended to vividly document the possibilities of non-hierarchical participation in the telecommunications media.

Christian Marquart

Vebacom ist Träger des nordrhein-
westfälischen Multimedia-Pilotprojekts
„Infocity NRW". Dies stand auch im
Vordergrund des Messeauftritts der Vebacom: Der Messestand sollte die Infocity –
die digitale Stadt – mit den privaten,
öffentlichen und geschäftlichen Anwen-
dungsbereichen von Multimedia und Telekommunikation in nuce abbilden.
Daneben sollte der Stand einen Überblick
über die derzeitigen Vebacom-Aktivitäten
geben, mit Schwerpunkt bei den Angeboten für Geschäftspartner.

Vebacom is acting as a sponsor of the
North Rhine-Westphalian multimedia pi-
lot project "Infocity NRW". This was also
placed in the foreground of Vebacom's
trade-fair appearance. The company's
stand was to be a nutshell representation
of Infocity – the digital city – showing

Der Entwurf des Vebacom-Messestandes
vom Team Rolf und Tim Heide (Hamburg /
Berlin) setzte das Thema Vernetzung /
Verknüpfung in eine sinnfällige architektonische Metapher um. Kernstück des
Entwurfs ist ein gegenläufiges Treppen-
system, gehüllt in zwei auf- bzw. ab-
steigende Röhren, die auf halber Höhe
einen „Knoten" bilden. Dem körperlosen,
virtuellen Thema setzt die Architektur
eine klare Form und eine entschiedene
Körperlichkeit entgegen. Obwohl für die
nötigen Räume – für das offene Foyer
im Erdgeschoß, einen Bühnenraum im
Obergeschoß und auch für abgeschlossene
Einheiten – gesorgt war, handelte es sich
in der Erscheinung doch um eine Architektur der Wege, eine Promenade. Die
Besucher wurden animiert, den Treppen
zu folgen, die Körpererfahrung des Publikums korrespondierte also dem Motiv des
bewegten Informationsflusses.

the private, public and commercial applications of multimedia and telecommunications. In addition, the stand was
intended to provide an overview of
current Vebacom activities with a main
focus on the products on offer to business
customers.

The initial design for the Vebacom trade-
fair stand by the team of Rolf and
Tim Heide (Hamburg / Berlin) converted
the theme of networking / interlinking
into an analogous architectonic metaphor.
The heart of the design was a contra-
rotating system of steps, enveloped in
two ascending and descending tubes,
intersecting half way up to form a "node".
The abstract virtual theme was contrasted
with an architecture of clear shapes and
a decidedly concrete appearance.

In seiner starken Plastizität und der gerichteten Verschränkung der Treppenläufe distanziert sich diese Architektur deutlich von dem, was gegenwärtig unter dem Begriff „Medienarchitektur"zur modischen Attitüde geworden ist. „Medienarchitektur" versucht, mit transparenten und optisch sich wandelnden Flächen, die als „Screens" und Monitore fungieren sollen, die Immaterialität der digitalen Medien nachzuahmen – letztlich ein vergebliches und am Ende meist peinliches Unterfangen. Rolf und Tim Heide fanden hingegen eine architektonische Figur, die – wenn man schon eine Anspielung vermuten will – eher als Hommage an den Zeichner M.C. Escher zu verstehen ist. Berühmt wurde seine Darstellung eines Klosters, dessen Kreuzgang sich auf dem Dach befindet: eine Treppe, deren Stufen je nach Richtung endlos hinauf bzw. hinab führen, und die doch nur um den Lichthof herumführt. Diese Architektur ist selbstverständlich nicht realisierbar – aber die Anspielung von Heide & Heide funktioniert dennoch. Besser könnte man die Schwierigkeit und die Herausforderung nicht illustrieren, die sich aus dem selbstreferentiellen Problem der Information über Information ergibt.

Im Kontrast zu dieser Architektur, die das informelle Paradox der immer noch schwer durchschaubaren neuen Medien thematisierte, standen die Show-Elemente des Event-Konzeptes:

Although enough space was left for the rooms which were needed – for the open foyer on the ground level, a stage area on the upper floor and for the closed-off units as well – the main feature of the stand was an architecture of pathways, a promenade. The visitors were encouraged to follow the steps so that the bodily experience of the public corresponded to the motif of a mobile flow of information.

In den „Röhren" wurde das Publikum buchstäblich beiläufig mit Bildern aus der Welt der Telekommunikation vertraut gemacht; avcontext hatte hier in Zusammenarbeit mit Michael Schirner ein synästhetisches Erlebnis aus Klang- und Bildwelten inszeniert, in Anlehnung an die populären Slotmachines. Tenor der Inszenierung: Multimedia ist ein gemeinsam erlebbares Ereignis, nicht vernetzte Isolation. Genauso sollte die Medienzukunft aussehen.

With its powerful vividness and the strategic intersecting of the staircases, this architecture clearly distanced itself from that which has now become a fashionable attitude under the heading of "media architecture". "Media architecture" tries to copy the immateriality of the digital media by using transparent and optically varying surfaces which are intended to act as "screens" and monitors. But this is a hopeless and, in the end, usually embarrassing undertaking. Rolf and Time Heide, in contrast, found an architectonic figure of speech which – if one wishes to suspect an allusion to something else – was rather to be understood as a homage to the artist, M.C. Escher. His portrayal of a monastery with its cloister on the roof is known universally: a staircase whose steps – whatever their direction – lead upwards and downwards without ever coming to an end but only circling a courtyard. This architecture, of course, cannot be actually built – but the allusion by Heide & Heide still works. It would not be possible to give a better illustration of the difficulty and the challenge involved in the self-referring problem of information about information. The show elements contained in the design concept for the event stood in stark contrast to this architecture which picked out as a central theme the informal paradox of the new and still difficult-to-comprehend media:

In the "tubes", the public was familiarised with images from the world of telecommunications in an almost by-the-way manner. avcontex had worked with Michael Schirner to stage a synaesthetic experience of the worlds of sound and image in a fashion somewhat similar to the popular slot machines. The tone of the setting was that multimedia is an adventure which can be experienced with others and not a world of networked isolation. This, according to the message, was just how the media should appear in future.

**Vernetzung und Verknüpfung
– die digitale Stadt**

Aussteller
Vebacom GmbH, Düsseldorf
Messe
CeBIT
Jahr
1996
Ort
Hannover

Networking and Interlinking
– the digital City

Exhibitor
Vebacom GmbH, Düsseldorf
Trade fair
CeBIT
Year
1996

Größe
Standfläche 800 qm
(nur Erdgeschoßfläche)
begehbare nutzbare Obergeschoßfläche
501,24 qm
(ohne Grundfläche der Treppen)
Tragkonstruktion 637,80 qm
(Grundfläche von Treppen, Dächern,
Decken u.ä.)
Konzept
Rolf Heide, Hamburg, Tim Heide, Berlin
Mitarbeiter
Peter Kräling, Rainer Schmitz,
Andreas Glücker, Hjördis Klein
Bauten
Ernst F. Ambrosius & Sohn, Frankfurt
Medien
avcontext, Stuttgart
Michael Schirner, Düsseldorf
Fotos
avstudios
Vaclav Reischl

Location
Hanover
Size
Stand area 800 sq. metres
(only ground-level area)
Useable area of upper level which
could be walked on 501.24 sq. metres
(without steps)
Load-bearing construction 637.80 sq. metres
(area of steps, roofs, ceilings etc.)
Design concept
Rolf Heide, Hamburg, Tim Heide, Berlin
Collaborators
Peter Kräling, Rainer Schmitz,
Andreas Glücker, Hjördis Klein
Construction work
Ernst F. Ambrosius & Sohn, Frankfurt
Media
avcontext, Stuttgart
Michael Schirner, Düsseldorf
Photos
avstudios
Vaclav Reischl

Würfelspiele in Primärfarben

Dieter Thiel für Ansorg
Dieter Thiel for Ansorg

Games of Dice in Primary Colours

Can a coloured game of dice function as a trade-fair stand for a lamp manufacturer? Can the trade-fair visitor adjust to a change in scale which plunges him into a building-block model through whose alleyways, galleries and squares he has to struggle, beneath clouds of metal grids?

Funktioniert ein buntes Würfelspiel als Messestand für einen Leuchtenhersteller? Funktioniert der Maßstabssprung des Messebesuchers, der in ein Baukastenmodell versetzt wird, durch dessen Gassen, Galerien und Plätze er sich unter Wolken aus Metallgittern zwängen muß?

„Mir schwebte als Messestandkonzept
eine Stadt vor. Mehr Altstadt als Neustadt.
Winklige Gassen, Unregelmäßigkeiten,
Widersprüche, eher Neapel als Manhattan". Die Umsetzung derartiger Vorstellungen erfolgt bei Thiel nicht konkret,
sondern methaphorisch als farbiges Raum-
gebilde. Deshalb funktioniert das Konzept,
wird zum preisgekrönten Erfolgsent-
wurf. Dieter Thiel: „Faszinierend wird für
mich Messebau erst, wenn er zur experimentellen Kunstform wird".

"I imagined a city as a concept for the
trade-fair stand. More an old city than a
new one. Angular alleyways, irregularities,
contradictions – more like Naples than
Manhattan." Thiel puts these ideas into
practice, not concretely but metaphori-
cally, in the form of a coloured spatial
arrangement. This is why the design works
and was finally awarded a prize. As Dieter
Thiel says, "Trade-fair construction only
becomes interesting for me when it
becomes an experimental art form."

Das Briefing: Leuchtenhersteller kämpfen um einen engen Markt. Eine wichtige Rolle spielen dabei Aussage und Gestaltung des Messestandes auf Fachmessen. Ziel des Auftrittes ist es, stilistische und technische Kompetenz in Licht in Szene zu setzen und sich als profilierter Partner von Messearchitekten, Schaufensterplanern und Innenarchitekten auszuweisen. Die Metapher einer Stadt mit engen Gassen aus farbigen, nutzbaren Kuben in Primärfarben zielt auf dieses bildorientierte Publikum. Die kräftige Farbgebung – grün und grüngelb für zwei Besprechungsblöcke, rot für eine Galerie, blau für die Präsentation von Sonderanfertigungen, gelb für die Demonstration von Lichtqualität, und orange für den Küchen / Barbereich – dient der Orientierung und künstlerischen Aussage. Die clever inszenierte „Toystory" ist von außen mit einem schwarzen Vorhang wie ein „Christo" zugehängt, der neugierig macht und wiederum den bunt zerklüfteten Messestand zum schwarzen Block ergänzt.

The Briefing: Manufacturers of lamps and luminaires compete with each other within a narrowly defined market. An important role in this activity is played by the statement and design of the exhibition stand at specialist trade fairs. The aim is to illustrate stylistic and technical expertise in lighting and to demonstrate that the company is of distinctive importance for trade-fair architects, display-window planners and interior designers. The metaphor of a city of narrow alleyways consisting of coloured, useable cubes in primary colours is aimed at an image-oriented public. The powerful colours – green and green-yellow for discussion blocks, red for the gallery, blue for the presentation of special products, yellow for the demonstration of light quality and orange for the kitchen / bar area – serve to orient the visitor and to make an artistic statement at the same time. The cleverly staged "Toystory", like one of Christo's works, is concealed from the outside by a black curtain which makes people curious and complements the colourfully fractured stand for the black block. Dieter Thiel characterises the work with his client by explaining that "the complex project was only possible because the decision-making procedure during consultations with the client was direct and uncomplicated. The positive aspect of this way of working is the continuity of co-operation which leads to free and highly expressive solutions".

„Das komplexe Projekt war durch die schnellen Entscheidungswege im Gespräch mit dem Auftraggeber möglich. Das positive bei dieser Arbeitsweise ist die Kontinuität der Zusammenarbeit, die zu freien und ausdrucksstarken Lösungen führt", charakterisiert der Designer Dieter Thiel die Zusammenarbeit mit dem Auftraggeber.

Trotz aller formalen Freiheit erfüllt diese freie Form einer Messearchitektur die Wünsche des Kunden und bietet eine Plattform für alle Aufgaben: Präsentation neu entwickelter Modelle, die Inszenierung von Lichtwirkungen (hier an 5 gleichen Objekten in der Galerie), Kommunikation des Firmenprofils, Anwendungsbeispiele von Schaufenstersituationen. Dabei gliedert sich das Raum- und Farbkonzept wie ein Leitsystem. Eine Fachjury honorierte die Verbindung aus Funktion und künstlerischem Ausdruck mit der auf dieser Messe vergebenen höchsten Auszeichnung, dem ersten Preis für eine vorbildliche und richtungsweisende Standgestaltung.

In spite of all the formal freedom, this free form of trade-fair architecture satisfies the desires of the client and provides an all-purpose platform: presentation of newly developed models, the staging of light effects (here for 5 identical objects in the gallery), communication of the company's corporate image and examples of applications in display-windows. The spatial and colour layout is arranged like a guide system. An expert jury gave this combination of functionality and artistic expression the highest award issued at the trade fair, namely first prize for a stand design which sets new standards and points the way into the future.

The designer's preferred method of working is also especially suitable for a regular client such as Ansorg. It begins with an experimental clarification of the task using a cardboard model and various outlines of possible ideas. Finally, in an assembly hall during the precompletion stage, there is a final inspection of the full-scale design with an experienced team of workers.

Für einen „Stammkunden" wie Ansorg eignet sich auch die bevorzugte Arbeitsweise des Entwerfers: Sie beginnt bei der experimentellen Problemklärung am Pappmodell und zahlreichen Ideenskizzen bis zur endgültigen Kontrolle bei der Vorfertigung 1:1 mit einem eingespielten Team in einer Montagehalle.

Würfelspiele in Primärfarben

Aussteller
Ansorg GmbH Lichttechnik,
Mülheim an der Ruhr
Messe
EuroShop
Jahr
1996
Ort
Düsseldorf
Grundfläche
256 qm
Architektur
Dieter Thiel, Basel
Generalunternehmer Messebau
Kunzweiler International,
Weil am Rhein
Fotos
H.G. Esch

Games of Dice in Primary Colours

Exhibitor
Ansorg GmbH Lichttechnik,
Mülheim an der Ruhr
Trade fair
EuroShop
Year
1996
Location
Düsseldorf
Floor area
256 sq. metres
Architecture
Dieter Thiel, Basel
General contractor Construction Work
Kunzweiler International,
Weil am Rhein
Photos
H. G. Esch

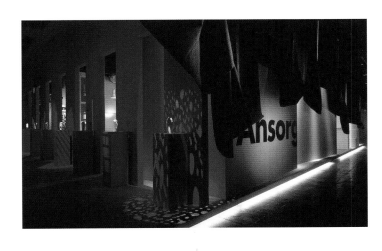

Tempel und Nomadenzelt
als Medienstars

Dieter Thiel / Philippe Starck
für Thomson Multimedia
Dieter Thiel / Philippe Starck
for Thomson Multimedia

A Temple and a Nomad's Tent
as Media Stars

Wie Filmarchitektur folgt Unterhaltungs-
architektur im Messebau eigenen Ge-
setzen. In dieser Illusionsindustrie spielen
heute Emotion, Mystik, Ethno, surreale
Kommunikation, Traumbilder, Poesie eine
wichtigere Rolle als die Abbildung von
Nüchternheit und Realität. Eher über
psychologische als über reale Werte findet
der wirkungsvolle und einprägsame Dialog mit dem Publikum statt.

Like film architecture, entertainment architecture in trade-fair construction
follows its own laws. In an illusion industry such as this, emotion, mysticism, eth-
nicity, surreal communication, dream
images and poetry play a more important
role than an illustration of sobriety and
reality. An effective and memorable
dialogue with the public can be better
achieved by psychological rather than
concrete means.

Das Briefing des Marketings der Abteilung
Consumer Elektronik des französischen
Thomson Konzerns war eher nüchtern
und zweckorientiert: Die zum Konzern
gehörenden drei deutschen Marken Telefunken, Nordmende und Saba sollten
auf der Berliner Funkausstellung als „drei
Marken – aber eine (Thomson-) Performance" vorgestellt werden.

The briefing by the marketing department
in the consumer-electronics division
of the French Thomson concern was, in
contrast, sober and goal-oriented.
The three German makes of product belonging to the company, Telefunken,
Nordmende and Saba, were to be introduced at the Berlin broadcasting exhibition as "three manufacturers but one
(Thomson-) performance".

Das Designteam Dieter Thiel / Philippe
Starck löste die schwierige Aufgabe mit
einem qualitativen Quantensprung.
Dabei waren Medienwirksamkeit und ma-
gische Beeinflussung des Publikums
von Anfang an Bestandteil des Entwurfs-
konzepts.

The design team of Dieter Thiel and
Philippe Starck solved the problem they
were given with a qualitative quantum
leap. Media effectiveness and magical
influence were components of the design
concept from the very beginning.

Wie eine moderne Tempelstadt gruppier-
ten die Designer die den Marken zuge-
ordneten Häuser in der blau ausgeschla-
genen 5.000 qm großen Halle. „Es ging
darum, die einzelnen Qualitäten der
Marken zunächst durch verschiedene
Architekturen zu charakterisieren", be-
schreibt Dieter Thiel die Idee des mit Philippe Starck zusammen entwickelten
Projekts, das in einer Rekordzeit von
knapp 6 Monaten vom ersten Gespräch
und Ortstermin im Frühjahr bis zur Pre-
miere im Spätsommer fertiggestellt
werden mußte.

The designers arranged the buildings into
a kind of modern temple city whereby
each structure was assigned to a different
make of product in the blue-decorated
5000 sq. metres hall. Dieter Thiel explains
the idea of the project which he developed in co-operation with Philippe
Starck: "The initial aim was to characterise
the individual qualities of the makes
of product by using different architecture
in each case". Everything had to be completed in a record time of just over
6 months, lasting from the first discussion
and on-site meeting in spring up to
the première in late summer.

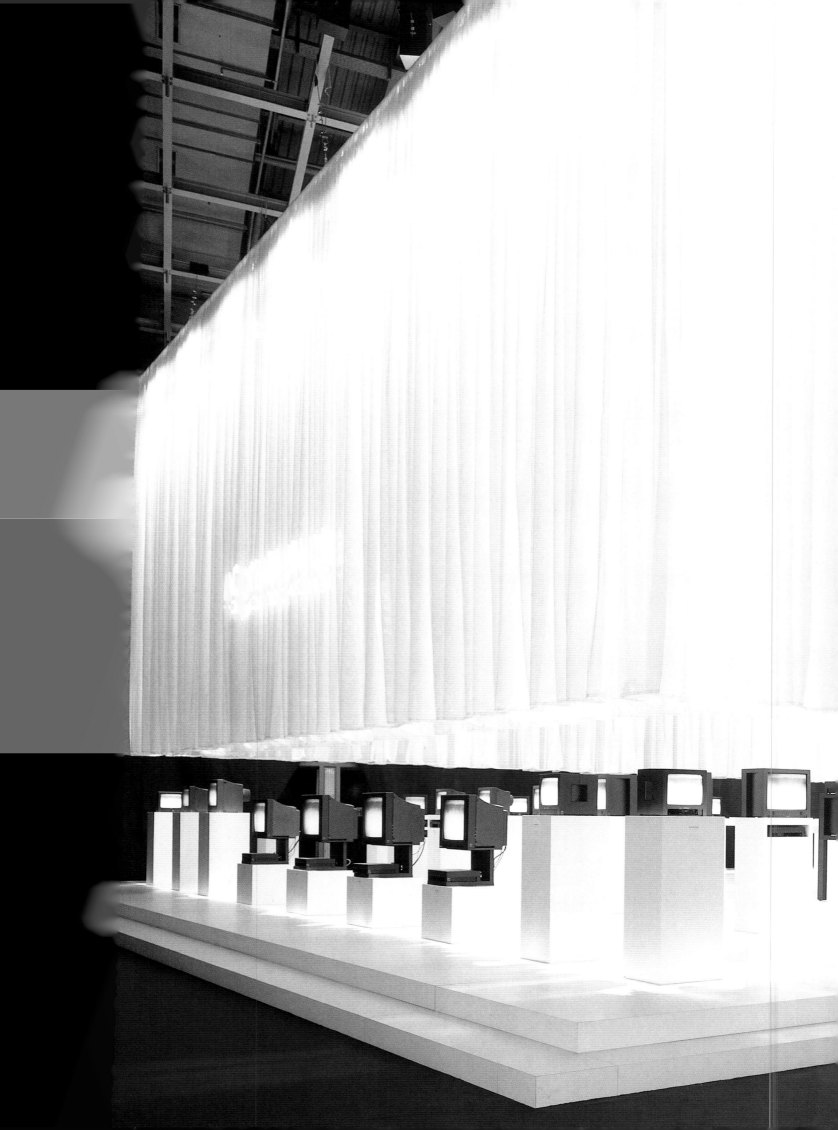

„Telefunken war für uns seriös, elegant, reich, klassizistisch, die Umsetzung in eine Architektur erfolgte deshalb streng stilisiert mit klassischen Bögen, Stufen und Gesimsen. Mehr monumentales Tempelhaus mit Stufen als trivialer Media-Markt. Aus dem Telefunkenblau machten wir kurzerhand ein dunkles Weinrot. Als Kontrastprogramm zum Telefunken-Tempel schufen wir im gleichen Umfeld plaziert das Saba-Zelt: Ein Nomaden-zelt aus roh zusammengeschlagenem Material in ornamentaler Bemalung in terrakotta, schwarz und weiß. Für Nord-mende schufen wir ein 'Nichtgebäude', einen rechteckigen Sockel mit einem von der Decke bis zwei Meter über den Boden hängenden Doppelvorhang, der von einer Windmaschine bewegt wurde." (Thiel)

"For us, Telefunken was serious, elegant, rich and classicist. These qualities were therefore illustrated in the architecture in a highly stylised manner with classical arches, tiers and ledges. The result was more of a monumental temple building with tiers than a trivial media market. We quickly decided to change the Telefunken blue into a dark wine red. As a contrasting programme to the Telefunken temple, we created the Saba tent placed in the same surroundings: a nomad's tent made of materials roughly thrown together and painted ornamentally in terracotta, black and white. For Nordmende, we created a 'non-building'; a rectangular podium which was enveloped in a double curtain suspended from the ceiling. This reached down to two metres above the floor and was kept in motion by a wind machine." (Thiel)

Additional theatrical effects made the blue room into a chamber of wonders: wafts of mist from dry ice spilled out of the nomad's tent, kinetic and projected effects interpreted the situations and placed modern technology in an extended cultural context. Presentation tricks such as a monumental moving table drew the public into the stand area. The portable Zéo TV's wobbled backwards, forwards and sideways alternately against a background of playground noises and bulbous-eyed videos. In such a presentation, television does not become abstract technology but a toy you can play with and a friend.

Zusätzliche Theatereffekte machten aus dem blauen Raum eine Wunderkammer: Nebelschwaden aus Trockeneis quollen aus dem Nomadenzelt, Kinetik und Projektionen interpretierten die Situationen und setzten moderne Technik in einen erweiterten kulturellen Kontext. Präsentationskunststücke, wie ein monumentaler sich bewegender Tisch zogen das Publikum in die Stände. Auf ihm wackelten im Takt nach hinten, vor- und seitwärts die tragbaren TV-Geräte Zéo zu Spielplatzgeräuschen und Kulleraugenvideos. Fernsehen wird in einer solchen Präsentation nicht zur abstrakten Technik, sondern zum faßbaren Spielzeug und Kumpel.

Derartige Zaubertricks von Ethno bis Klassik, von Surrealismus bis High-Tech schlagen sich auch in der Medienbilanz der Unternehmenspräsentation nieder: die Erlebnisinszenierung für Thomson von Thiel / Starck besetzte mit Abstand die Top-Plazierungen der Berichterstattung national und international. Der „Wackeltisch" mit den Kulleraugen-TV's – also eine ideenreiche Produktpräsentation und Designinszenierung – wurde zur meistverbreiteten Ikone der gesamten Funkausstellung 1995.

This wizardry, incorporating features ranging from the ethnic to the classic, from the surreal to high-tech, also found expression in the media balance of the company's presentation: the adventure-like stage-setting created for Thomson by Thiel and Starck was given by far the best reviews by reporters in the national and international press. The "wobbling table" with the bulbous-eyed TV's – an extremely imaginative product presentation and design setting – became the most widespread icon of the whole 1995 broadcasting exhibition.

Tempel und Nomadenzelt als Medienstars

A Temple and a Nomad's Tent as
Media Stars

Aussteller
Thomson Multimedia, Paris
Messe
IFA – Internationale Funkausstellung
Jahr
1995

Exhibitor
Thomson Multimedia, Paris

Ort
Berlin
Grundfläche
5.000 qm
Architektur
Dieter Thiel, Basel; Philippe Starck, Paris
Generalunternehmer Messebau
Kunzweiler International,
Weil am Rhein
Fotos
H.G. Esch, Urbschat Profi Foto

Trade fair
IFA – international broadcasting exhibition
Year
1995
Location
Berlin
Size
5000 sq. metres
Architecture
Dieter Thiel, Basel; Philippe Starck, Paris
General contractor Construction work
Kunzweiler International, Weil am Rhein
Photos
H. G. Esch, Urbschat Profi Foto

Laufstege zur Piazza

Stefan Zwicky
für das Forum kreativer Fabrikanten
der Schweiz
Stefan Zwicky
for the Forum of Creative Manufacturers
of Switzerland

Catwalks to the Piazza

Das Forum kreativer Fabrikanten der
Schweiz, eine lose Verbindung zwischen
22 Herstellerfirmen aus den Bereichen
Möbel, Textil und Beleuchtung, hatte sich
zum Ziel gesetzt, seine Produkte auf der
Schweizer Möbelmesse gemeinsam zu
präsentieren. Das an Messen atypische

The forum for creative manufacturers
of Switzerland, a loose association of 22
manufacturing companies in the sectors
of furniture, textiles and lighting, had
decided to jointly present their products
at the Swiss furniture exhibition. The
principle, an atypical one for trade-fairs,
of "seeing and judging all exhibited

Prinzip „des Sehens und Beurteilens aller ausgestellten Produkte unter gleichen Bedingungen", das heißt, mit dem Verzicht auf Abschirmung gegenüber der Konkurrenz, wurde vom einkaufenden Fachhandel positiv aufgenommen. Im Forum entstand durch die geschaffene Atmosphäre eine für Schweizer Verhältnisse ungewohnt offene Begegnung zwischen Herstellern, Einrichtungshäusern, Designern und Publikum.

Vorgabe für die Forum-Architektur in der stützenlosen, 10 m hohen „alten Festhalle" in Bern, war ein knapp bemessener Kostenrahmen, der mit der Auflage verbunden war, flexiblere Elemente zu schafen, die auch für zwei weitere Male verwendet werden sollten. Dementsprechend rechnete man auch mit einem Minimum an Einlagerungsvolumen. Der quadratische Grundriß von 1.000 qm wurde durch ein orthogonales Achsenkreuz erschlossen. Damit entstanden vier Ausstellungsflächen, die auf ihren Außenseiten durch 6 m hohe Tuchpaneele abgeschirmt wurden. Von außen gesehen, wurde das Forum als textiler, dünnwandiger zweigeschoßiger Kubus mit einer Seitenlänge von 31 m wahrgenommen. Neben den Erschließungsachsen erlaubten auch die vier offenen Ecken von außen her Einblick in die Ausstellung.

products under the same conditions", in other words without screening off the competition, was positively received by visitors from the specialist trades. Due to the atmosphere created in the forum, there was an open meeting of manufacturers, furnishing companies, designers and the public, a situation unusual for the Swiss.

A stipulation for the forum architecture in the 10-metre-high "old festival hall" in Bern was that a tight budget had to be kept to. This was accompanied by a condition that flexible elements were to be created which were to be used again two more times. A minimum of storage volume was thus to be expected as well. The square floor area of 1000 sq. metres was accessed by an orthogonal intersection of pathways. This created four exhibition areas which were screened at their edges by 6-metre-high cloth panels. Seen from the outside, the forum looked like a thin-walled two-level cube made of cloth with a side length of 31 metres. In addition to the access pathways, the four open corners allowed a view of the exhibition from the outside.

Im Inneren führten die als Laufstege
gebauten Mittelachsen zur zentralen,
ebenfalls erhöhten Piazza mit der
gemeinsamen Cafeteria aller Aussteller.

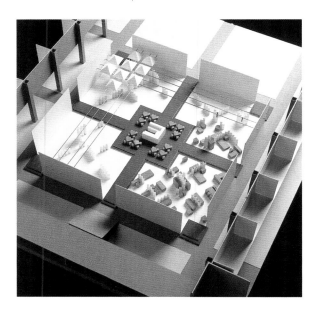

Aus der Absicht, für alle Exponate gleich
optimale Lichtverhältnisse zu schaffen,
ohne mit individuellen Beleuchtungs-
aggregaten zu operieren, entstand die
Idee, die Decke als aufgehängte, stützen-
lose Lichtdecke zu konstruieren, wie man
sie zum Beispiel in Großfotostudios für
Automobilfotografie antrifft. Zu diesem
Zweck wurden über den vier Ausstellungsflächen je 140 qm quadratische Flächen-
leuchten in Leichtbauweise konstruiert.
Die mit je 1.000 Watt Halogen ausge-
rüsteten Deckenelemente geben durch
ein gespanntes Diffusionstuch ein regel-
mäßiges, markantes aber weiches Licht
ab. Zusammen mit dem wollweißen Tep-
pichboden bildet diese souveräne Licht-
führung eine dominante und für die
verschiedenartige Materialbeschaffenheit
der Exponate auch verbindende
Atmosphäre.

Zur neutralen und doch nicht farblosen
Grundstimmung dieser Basisarchitektur,
gehören auch die graugebeizte Zim-
mermannsarbeit für Laufstege, die Bar-
theke aus roh gesägten Tannenbrettern
und schwarzer Eternitabdeckung sowie
die mineralgrauen „Paravents" aus
Eternitplatten. Diese mit rohmetallenenen
Beschlägen in Zick-Zack-Anordnung
standfest verketteten Raumteiler waren
auch Träger der einheitlichen Firmen-
beschriftung. Ebenfalls wurde jegliches
Ausstellungsgut wie Möbel, Stoffe,
Teppiche und Beleuchtungskörper mit
einer einheitlichen Grafik beschriftet.

In the inside, central pathways were
constructed as catwalks leading to the
central "piazza", also elevated, containing
the cafeteria for all the exhibitors.

The intention to create the same advantageous lighting conditions for all the
exhibits without the use of individual
lighting generators resulted in the idea
of building the ceiling as a suspended
lighting roof without supports as is seen,
for example, in large photo studios for
automobile photography. To this end, 140
sq. metres of square surface-lighting
luminaires were fitted above each exhibition area. The ceiling elements, each
equipped with 1000-Watt halogen lamps,
gave off a regular, striking but soft light
through a stretched, light-diffusing
sheet of material. Together with the
white-wool carpeting, the sophisticated
lighting produces a dominant atmosphere
which also links together the different
types of product.

The neutral but not colourless basic
mood of this underlying architecture includes the grey-stained carpentry for the
catwalks, the bar counter made of roughly
sawn pine planks with a black Eternit
covering as well as the mineral-grey
"screens" made of Eternit panels. All the
exhibition fittings such as furniture,
textiles, carpets and luminaires are inscribed with a uniform graphic.

Laufstege zur Piazza

Aussteller
Forum kreativer Fabrikanten der Schweiz:
Anderegg, Belux, Création Baumann,
Denz, Dietiker Switzerland, Glaströsch Design,
Greter, Keramik Mobil, Lehni, Lantal Textiles,
Kollektion Röthlisberger, Ruckstuhl, Sele 2,
Swiss Seats hm, Team by Wellis, Thut Möbel,
USM, Victoria, Vitra, Atelier Vorsprung,
Wogg, Zumsteg
Messe
SMI – Schweizer Möbelmesse International
Ort
Bern
Jahr
1989
Größe
1.000 qm
Konzept & Gestaltung
Stefan Zwicky, Zürich
Alfred Hablützel, Basel
Ausführende Firmen
Strickler Reklame, Zürich
Fotos
Alfred Hablützel
Stefan Zwicky

Catwalks to the Piazza

Exhibitor
Forum of Creative Manufacturers of
Switzerland:
Anderegg, Belux, Création Baumann, Denz,
Dietiker Switzerland, Glaströsch Design,
Greter, Keramik Mobil, Lehni, Lantal Textiles,
Kollektion Röthlisberger, Ruckstuhl, Sele 2,
Swiss Seats hm, Team by Wellis, Thut Möbel,
USM, Victoria, Vitra, Atelier Vorsprung,
Wogg, Zumsteg
Trade fair
Schweizer Möbelmesse International SMI
(Swiss international trade-fair for furniture)
Location
Bern
Year
1989
Size
1000 sq. metres
Conception and design
Stefan Zwicky, Zurich
Alfred Hablützel, Basel
Work done by
Strickler Reklame, Zurich
Photos
Alfred Hablützel
Stefan Zwicky

Kabinettstück(e) in (als) Raum- und Themenfolge

merz sauter zimmermann
für Waldner
merz sauter zimmermann
for Waldner

Showcase(s) in (as) a Sequence of Rooms and Themes

Das Raumangebot auf der Messe ist in diesem Fall etwas ungewöhnlich, da zwei nicht zusammenhängende Standflächen zur Verfügung stehen: ein von allen Seiten einsehbarer Inselstand und gegenüber ein Wandstand, eigentlich eine Rampe, aus der durch Überdeckelung eine Podesterie (bis ca. 90 cm Höhe) errichtet wurde. Beide Stände sind gestalterisch so aufgebaut, daß eine signifikante Verbindung zwischen ihnen besteht, sie kommunizieren durch 9er-Split, Großbilder und Logos.

In this case, the space provided at the trade fair is somewhat unusual as two separate stand areas are available: an isolated stand which can be seen into from all sides and, opposite, a wall stand, actually a ramp which, when covered, creates a platform (up to approx. 90 cm high). Both stands are designed so that there is a meaningful link between them; they communicate through a projection screen with 9 video cubes, outsize images and logos.

Common to both stands is the "showcase" layout. The products of Waldner Laboreinrichtungen can be used for creating specific indoor situations. Six individual rooms have been developed therefore which appear to be closed off but the adjacent rooms can be partially seen into as they are only separated from each other by wall partitions. Each showcase represents a particular theme such as laboratory automation, safety workbenches, disposal and ventilation systems etc., loosened up by a media traffic-light and a media cell. The visitors thus pass through a simulated laboratory world.

Gemeinsam ist beiden Ständen die „Kabinett"-Konstruktion: Das Produkt der Waldner-Laboreinrichtungen bietet sich dazu an, Innenraumsituationen zu schaffen: So wurden sechs Einzelräume entwickelt, die geschlossen wirken, wobei jedoch die anliegenden Räume teilweise einsehbar sind, denn nur Wandscheiben trennen sie voneinander. Jedes Kabinett repräsentiert einen inszenierten Themenbereich, wie z.B. Laborautomatisation, Sicherheitswerkbänke, Entsorgung, Lüftungssysteme etc., aufgelockert durch eine Medienampel sowie eine Medienzelle. So gehen die Besucher durch eine simulierte Laborwelt.

Diese Laborwelt der Waldner-Produkte wurde von einer Gegenwelt umgeben: Für den Standaufbau wurden ausschließlich Materialien eingesetzt, die der Aussteller selbst in seinen Möbeln nicht verwendet, wodurch die Trennung von Standgestaltung und Produkt immer präsent ist. Die Bauelemente wurden in der Waldner'schen Schreinerei gefertigt und später für einen Schauraum wiederverwendet.

This laboratory world of Waldner products is surrounded by a contrasting environment. For the stand construction, only materials are employed which the exhibitor does not use for furnishings so that the separation of stand design and product is always apparent. The construction elements were manufactured in Waldner's joinery workshop and later re-used for a showroom.

Eine Materialbesonderheit stellen die üblicherweise im Fassadenbau verwendeten Faserzementplatten dar, die hier als kostengünstige „Stellwände" fungieren und plakativ zur Geltung kommen, da sie besonders wirkungsintensiv eingefärbt werden konnten.

A special feature of the materials used is the fibre-cement panels generally used for facades. Here, they function as inexpensive "partition walls" and have a distinctively striking effect as their colours are especially intensive.

**Kabinettstück(e) in (als)
Raum- und Themenfolge**

Showcase(s) in (as) a Sequence of
Rooms and Themes

Exhibitor
Waldner Laboreinrichtungen, Wangen i.A.
Trade fair
Achema
Year
1994
Aussteller
Waldner Laboreinrichtungen, Wangen i.A.
Location
Messe
Frankfurt
Achema
Size
Jahr
206.6 sq. metres
1994
Conception and design
merz sauter zimmermann, Stuttgart

Ort
Frankfurt
Größe
206,6 qm
Konzept und Gestaltung
merz sauter zimmermann, Stuttgart
Bauten
Firma Waldner
Fotos
merz sauter zimmermann

Construction work
The Waldner company
Photos
merz sauter zimmermann

Textile Häute

atelier holste
für Philips Consumer Electronics
atelier holste
for Philips Consumer Electronics

Textile Skins

The cubic shell of the trade-fair stand for
Philips Consumer Electronics appears
brusque and off-putting to the visitors at
the CeBIT 1992.

On the outside, textile skins – subordina-
ted to the strict grid pattern of a square
– block the view and stimulate curiosity.
On the inside, the skin, which is animated
by a sophisticated play of light, cuts off
the visitor from the bustle and noise of
the trade-fair. The clear presentation
of selected office-system products from

Schroff und abweisend stellt sich die
kubische Hülle des Messestands der Firma
Philips Consumer Electronics dem Besucher
der CeBIT 1992 dar.

Außen verwehren textile Häute, dem
strengen Raster des Quadrats unterwor-
fen, den Einblick und erzeugen Neugier.
Innen entreißt die durch eine ausgeklü-
gelte Lichtdramaturgie animierte Hülle
den Besucher der lärmenden Messe. Die
klare Präsentation ausgesuchter Philips-
produkte aus dem Bereich Officesystems
im Erdgeschoß, die großzügige Möglichkeit zum Reden und Verhandeln im
Obergeschoß sowie die emotional an-
sprechende Gesamtatmosphäre des Stands
enthüllen ein neu definiertes Verständnis
der Beziehung Mensch - Computer.

Philips on the floor level, the generous
facilities for talks and negotiations on the
upper level and the emotionally stimu–
lating overall atmosphere of the stand
unfold a newly defined understanding of
the person-computer relationship.

Textile Häute

Aussteller
Philips Consumer Electronics, Hamburg
Messe
CeBIT
Jahr
1992
Ort
Hannover
Standkonzeption, Entwurf, Gestaltung
atelier holste, Isernhagen
Mitarbeit
Dirk Spork, Michael Grüter
Größe
270 qm
Doppelgeschoßiger Aufbau zuzügl. 45 qm,
doppelgeschoßiger Kabinentrakt 45 qm
Bauten
Zeisig, Völksen
Beleuchtung
Showtec, Köln
Fotos
Heiko Wrensch, Dirk Spork

Textile Skins

Exhibitor
Philips Consumer Electronics, Hamburg
Trade fair
CeBIT
Location
Hannover
Year
1992
Stand conception, layout and design
atelier holste, Isernhagen
Collaborators
Dirk Spork, Michael Grüter
Size
270 sq. metres
Double-level structure plus a 45 sq. metres
double-level cabin wing 45 sq. metres
Construction work
Zeisig, Völksen
Lighting
Showtec, Cologne
Photos
Heiko Wrensch, Dirk Spork

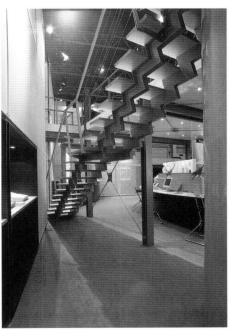

Inszenierter Raum

Interdisziplinäre Inszenierung auf der Messebühne

merz sauter zimmermann

Interdisciplinary Stage-Management on the Trade-Fair Platform

Temporäre ausdrucksvolle Impressionen „Realisierbare Utopien"

„Raum ist der Ausdruck der Gesellschaft. Da sich unsere Gesellschaften einer grundlegenden und strukturellen Transformation unterziehen, ist es also eine vernünftige Hypothese anzunehmen, daß gegenwärtig neue räumliche Formen und Prozesse entstehen" (Manuel Castells). Diese Veränderungen für Architektur und Design wirken sich naheliegenderweise auch auf den temporären Bau, auf die Ausstattung von Events und die Inszenierung von Veranstaltungen aus. Das bedeutet, daß in die Konzepte solcher Bauten oder Aktionen aktuelle Zeitgeist-Strömungen, Trends, ja gewisse Lebensgefühle mit einfließen, sie müssen mit den gewünschten Emotionen und Informationen austariert und schließlich adäquat verbunden werden. Daher bedarf ein veranstalterisches Gesamtkonzept einer gewissen interdisziplinären „Zeitdiagnostik" (Peter Sloterdijk). Sie findet ihre Umsetzungen in allen Teilen des gesamten Projekts, schließlich auch in seinen Aktionen (wie Erlebnisparcours, Medienspektakel oder Showdance), Möbeln, Kostümen, Speisen, bis hin zu kleinen Details.

Temporäres wird mit Zeitlosem kombiniert. Neue Medien, alle technischen Möglichkeiten wie Großrechner, Großprint und Internet ermöglichen solch ein Unterwegs-Sein, Sich-Ändern-Können, allerdings auf der Basis von Statik und Sicherheit in der Bautechnik und absoluter Produktbezogenheit.

Doch im Gegensatz zum Theater verzichten hier die Regisseure auf eine individuelle Handschrift. Individuell auf das Ereignis, auf die Firmenphilosophie oder auf das Produkt zugeschnittene Deutlichkeit wird nur durch Vermeiden fester Strukturen und einheitlicher Linien erreicht. Auf dieser Bühne muß Besonderes geschaffen werden, die Baukörper allerdings sollen paradoxerweise dezent und dennoch auffällig wirken.

Interdisciplinary Stage-Management on the Trade-Fair Platform

Temporary and expressive impressions "Attainable Utopias"

"Space is the expression of a society. As our societies are at present being subjected to a fundamental and structural transformation, it is a reasonable hypothesis to assume that new spatial forms and processes are now being created." (Manuel Castells). These changes concerning architecture and design also have an effect on temporary buildings and on the furnishing and stage-management of events. This means that currents of the Zeitgeist, trends, yes even attitudes to life are incorporated in the design of such constructions or activities; these currents have to be balanced against and, finally, adequately linked to the emotions to be mediated and the information to be provided. An overall concept for an event thus requires a certain interdisciplinary "diagnostics of the time" (Peter Sloterdijk). It can be implemented in all parts of the project and also in the activities (such as a guided adventure tour, a media spectacle or show-dancing), the furniture, costumes, meals, right down to the smallest details.

The temporary is combined with the timeless. New media and all the technical possibilities such as mainframe computers, large-scale printing and the Internet enable such movement, such ability to change. But they must be based on reliable and safe structural engineering and exclusively oriented to the product.

In contrast to the theatre, however, the directors here have no desire to stamp a production with their own signature. A clarity which is individually tailored to the event, to the company's philosophy or to the product can only be achieved through the avoidance of fixed structures and uniform lines. At trade fairs, something special has to be created but, paradoxically, the structures should be discreet while still being highly noticeable.

Dabei hilft kreative Experimentierfreudigkeit im Umgang mit Materialien, Grafik und Dekoration: Von neuen Techniken und Verfahren werden Muster hergestellt, Materialien auf Sicherheit und Belastbarkeit in ihrem neuen Einsatzgebiet geprüft. Außergewöhnliche Bodenbeläge, Regalverkleidungen, Wandabhängungen und ähnliches sind so zum Einsatz gekommen. Das ist besonders für low-budget-Aufträge interessant. Bisweilen werden Stilbrüche als Stilmittel eingesetzt (z.B. Bodenbelag aus rohen, warmgewalzten Stahlplatten unter Hochglanzlimousinen).

Der Zuschauerraum ist oft gleichzeitig die Bühne und umgekehrt: Messestände sind betretbare Bühnen mit durchsichtigen Kulissen. Oft sind sie von allen Seiten zugänglich und einsehbar. Hier kann mit verschiedenen Perspektiven gearbeitet werden, z.B. sind die Motorräder (IFMA Köln) in verschiedenen Höhen von allen Seiten sichtbar. In begehbarer Bühne werden Innenräume komponiert (Waldner), abdrehbare Bühnen lassen optimale Raumnutzung zu.

Ganzheitliche interdisziplinäre Inszenierungen, das heißt hier, daß auf der Basis der Architektur und Ingenieursarbeit für den kreativen Entwurf sowie für die speziellen Anforderungen von fliegenden Bauten, Zeltträgern oder Tribünen (auch im Genehmigungsrecht), in Zusammenarbeit mit freien Mitarbeitern aller möglichen Disziplinen (Innenarchitekten, Drucker, Künstler, Video-Spezialisten, Handwerker, Schneider, Kostümbildner, Werbefachleute u.a.) die Gestaltung ausgeführt wird: Schon während der Vorbesprechungen sind neben den Architekten entsprechende Fachleute von Anfang an dabei und betreuen das Projekt in jedem Stadium mit. Das gibt den Projekten die Chance, „aus einem Guß" zu sein. merz sauter zimmermann agiert als Zentrale, als Dreh- und Angelpunkt für die Zusammenarbeit mit diesen vielen Mitarbeitern.

A creative willingness to experiment with materials, graphics and decoration is of help here. Examples of new technologies and procedures are put together and materials are tested to ensure that they are safe and strong enough to cope with new conditions of use. Unusual floor coverings, shelf coatings, wall hangings and similar have thus been made use of. This is especially interesting for low-budget projects. From time to time, stylistic incongruency is used as a means of creating style (e.g. a floor covering made of rough, hot-rolled steel plates on which spotless shiny limousines are exhibited).

The audience area is often the stand at the same time and vice versa. Trade-fair stands are stages you can walk onto with a transparent backdrop. They are often accessible or can be looked into from all sides. Different perspectives can be worked with here. The motorbikes at the IFMA Cologne, for example, are visible at different heights and from all sides. Interior rooms are "composed" (Waldner) on accessible stages and platforms which can be moved to allow an optimum use of space.

Holistic interdisciplinary "stage" production means that, on the basis of the architecture and engineering, the design work is done for the initial creative idea and also for the special requirements of temporary buildings, tents or podiums in co-operation with freelance contributors from all possible disciplines (interior designers, printers, artists, video specialists, handworkers, tailors, costume designers, advertising experts etc.). From the very beginning, the appropriate specialists as well as the architects are present, even during the preliminary discussions, and provide their services for the project during every stage of completion. This enables projects to come from a "single mould" as it were. The merz sauter zimmermann company acts as a control centre, as a pivot for all the people working together.

Besondere Wichtigkeit hat die Gestaltung der „Fassade" im Messebau. Sie hat, mehr als die städtebauliche Fassade, die Zusatzanforderung des Eye-Catchers sowie, daß bereits in der Fassade Firmen- oder Produktname, Logo und eventuell Informationen erscheinen. Das Äußere des Messebaus muß schon Spuren dessen zeigen oder darauf anspielen, was sich in seinem Inneren befindet. Es muß mit dem Inhalt korrespondieren.

Vilém Flusser spricht von der Fassade als „Gesicht, und zwar jenem Gesicht, unter dem sich Gebäude maskieren, um ein öffentliches Ansehen zu haben und um eine Rolle zu spielen". Doch Fassaden sind „nicht einfach jene Seite des Gebäudes ..., dank derer sich die Gebäude nach außen, an die Öffentlichkeit wenden", sondern Gebäude kommen „erst dank Fassaden zu sich selbst", werden „gewissermaßen aus anonymen Stoffen zu Personen ... Fassaden werden nicht etwa im nachhinein einem Gebäude aufgesetzt, um es ansehnlich zu machen", sondern Architekten entwerfen „(ähnlich wie Dramaturgen) Gebäude in Funktion von Fassaden, Handlungen in Funktion von Rollen". Die Form kann der Funktion folgen und umgekehrt. Die Spannung zwischen Fassade und Funktion ist im Messebau eine besondere Herausforderung. Die Dialektik zwischen Fassade und Funktion könnte man gerade in der Polarität, die fliegende Bauten darstellen, wiedergespiegelt sehen darin, daß wir, so Martin Pawley, „in einer Zeit der Doppelexistenz von 'architektonischen Körpern' und 'Informationskörpern'" leben.

Optimal ist, wenn das Spielen mit den Grenzen der Darstellungskraft in Klarheit und eine gewisse Bestimmtheit mündet. Das heißt auch: Spezialeffekte einsetzen ohne „Effekthascherei"; Informationen vermitteln; Erinnerungen schaffen; Aktualität und Traditionen in Verbindung setzen und dennoch die Wirkung einer optimierten Komplettkomposition zu erreichen; das Gewollte dezent unterstreichen; Besucher in ein Medium zu entführen, zu faszinieren, aber niemals abgleiten zu lassen.

In trade-fair construction, the design of the facade is of special importance. More than the facades in urban architecture, there is the additional requirement that it should be an eye-catcher and that the company or product name, the logo and perhaps information as well should be included in the facade. The outside of a trade-fair structure must show traces of or hint at what is on the inside. It has to correspond to the contents.

Vilém Flusser speaks of the facade as a "face, a face which acts as a mask for the building so that it can acquire public prestige and play a specific role". But, he says, a facade is "... not simply that side of the building ... which faces the outside and the public". On the contrary, buildings "only become alive and from anonymous materials, acquire a personality of their own thanks to the facade. Facades are not just stuck onto buildings as an afterthought to make them look nice" but architects "design buildings as a function of facades like a dramatist directs actions as a function of roles". Form can follow function and vice versa. The tension between facade and function in trade-fair construction is a special challenge and this dialectic is reflected in the polarity of temporary buildings so that we, like Martin Pawley, "live in a time when 'architectonic entities' are at the same time 'objects of information'".

The best results are achieved by playing with the limits of the possibilities inherent in presentation but ending with clarity and a particular kind of certitude. This also means that special effects should be used without gimmickry, that information should be passed on, memories created, the modern and the traditional linked together, but that the effect is achieved of a balanced overall 'composition'. Emphasis, where necessary, should be discreet and visitors should be enticed and fascinated but never allowed to slip away.

Szenario und Parcours

merz sauter zimmermann
für BMW Motorrad
merz sauter zimmermann
for BMW motorcycle division

Scenario and Guideway

Dieser Messestand besteht aus zwei Teilen, die sich ergänzen, aber dennoch voneinander völlig unterscheiden: eine „Kurven-Hochbahn" aus Stahlträgern sowie der für BMW exklusiv entworfene „serienmäßig" als Messestand eingesetzte Pavillon-Baukörper, ein zweigeschossiger elliptischer Stahlbau mit Aluminium-Streckmetallüberdachung (Grundfläche ca. 106 qm, Höhe über 6 m).

Auf einer von 2,5 m bis 4 m ansteigenden Kurvenbahn sind Motorräder auf Stahlträgern plaziert, die wie Standbilder eines Geschwindigkeitsfilms wirken. Diese „Bühne" für die Motorräder befindet sich also über den Köpfen der Besucher, kann aber von allen Seiten gesehen werden, z.B. vom 2. Stock des Pavillons aus. Die Kurven-Hochbahn ergänzt in ihrer Form den elliptischen Pavillon-Baukörper: Ebenfalls elliptisch, ist sie gleichzeitig sein Ausläufer und seine Erweiterung im Sinne einer Umlaufbahn. Dadurch wurde der relativ kleine, zur Verfügung stehende Raum nicht nur optisch nach oben erweitert, sondern zugleich auch eine besonders auffällige Fernwirkung geschaffen.

Im Pavillon befinden sich im Obergeschoß Büros, Cafeteria und Barbereich. Im Erdgeschoß sind um 21 Motorräder herum strukturierte Themen-Exponate in Form von Glas- und Metalltafeln arrangiert, komplexe Informationseinheiten, die mit Stahlseilen von dem gebogenen Träger der Kurven-Hochbahn abgehängt sind (am Boden gegen Schwingung gesichert). Motorradexponate sowie Kurvenbahnstützen bilden mit ihrer vertikalen Komponente Pylone, die einen unsichtbaren Parcours abzustecken scheinen.

The trade-fair stand consists of two sections which complement each other but are nevertheless completely different to each other: a "curving elevated track" made of steel beams and a pavilion

exclusively designed as a standard trade-fair stand for BMW; a two-level elliptical steel construction with an aluminium expanded-metal roof (floor area: approx. 106 sq. metres; height: over 6 m).

Motorbikes are arranged on steel beams on a curved track rising from 2.5 m to 4 m and give the impression of freeze frames in a film about speed. This "stage" is therefore above the heads of the visitors but can be seen from all sides, e.g. from the upper level of the pavilion. The shape of the curved elevated track complements the elliptical pavilion. The arms of the track and its extension are also elliptical like an orbit. In this way, the relatively small amount of space available is not only extended upwards from an optical point of view but an especially distinctive effect at a distance is also created.

The pavilion contains offices, a cafeteria and a bar area on the upper level. On the lower level, theme exhibits in the form of glass and metal boards are arranged around 21 motorcycles. These boards are complex units of information which are suspended by steel cables from the curved beams of the elevated track (on the floor they are secured against vibration). The vertical components of the motorcycle exhibits and the supports for the track form pylons which mark out an invisible guideway.

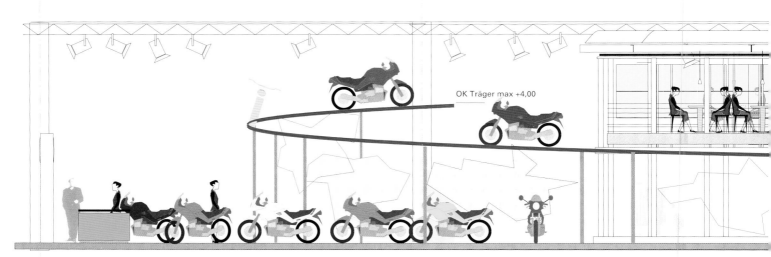

OK Träger max +4,00

Die Besucher wandeln von außen nach innen und (im Pavillon) von unten nach oben. Der Weg führt durch die verschiedenen Informations-Stationen, die jeweils verschiedene Themen behandeln. Das Gesamtbild transportiert die Sprengung der üblichen Dimensionen, worin die Kurvenbahn ein Symbol für Dynamik ist, für die große Freiheit auf dem Zweirad- „Ritt in grenzenlose Weiten".

Unentbehrlich ist die Einbindung umweltschützender Maßnahmen für die fliegenden Bauten. Recycling und Wiederverwendbarkeit einzelner Bauteile lassen sich mit dem Novitätenanspruch der Messe vereinbaren: flexible und modifizierbare Elemente werden hergestellt. Zum Beispiel läßt sich der für BMW exklusiv entworfene Pavillon, ein Unikat, das seitdem von BMW als Dauereinrichtung auf Messen verwendet wird, immer wieder neu variieren: Man kann ihn in Längs- und Querachse unterteilen. Man kann zwei Podesterien entfernen bzw. hinzufügen. Man kann ihn mit oder ohne Dach aufbauen, auch können die Wände durchsichtig oder geschlossen installiert werden, oder man kann dem Pavillon eine Bauchbinde umlegen, ein Großbild oder anderes.

The visitors wander into the inside from the outside and (in the pavilion) from the lower to the upper level. They pass through different information stations, each of which deals with a different topic, but the overall picture conveys the breaking down of normal dimensions, the curved track being a symbol for dynamism, the unlimited freedom of two-wheel transportation, "a ride into the endless distance".

The incorporation of ecological measures for the temporary buildings is indispensable. Recycling and the re-useability of individual components can be reconciled with the demand for innovation associated with trade fairs by using the flexible and modifiable elements which are now available. The pavilion exclusively designed for BMW, for example, a unique specimen which has since then been used by BMW as a permanent feature at trade fairs, can be varied again and again: it can be divided on longitudinal and diagonal axes, two platforms can be removed or added, it can be erected with or without a roof, the walls can be transparent or opaque or a 'cummerbund', a large-scale photo or other items, can be placed around the pavilion.

Szenario und Parcours

Scenario and Guideway

Exhibitor
BMW AG (motorcycle division), Munich
Trade fair
IFMA – international bicycle and
motorcycle exhibition

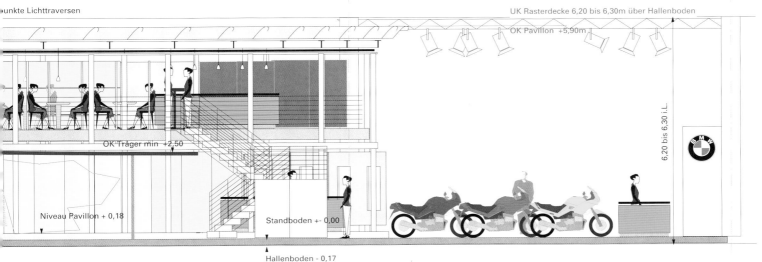

punkte Lichttraversen

UK Rasterdecke 6,20 bis 6,30m über Hallenboden

OK Pavillon +5,90m

OK Träger min +2,50

6,20 bis 6,30 i.L.

Niveau Pavillon + 0,18

Standboden +- 0,00

Hallenboden - 0,17

Aussteller
BMW AG Sparte Motorrad, München
Messe
IFMA – Internationale Fahrrad- und
Motorradausstellung
Jahr
1994
Ort
Köln
Größe
738 qm
Konzept und Gestaltung
merz sauter zimmermann, Stuttgart
Bauten
Brunnner & Eisenreich, Puchheim
Fotos
merz sauter zimmermann

Year
1994
Location
Cologne
Size
738 sq. metres
Layout and design
merz sauter zimmermann, Stuttgart
Construction work
Brunner & Eisenreich, Puchheim
Photos
merz sauter zimmermann

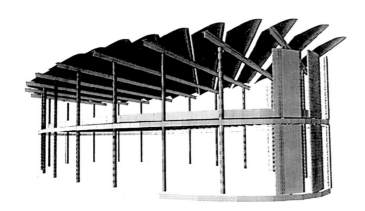

Mit Auge und Fuß

Alfred Hablützel für Villeroy & Boch
Alfred Hablützel for Villeroy & Boch

With Eye and Foot

Die vom Studio Hablützel gestalteten Messestände für den Bereich Architekturfliesen von Villeroy & Boch waren schon in den Jahren 1991 und 1993 nicht als ein an die Messe translozierter Showroom konzipiert. Einmal war es ein Museumsraum, einmal ein imaginärer Bauplatz in Renaissance-Manier. Die Marketingstrategie für die Baumessen München und Basel 1995 bestand wiederum darin, Kommunikation zu Architekten und Anwendern über ein assoziatives Medium herzustellen.

The trade-fair stands created by the Hablützel studio for the architectural-tiles division of Villeroy & Boch were not designed in 1991 and 1993 to be just showrooms relocated to a trade fair. On one occasion, a museum area was created and, on another, an imaginary building site in the Renaissance manner. The marketing strategy of the Munich and Basel trade fairs in 1995 was to create an associative medium which would act as a communicative link to architects and users.

Blickwinkel

1995 wurde für die Botschaft, mit dem Schwerpunktthema „Bodenfliesen", eine neue, visuell-räumliche Gestaltungssprache entwickelt. Die beiden Wörter des Leitmotivs „Blickwinkel Fußboden" waren Auslöser der Idee einer lapidaren, fotografischen Umsetzung von Blick(winkel) und Fuß(boden) mittels typischer schwarz/weiss-Fotografien – sinnbildlich für Beschäftigung und Erleben von Bodenkeramik mit dem Auge (durch den Kopf) und mit dem Fuß (durch den Körper). Die fünf variierten Aufnahmepaare „Auge und Fuß" wurden in Zusammenarbeit mit dem Künstler und Fotografen Balthasar Burkhard realisiert.

In 1995, a new visual-spatial design language was developed for conveying the message, the main theme of which was "floor tiles". The two concepts of the leitmotif "angle of vision and floor" triggered an idea involving succinct, photographic representations of the angle of vision and the floor using standard black-and-white photographs. The aim was to produce a symbol for how the floor ceramics are experienced with the eye (angle of vision) and with the foot (floor). The five different pictures "Eye and Foot" were created in co-operation with the artist and photographer, Balthasar Burkhard.

Project implementation:
five staggered cubic rooms

The long narrow stand consists of five square rooms which are rotated away from the longitudinal axis and whose side length is four metres. The resulting triangular areas of left-over space at the back of the stand accommodate the whole infrastructure and the collection of samples. On the front longitudinal side, the rooms are staggered with four passageways leading to the second stand opposite belonging to V&B Sanitär.

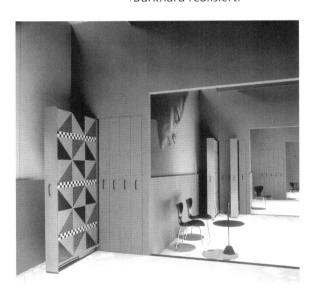

Projektrealisation:
fünf gestaffelte Raumkuben

Der schmal-lange Standgrundriß besteht aus fünf zur Längsachse abgedrehten quadrischen Räumen von vier Metern Seitenlänge. Die dadurch entstehenden dreieckigen Resträume nehmen an der Rückwand des Standes die gesamte Infrastruktur und die Musterkollektion auf. An der vorderen Längsseite entsteht eine räumliche Staffelung mit vier Durchgängen zum gegenüberliegenden zweiten Stand von V&B Sanitär.

Die „Außenfassaden" der fünf zum Messegang angeschrägten Räume sind im unteren Drittel als Glasband gestaltet. Ähnlich einem Diapositiv sind die Glas-

The bottom third of the "exterior facades" of the five rooms which are at an angle to the visitors' pathway are composed of glass "bands". Similar to slides, the glass bands carry five huge serigraphy photos of naked feet. This results in a diffusely perforated low-level view into and out of each room.

bänder Träger von fünf riesigen, fotografierten, nackten Füßen in Serigraphiedruck. Es entsteht dadurch – unter der Augenhöhe – ein diffus durchbrochener Ein- und Ausblick.

Analog dazu ist das zum Fuß entsprechende Gesichtsprofil in den oberen zwei Dritteln der Gegenseite mit Blick zum Boden gerichtet.

Entsprechend zur räumlichen Staffelung sind auch die einzelnen Bodenflächen leicht geneigt, was zur bewußteren Wahrnehmung der fünf keramischen Bodenthemen beiträgt. Jeder Raum wird dadurch über eine Stufe betreten.

An der Decke sind Spiegelflächen montiert, die dem Besucher einen mehrfachen Betrachtungsabstand zur Beurteilung der Bodenwirkung erlauben. Jeder der fünf Böden ist mit einem einzigen, maskierten Scheinwerfer beleuchtet. Das Raumlicht resultiert einzig durch die Lichtreflexion des Bodens.

Analogous to this is the profile of a face to match the foot. The former is located in the upper two-thirds of the opposite side with the eye looking at the floor.

Matching the staggered rooms, the individual floor surfaces are also slightly inclined which makes for a more conscious perception of the five ceramic floor themes. Each room is therefore entered by a step.

Mirrored surfaces are fitted on the ceiling which allow the visitor to judge the effect of the floor at a distance several times farther away than if viewed by direct inspection. Each of the five floors is lit with a single, masked spotlight. The light in the rooms is the sole result of light reflected from the floors.

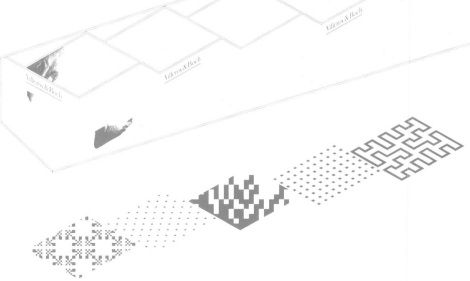

Mit Auge und Fuß

Aussteller
Villeroy & Boch AG, Mettlach
Messen
Bau 1995, München;
Swissbau 1995, Basel
Größe
120 qm
Idee, Konzept und Gestaltung
Alfred Hablützel, Thomas Petraschke, Basel
Mitarbeit
Stefan Zwicky, Zürich
Balthasar Burkhard, Fotografie
Boisset et Gaujac (F)
Fotos
Alfred Hablützel

With Eye and Foot

Exhibiton
Villeroy & Boch AG, Mettlach
Trade fairs
Bau 1995, Munich;
Swissbau 1995, Basel
Size
120 sq. metres

Idea, layout and design
Alfred Hablützel, Thomas Petraschke, Basel
Collaborators
Stefan Zwicky, Zurich
Balthasar Burkhard, Photographer,
Boisset et Gaujac (F)
Photos
Alfred Hablützel

Im Anfang war der (das) (W)Ort

Adolf Krischanitz
für den Österreichischen Buchhandel
Adolf Krischanitz
for the Austrian book dealers

The Word as Construction and the Construction as Word

Zur Idee
Nicht nur temporäre Pavillons stellen die Schönheit des Vergänglichen (fast eine antropomorphe Dimension) dar und stilisieren sich zur transitorischen Erscheinung am „falschen" Ort, erzeugen aber damit möglicherweise ein richtiges Bewußtsein. Die Physis des Gebäudes verschwindet

About the idea
Temporary pavilions illustrate the beauty of the transitory (almost an anthropomorphic dimension) and are stylised as "dislocated" fleeting apparitions.

zugunsten des Sinns. Dies ist vergleichbar mit dem Phänomen der Schrift. Das geschriebene (getippte, gemalte, gemeißelte) Schriftzeichen entbehrt nicht einer gewissen Monumentalität, die, reiht man die Buchstaben aneinander zu Wörtern, Sätzen etc., zugunsten der Sinnerkenntnis schwindet. Pavillon und Schrift stehen also in einem sinnstiftenden Zusammenhang.

Nevertheless, they still, perhaps, generate the required type of awareness. The physicalness of a tem-porary construction disappears to be replaced by its meaning. This is comparable to the phenomena of writing. The written (typed, painted, chiselled) characters do not lack a certain monumentality but this fades away to be replaced by the recognition of meaning when the letters are placed in rows (constructed) to form words, sentences and so on. Pavilions and writing as constructions are thus related in the way they carry meaning.

Zum Ort

Im Anfang war der (das) (W)Ort. Der Ort ist bestimmt durch seine Mitte (Obelisk), seine Peripherie (Pavillon) und seinen Kontext (Hof). Die einzelnen Schichten stellen jeweils das Rahmenwerk (Fond) für die nächstfolgende Schicht dar. Die ideelle (geometrische) Besetzung des Ortes erfolgt durch den Mittelpunkt des kreisförmig gekrümmten Raumes. Dieser Mittelpunkt ist markiert durch die Nadelform des bestehenden Obelisken. Dieser trägt den Namen „Österreich" in Form einer vertikal angeordneten Schrift. Der eigentliche Raum wird gebildet durch in Krümmung gestellte, plane, beidseitig mit Schrift bedruckte Flächen (Buchseiten), dies alles wird gebunden durch das kompakte Dach (Rücken). Der Pavillon ist Synthese zwischen Ausgestelltem und Ausstellendem, zwischen Gefäß und Objekt, zwischen Form-Form und Inhalts-Form. Der Pavillon als Zirkulationsapparat steht für Bewegung, Wiederholung, virtuelle Anwesenheit und für das Kontinuum strömender Zeit. Text außen (weiß): Umlaufendes Textfragment aus den Tagebüchern von Robert Musil. Texte innen (schwarz): Jedes Paneel enthält bestimmte Textproben aus der österrreichischen Literaturgeschichte: z.B. Grillparzer, Joseph Roth, Wiener Gruppe, Thomas Bernhard u.ä.

Zum Gebäude

Für den „Schwerpunkt Österreich" zur Frankfurter Buchmesse 1995 wurde ein ca. 1.100 qm großer temporärer Ausstellungspavillon errichtet.

Das Gebäude wurde in neun Tagen aufgebaut, während der fünf Tage dauernden Buchmesse benutzt und danach in vier Tagen abgebaut. Es ist auch vorgesehen, daß der Pavillon immer wieder für eine temporäre Nutzung aufgebaut wird.

Der eingeschossige, ringförmige Pavillon (Außendurchmesser 46 m, Ringbreite ca. 10 m, Höhe 4 m) besteht aus 24 Bausegmenten und 4 Eingangsrampen, die mit Stahlprofilrahmen und vorgefertigten Dach- und Bodenelementen zusammengebaut sind. Die Außen- bzw. Innenfassaden sind völlig verglast, gleichzeitig ist die Außenfassade beidseitig mit Folienbeschriftung (Text) bedruckt.

About the location

The word as construction. The location of the stand is determined by its centre (obelisk), its peripherals (pavilion) and its context (courtyard). Each layer acts as a framework (background) for the next. The non-material (geometrical) occupation of the location is effected through the centrepoint of the circular area. This centrepoint is marked by the needle shape of the obelisk there which bears the name "Austria" in the form of a vertically arranged inscription. The actual room is formed by plane surfaces inscribed on both sides (book pages) placed in a curve and these are joined together by the compact roof (the spine of the book). The pavilion is a synthesis of exhibit and exhibitor, of vessel and object, of the form of form and the form of content. The pavilion promotes circulation and represents movement, repetition, virtual presence and the continuum of the time flow. Outside text (white): extracts from the diaries of Robert Musil. Inside text (black): each panel is covered with specific extracts from Austrian literary history, e.g. Grillparzer, Joseph Roth, the Viennese Group, Thomas Bernhard and so on.

About the building

A temporary exhibition pavilion approximately 1100 sq. metres was erected specially for Austrian literature at the 1995 Frankfurt book fair.

The building was constructed in nine days, used during the five days of the book fair and then dismantled in four days. The pavilion can be erected repeatedly for temporary use.

The single-level ring-shaped pavilion (external diameter 46 m, breadth of ring approx. 10 m, height 4 m) consists of 24 segments and 4 entry ramps which are joined together with shaped-steel frames and prefabricated roof and floor elements. The outer and inner facades are all glass and, at the same time, there are printed transparencies (text) on both sides of the outer facade.

Der Pavillon wurde auf einem gepflasterten Platz im Messegelände Frankfurt um einen bestehenden Obelisken errichtet. Er schwebt ca. 48 cm über dem Gelände, auf verstellbaren Teleskop-Beinen.

Das Raumprogramm umfaßt einen Ausstellungsbereich und ein Café / Veranstaltungsbereich, wo auch Radio- und Fernsehübertragungen stattfinden können. Außerdem sind ein Büroraum, Küche und ein Rundfunkstudio vorhanden.

Der gesamte Innenraum wird über 5 cm breite Schlitze im Fußbodenbereich an den Außen- bzw. Innenfassaden natürlich belüftet. Die Entlüftung erfolgt über elektrisch betriebene Ventilatoren im Dachbereich.

Das Gebäude kann über vier Öffnungen betreten und verlassen werden, an die sich, den vier Hauptachsen des Platzes gemäß, tangential Rampen anschließen. Die Ringform ermöglicht eine rotierende Bewegung des Besucherstromes mit Bereichen der schnellen Bewegung und der Langsamkeit.

The pavilion was constructed on a paved square around an already existing obelisk on the trade-fair site in Frankfurt. It hovers 48 cm above the ground on adjustable telescopic supports.

The area accommodates an exhibition area and a café / event area where radio and television broadcasts can be made. There is also an office, a kitchen and a radio studio.

The whole interior is naturally ventilated through 5 cm slits near floor level in the outer and inner facades. Air is removed by electrically operated fans in the roof.

For entering and leaving the building, there are four 'doorways' leading out to tangential ramps corresponding to the four main axes of the square. The ring shape allows visitors to move in a circle with areas where they can walk quickly or slowly.

Im Anfang war der (das) (W)Ort

The Word as Construction and
the Construction as Word

Exhibitor
Hauptverband des Österreichischen
Buchhandels
(main association of Austrian book dealers)
Trade fair
Book fair

Aussteller
Hauptverband des Österreichischen
Buchhandels

Year
1995
Location
Frankfurt
Size
1100 sq. metres
Messe
Architect
Buchmesse
Adolf Krischanitz
Jahr
Collaborator
1995
Eric Red
Ort
Statics
Frankfurt
Manfred Gmeiner & Manfred Haferl
Größe
Construction work
1.100 qm
Ernst F. Ambrosius & Sohn, Frankfurt
Architekt
Photos
Adolf Krischanitz
Margherita Spiluttini
Mitarbeit
Eric Red
Statik
Manfred Gmeiner & Manfred Haferl
Bauten
Ernst F. Ambrosius & Sohn, Frankfurt
Fotos
Margherita Spiluttini

Die Light-Pipe unter der Kuppel

Kauffmann Theilig & Partner
für Mercedes Benz
Kauffmann Theilig & Partner
for Mercedes Benz

The Light-Pipe Under the Cupola

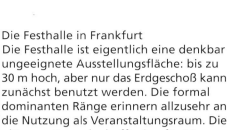

Die Festhalle in Frankfurt
Die Festhalle ist eigentlich eine denkbar ungeeignete Ausstellungsfläche: bis zu 30 m hoch, aber nur das Erdgeschoß kann zunächst benutzt werden. Die formal dominanten Ränge erinnern allzusehr an die Nutzung als Veranstaltungsraum. Die gläserne Kuppel schafft eine für Messe- und Ausstellungszwecke unkontrollierbare Tageslichtsituation.

The festival hall in Frankfurt
The festival hall is an extremely unsuitable exhibition area. It is up to 30 m high but, at first sight, only the ground level can be used. The formally dominant seating stands are a strong reminder of its use as an arena for various kinds of event and the daylight coming through the glass cupola cannot be adequately controlled for trade-fair and exhibition purposes.

Given the space available, it seemed a good idea to use the existing space to build on several levels, to hide interfering structures and their functions and to guide and co-ordinate the daylight to make it suitable for an automobile exhibition.

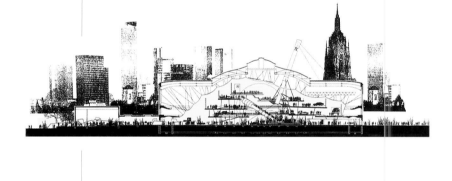

Die Interpretation der räumlichen Gegebenheiten hat es nahegelegt, den vorhandenen Luftraum mit dem Einbau von mehreren Geschossen zu nutzen, optisch und funktional störende Einbauten auszublenden, und das Tageslicht so zu lenken und zu koordinieren, daß es der Absicht des Ausstellens von Autos gerecht wird.

Automobilausstellung
Was heißt das? Die Aufgabenstellung ist vielleicht ähnlich der eines Museums: der Weg des Besuchers muß eindeutig sein, Ausstellungsgegenstand und Ausstellungshintergrund müssen eindeutig erkennbar werden, der Ausstellungsort muß räumlich, lichttechnisch, akustisch usw. auf den Ausstellungsgegenstand vorbereitet sein. Der gedankliche Zusammenhang zum Guggenheim-Museum in New York ist nicht falsch; oder zu einem guten Warenhaus: große Menschenmengen, dennoch übersichtliche Präsentation der Waren – auch hier könnte man einige Vergleiche zur modernen Baugeschichte ziehen.

Automobile exhibition
What does this actually entail? The problem is similar to that of a museum: the visitor has to be clearly guided through the exhibition, the exhibits and the background have to be clearly detectable, the location has to be prepared for the exhibits as regards space, lighting, acoustics and so on. A conceptual correlation with the Guggenheim Museum, for example, would not be inappropriate or to a good department store: large crowds of people but a clear presentation of the goods. A comparison to modern architectural history could also be drawn here.

The advantages of the multi-level structure are as follows: The degree to which the different levels jut out into the upper central area varies and the resulting surfaces can be used in different ways to suit the varying requirements of the exhibition. The viewpoint enjoyed by the visitor changes constantly and arouses his interest. He has a general view of the exhibits while ascending on the escalator and also while descending to floor level, a distance of 600 m by foot. The black curtains keep out any disturbing features of the hall and attempt to seduce the visitor into a private world with its own special atmosphere.

Die mehrgeschossige Installation leistet das: die Ebenen ragen unterschiedlich weit in den zentralen Luftraum, die so entstehenden Flächen reagieren individuell auf die Anforderungen der Ausstellung. Es entstehen stets wechselnde und spannende Blickbeziehungen. Der Besucher erhält nicht nur während der Fahrt mit der Rolltreppe nach oben einen Überblick über das Dargebotene, sondern auch während seines 600 m langen Wegs zurück ins Erdgeschoß. Die schwarze Hülle blendet alles Störende aus und versucht, den Besucher in eine in sich stimmige (Traum-) Welt zu verführen.

Die Materialien

Die hölzernen Oberflächen der Ebenen dominieren den Raumeindruck. Es entsteht ein Werkstattcharakter. Ein Charakter, der die Qualität eines temporären Bauwerks unterstützt. Es entsteht ein homogener Hintergrund, welcher zu den glänzenden und technisch bestimmten Produkten kontrastiert. Die stählernen Stützen, welche notwendigerweise die Ebenen tragen, sind mit einer ganzen Reihe von gezielten Maßnahmen (Farbe, Geometrie) in den Hintergrund gedrängt. Auch das Tragwerk der einzelnen Ebenen besteht aus Stahl (insgesamt 600 t). Die hölzernen Decken auf der Ober- und Unterseite verdecken diese Konstruktionen jedoch gänzlich. Die schwarze Hülle ist mit Spannseilen vom Dachtragwerk abgehängt und kann auf individuelle räumliche Anforderungen reagieren.

Die Light-Pipe

Die Light-Pipe hat drei Funktionen: Tageslichtlenkung, Abluftkamin und sichtbares Zeichen im Innen- und Außenraum.

Die Frankfurter Festhalle bietet mit der doppelschaligen, gläsernen Kuppel an sich gute Tageslichtbedingungen. Diese sind jedoch so ohne weiteres für eine Automobilmesse nicht zu verwenden. Die schwarze Hülle blendet das Tageslicht aus, die Light-Pipe bündelt das Tageslicht und bringt es an gezielten Stellen in die Halle. Heliostaten und Umlenkspiegel sowie die hochreflektierende Innenfläche der Röhre leisten das.

Materials

The wooden surfaces of the different levels dominate the overall impression. A kind of workshop feeling is created – something which a temporary structure underlines – and a homogenous background is provided which contrasts with the shiny products of automobile engineering. The steel pillars needed for supporting the levels are deliberately made into a part of the background by the use of various techniques (colour, geometry). The load-bearing structure of the individual levels is also made of steel (altogether 600 t) but is completely hidden by the wooden ceilings and floors. The black curtain is suspended from the roof structure by tension cables and can be altered to fit different spatial requirements.

The Light-Pipe

The light-pipe has three functions: to guide the daylight, to remove used air and to act as a visible symbol on the inside and outside.

The double-layered glass cupola of the festival hall in Frankfurt provides good lighting conditions but, unfortunately, they are not suitable for an automobile exhibition. The solution was to use a black curtain to keep out the daylight while installing a light pipe to bundle the daylight and guide it to specific locations within the hall. This is done by means of heliostats and deflecting mirrors in conjunction with the highly reflective interior surface of the pipe.

The many lamps combined with the large number of people produce heat which rises. If one wishes to use the upper zones of the space available, good airconditioning is therefore necessary. This is achieved here using natural methods; the light-pipe simply acts as a chimney for removing the warm used air.

Viele Lampen und viele Menschen erzeugen Wärme. Die Wärme steigt in
einem Raum nach oben. Will man auch
die oberen Zonen dieses Raums benutzen,
muß man für eine vernünftige Klimati-
sierung sorgen. Dies geschieht auf natür-
lichem Wege. Die Light-Pipe wird als
Abluftkamin genutzt.

Schon von weitem erkennt der Besucher
die Light-Pipe, welche etwa 10 m aus dem
Dach der Festhalle herausragt; soweit,
wie es notwendig war, um die Aufgabe
Licht und Abwärme zu bewältigen.

Baukasten – Wiederverwendbarkeit
Alle Bauteile sind so konstruiert, daß sie
für weitere Messeereignisse in der Festhalle wieder verwendet werden können.

The light-pipe, which sticks out about
10 m from the roof of the festival hall,
can be seen by the visitor even from a
long way away. This height is also enough
for the pipe to perform its tasks of providing light and removing heat.

The re-useability of modules
All the components are designed so that
they can be used for other trade-fair
events in the festival hall.

Die Light-Pipe unter der Kuppel

Aussteller	**The Light-Pipe Under the Cupola**
Mercedes Benz AG, Stuttgart	
Messe	Exhibitor
IAA – Internationale Automobilausstellung	Mercedes Benz AG, Stuttgart
Jahr	Trade fair
1995	IAA – international automobile exhibition
Ort	Year
Frankfurt	1995

Größe
11.000 qm
Konzept & Mitarbeiter
Kauffmann Theilig & Partner, Ostfildern
Andreas Theilig, Dieter B. Kauffmann,
Rainer Lenz
Atelier Markgraph, Frankfurt
Projektarchitekten
Uwe Schindler (Projektpartner),
Heidrun Ferber, Veronika Mahlke,
Steffen Haas, Hermann Esslinger,
Stefan Nixdorf
Bauten
Ernst F. Ambrosius & Sohn, Frankfurt
Beratung Tragwerk
Pfefferkorn & Partner, Stuttgart
Beratung Lüftungskonzept
Transsolar Energietechnik GmbH, Stuttgart
Kommunikation & Medien
Atelier Markgraph, Frankfurt
Grafik
Designbüro Uli Helbing
Fotos
Vaclav Reischl

Location
Frankfurt
Size
11000 sq. metres
Design and collaborators
Kauffmann Theilig & Partner, Ostfildern
Andreas Theilig, Dieter B. Kauffmann,
Rainer Lenz
Atelier Markgraph, Frankfurt
Project architects
Uwe Schindler (project partner)
Heidrun Ferber, Veronika Mahlke,
Steffen Haas, Hermann Esslinger,
Stefan Nixdorf
Construction work
Ernst F. Ambrosius & Sohn, Frankfurt
Consultants for load-bearing structure
Pfefferkorn & Partner, Stuttgart
Consultants for ventilation
Transsolar Energietechnik GmbH, Stuttgart
Communications and media
Atelier Markgraph, Frankfurt
Graphics
Designbüro, Uli Helbing
Photos
Vaclav Reischl

Der Lattenwald

Kauffmann Theilig & Partner
für Mercedes Benz
Kauffmann Theilig & Partner
for Mercedes Benz

A Forest of Wooden Slats

Vielfalt und Einheit
Es wird eine Fülle von unterschiedlichen
Fahrzeugen präsentiert: gewohnte Pkws
in unterschiedlichen Ausstellungslinien,
T-Modelle, Kleintransporter für gewerb-
lichen und individuellen Einsatz, Designo-
Fahrzeuge, Linien- und Reisebusse.

Variety and Uniformity
An abundance of different vehicles is
presented: the usual saloon cars in different exhibition lines, T-models, pick-ups
for trade and private use, "Designo"-
vehicles, buses for public transport and
coaches.

Für ein Ausstellungskonzept ist dies ein Problem: Vielfältige, zum Teil völlig unterschiedlich dimensionierte und extrem individuelle Fahrzeuge stehen maßstabslos nebeneinander – fast wie auf dem Parkplatz einer Autobahnraststätte. Die Individualität der Exponate, Orientierung und Konzentration der Besucher auf die Produkte leiden darunter.

Wir haben nach einem Element gesucht, welches dieser Vielfalt einen einheitlichen Rahmen gibt. Ein Element, welches in der Lage ist, unterschiedliche Maßstäbe zusammenzubringen, ein Element, was zwar effizient ist, aber dennoch im Hintergrund bleibt.

Der Lattenwald
6.000 vertikal aufgestellte Holzlatten, 2 m, 4 m oder 6 m lang, im wesentlichen in gewohnten Dachlattenquerschnitten, naturbelassene Holzoberfläche. Diese Latten vermitteln zwischen kurzen und langen Exponaten, zwischen hohen und niedrigen Fahrzeugen, zwischen farbigen und nicht farbigen Lacken. Sie zonieren, bilden Räume unterschiedlicher Dichte und Größe und umspülen die Exponate förmlich.

Durch die Transparenz zwischen den Stangen ahnt der Besucher die nächste Ausstellungslichtung, unterschiedliche Farben und Lichtintensitäten schimmern durch und wecken den Reiz neuer Entdeckungen.

Funktionen
Alle notwendigen Einrichtungen, die baulich ausformuliert werden müssen wie z.B. Betreuungszone, Besprechungsräume, Küche etc. sind so eingefügt, daß sie nicht körperlich in Erscheinung treten: Transparentes, zum Teil bedrucktes Glas wird rahmenlos zwischen und in den Holzlatten aufgestellt, Raumabschlüsse sind zwar vorhanden, aber nicht erkennbar. Die einzelnen Funktionen sind wie Inseln in Waldlichtungen angeordnet, Mitarbeiter und Berater mischen sich ganz selbstverständlich unter die Besucher.

This is a problem for the exhibition design that there is a great variety of very individual vehicles, some of them being of completely different sizes, which are placed next to each other at random, almost like a parking lot at a motorway service station. The individuality of the exhibits also makes it difficult for the visitor to orient himself or concentrate on the products.

We looked for an element which could place this variety within a uniform context, an element which was able to link the differing dimensions of the exhibits, was effective but still remained in the background.

The forest of slats
The exhibition contains 6000 vertically arranged wooden slats, 2 m, 4 m or 6 m long, most of them having the usual cross-section of roof battens and an untreated surface.

The slats mediate between short and long exhibits, high and low vehicles, brightly coloured and not so brightly coloured paints. They create zones and

Angemessenheit

Insgesamt 18 km Dachlatten werden verwendet. Sie sind in einem 15 cm hohen Bodenpodest verankert, die oberste Schicht aus Schichtsperrholz ist gleichzeitig die Gehfläche. Die Holzlatten sind auch Träger der Standgrafik und wirkungsvoller Reflektor der Standbeleuchtung.

Alle Materialien sind nachwachsende Rohstoffe und hervorragend recyclingfähig. Viele Baumaterialien sind unbearbeitet, so daß sie in einen weiteren Produktionskreislauf zurückgegeben werden können.

Herstellung und Montage des Standes sind sehr einfach und insoweit auch einer Messedauer von zehn Tagen angemessen.

Facilities

All the necessary facilities which had to be included in the structure, such as a service area, discussion rooms, a kitchen and so on, are incorporated so that they are not, in fact, physically visible as such. Transparent frameless glass panes, in part bearing inscriptions, are placed between and in the wooden slats. The different areas are delimited but this is not immediately detectable. The individual facilities are arranged like islands in forest clearings so that exhibitor personnel and consultants mix easily with the visitors.

Suitability

A total of 18 km of roof slats is used. They are anchored in a 15 cm high floor platform and the upper layer made of layered plywood is simultaneously the walking surface. The wooden slats also carry the graphics and effectively reflect the lighting for the stand.

All the materials are self-regenerating raw materials and are excellently suitable for recycling. In addition, many of the construction materials are untreated so that they can be re-used in the production process.

The stand is very easy to manufacture and assemble, making it is highly suitable for a trade fair of ten days duration.

Der Lattenwald

Aussteller
Mercedes Benz AG, Stuttgart
Messe
Auto Mobil International
Jahr
1996
Ort
Leipzig
Größe
1.000 qm
Konzept
Kauffmann Theilig & Partner, Ostfildern
Andreas Theilig, Dieter B. Kauffmann
Rainer Lenz
Mitarbeiter
Julia Därfler
Bauten
Dietrich Display, Friolzheim
Beleuchtung
Rolf Derrer, Zürich
Grafik
Designbüro Uli Helbing
Fotos
Vaclav Reischl
Frank Kleinbach

A Forest of Wooden Slats

Exhibitor
Mercedes Benz AG, Stuttgart
Trade fair
Auto Mobil International
Year
1996
Location
Leipzig
Size
1000 sq. metres
Design
Kauffmann Theilig & Partner, Ostfildern
Andreas Theilig, Dieter B. Kauffmann
Rainer Lenz

Collaborator
Julia Därfler
Construction work
Dietrich Display, Friolzheim
Lighting
Rolf Derrer, Zurich
Graphics
Designbüro Uli Helbing
Photos
Vaclav Reischl
Frank Kleinbach

Die gebirgige
Ausstellungs-Landschaft

Kauffmann Theilig & Partner
für Mercedes Benz
Kauffmann Theilig & Partner
for Mercedes Benz

An Exhibition Landscape of Mountains

Here, a separate world has been created on a ground floor area of over 10.000 sq. metres. The unattractive surfaces of the hall construction are mostly concealed and,

Auf einer Grundfläche von über 10.000 qm entwickelte sich eine eigene Welt: Die schnöden Oberflächen der Hallenkonstruktion sind weitgehend ausgeblendet; eine gebirgige Landschaft, in zwei Ebenen organisiert, erzeugt Räume und Teilräume, unter der Erde und über der Erde. Das Konzept wird so der Vielfalt der Exponate gerecht. Ein grobmaschiges, hellfarbiges Sisalgewebe überzieht die Landschaft vollständig. Es erzeugt einen einheitlichen Ausstellungshintergrund für einen ganzheitlichen Messeauftritt der Nutzfahrzeuge von Mercedes Benz.

instead, there is a landscape of mountains organised on two levels into rooms and areas, both below and above the earth. The design does justice to the variety of the exhibits by means of a large-mesh, light-coloured sisal fabric which completely covers the landscape, thus creating a uniform background to the exhibition and ensuring an integral appearance by the utility vehicles of Mercedes Benz.

15 m lange Reisebusse stehen kühn auf einer Schrägen, sechs, sieben oder acht Zugmaschinen sind nebeneinander spielerisch auf einem Hochplateau angeordnet, vierrad-getriebene Spezialfahrzeuge sind plaziert in einer Nische.

Die spielerische Leichtigkeit, in der diese schweren Fahrzeuge fast selbstverständlich ihren Platz finden, erweckt den Eindruck von Unangestrengtheit, relativiert den Maßstab und nimmt die Massivität eines solchen Fahrzeugs für den Besucher.

Der Weg

Über die westliche Stirnseite der Halle betreten die Besucher, aus unterschiedlichen Richtungen kommend, die Ausstellungshalle von Mercedes Benz. Ein leichter textiler Vorhang verdeckt zunächst den Blick in die Halle, informiert über wesentliche Absichten und erhöht die Spannung.

So vorbereitet, betritt der Besucher die Halle über einen 200 m langen, diagonal über alle Bereiche geführten Steg. Dadurch gelingt es, allen Ausstellungsbesuchern einen hervorragenden Überblick zu verschaffen.

Vom Endpunkt des Steges aus ist ein spannender Weg durch die Ausstellung inszeniert. Dieser Weg führt durch alle Themen, die Mercedes Benz für seine Besucher vorbereitet hat. Das Ausstellungskonzept wird so dem ganzheitlichen Ansatz des Ausstellers gerecht. Ein Produkt/ein Thema kann vom Besucher aber auch gezielt aufgesucht werden.

15 m-long coaches are boldly presented on an inclination; six, seven or eight traction engines are playfully arranged next to each other on an elevated plateau and special four-wheel-drive vehicles look self-consciously for protection in a niche. The feeling of playful lightness imparted to these heavy vehicles invokes an impression of effortlessness, puts them on a more relative scale and diminishes their effect of massiveness on the visitor.

Visitor's pathway

The visitors, coming from different directions, enter the exhibition hall of Mercedes Benz through the west front side of the hall. A lightweight fabric curtain at first blocks off the view into the hall but gives a basic idea of what is to be expected and increases anticipation.

Thus prepared, the visitor enters the hall across a 200 m-long footbridge which passes diagonally over all the different sections of the exhibition. This gives him an excellent overview in the truest sense of the word.

At the end of the footbridge, there is a fascinating pathway leading through the different themes of the exhibition as prepared for the visitor by Mercedes Benz. In this way, the exhibition design complies with the holistic approach adopted by the exhibitor but visitors are still able to find the different themes or products they are interested in without having to search about.

Ausstellungs-Landschaft
Auf dem erhabenen Plateau werden
Weltneuheiten präsentiert. Kleine Ver-
werfungen bilden ganz selbstverständlich Brüstungen und Begrenzungen. In
einer Grotte abseits von Lärm und Licht
präsentieren sich Dinge, die mehr Konzentration benötigen. In einer Mulde

entsteht ganz selbstverständlich ein Forum. Unter einem Felsvorsprung ist ein
Produkt plaziert, um besonders beachtet
zu werden. In dem die Landschaft durch-
ziehenden Canyon / Tal präsentieren sich
rechts und links in dichter Folge immer
wieder neue Themen.

Die Analogie zum geografischen Land-
schaftsbegriff hilft uns, mit der Vielfalt,
mit den unterschiedlichen Maßstäben und
mit den unterschiedlichen Kommunika-
tionselementen differenziert umzugehen.

Das Sisalgewebe ist gleichsam die Vegetation, die alle Unterschiede und alle Teilräume wieder zusammenfaßt.

Exhibition landscape
On the eminent plateau, world innovations are presented. Small faults in the
landscape act as natural balustrades
and borders. In a grotto away from the
noise and light, there are items which
require more concentration. A forum is
created in a hollow and one exhibit is
placed beneath a ledge to attract the
attention. In the canyon passing through
the landscape, a series of new themes are
presented in rapid sequence.

The analogy to a geographical landscape helps us to handle the variety, the
different scales and the different communications elements.

The sisal fabric is at the same time a kind
of vegetation, providing a link between
all the different features and areas.

Die gebirgige Ausstellungs-Landschaft

Aussteller
Mercedes Benz AG, Stuttgart
Messe
IAA Nutzfahrzeuge
Jahr
1996
Ort
Hannover
Größe
12.000 qm Grundfläche
18.000 qm Ausstellungsfläche
Konzept
Kauffmann Theilig & Partner, Ostfildern
Andreas Theilig, Dieter B. Kauffmann,
Rainer Lenz
Atelier Markgraph, Frankfurt
Projektarchitekten
Almut Weinecke (Projektleitung)
Susanne Mim, Esther Hagenlocher
Bauten
Ernst F. Ambrosius & Sohn, Frankfurt
Beratung Tragwerk
Pfefferkorn & Partner, Stuttgart
Beratung Lüftungskonzept
Transsolar Energietechnik GmbH, Stuttgart
Kommunikation & Medien
Atelier Markgraph, Frankfurt
Grafik
Baumann + Baumann, Schwäbisch Gmünd
Fotos
Vaclav Reischl

An Exhibition Landscape of Mountains

Exhibitor
Mercedes Benz AG, Stuttgart
Trade fair
IAA utility vehicles
Year
1996
Location
Hanover
Size
12000 sq. metres floor area
18000 exhibition area
Design
Kauffmann Theilig & Partner, Ostfildern
Andreas Theilig, Dieter B. Kauffmann,
Rainer Lenz
Atelier Markgraph, Frankfurt
Project architects
Almut Weinecke (project management)
Susanne Mim
Esther Hagenlocher

Construction work
Ernst F. Ambrosius & Sohn, Frankfurt
Consultants for load-bearing structure
Pfefferkorn & Partner, Stuttgart
Consultants for ventilation
Transsolar Energietechnik GmbH, Stuttgart
Communications and media
Atelier Markgraph, Frankfurt
Graphics
Baumann + Baumann, Schwäbisch Gmünd
Photos
Vaclav Reischl

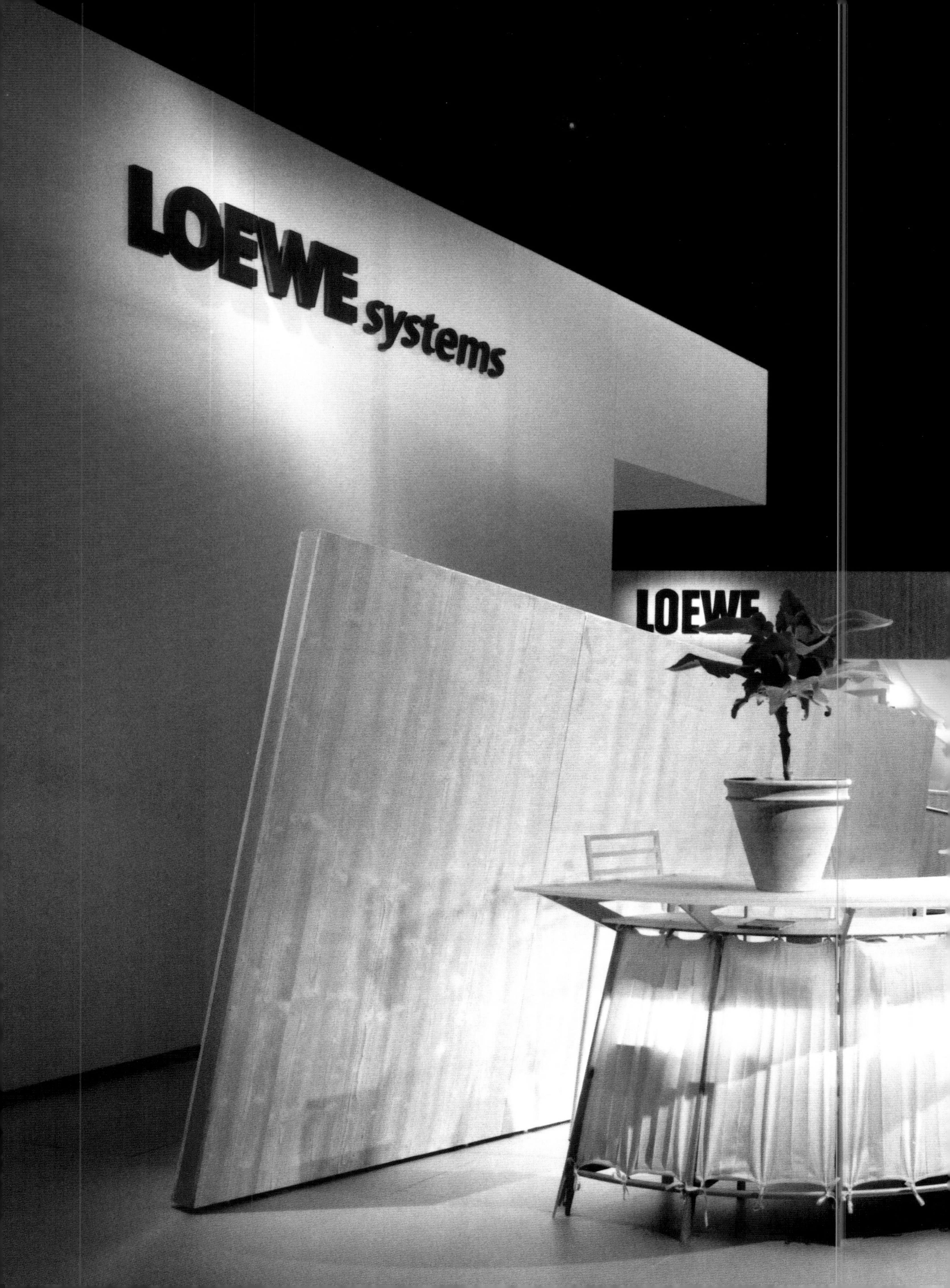
LOEWE systems
LOEWE

Film und Raum

Selbstinszenierung wird in dem Maße wichtiger, in dem die Austauschbarkeit der Produkte voranschreitet. Der Verbraucher kauft schon längst nicht mehr nur eine Ware, sondern vor allem die Aura, die es umgibt. Levi's sind etwas ganz anderes als nur Jeans, und eine Patek Philippe ist viel mehr als bloß eine Uhr. Solche Images müßen aber nicht nur in der klassischen Werbung, sondern auch auf Messen gelebt werden.

Produkte sieht der Messebesucher genug. Und sein Aufnahmevermögen läßt erfahrungsgemäß schon nach relativ kurzer Zeit im Gewühl und Trubel der Messe und unter dem Eindruck der Fülle der gebotenen Informationsreize deutlich nach. Ein perfekt entwickeltes Szenarium jedoch frischt das Aufnahmevermögen auf. Schönes sieht man eben lieber an als Ödes. Und etwas interessant Dargebotenes bleibt länger im Gedächtnis haften.

Film and Room

Self-presentation is becoming more and more important as the interchangeability of products increases. The consumer no longer buys just an article, he looks for an aura which it gives off: Levi's are not merely jeans and a Patek Philippe is much more than simply a watch. Such images, however, must also be brought to life at trade fairs and not just in classical advertising.

The trade-fair visitor sees a great variety of products. And as experience shows, his ability to take things in fades considerably after a relatively short time in the hustle and bustle of the fair and after being subjected to the floods of information. A perfectly developed scenario, however, can refresh the attention. People prefer to look at something beautiful than something ugly and an interesting presentation remains stuck in the memory for a much longer time.

 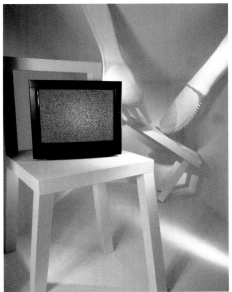 

So ist denn die Mischung von Information
und Unterhaltung auch keineswegs
Selbstzweck, sondern kalkulierter Bestandteil der jeweiligen Verkaufsstrategie.

The mixture of information and entertainment, therefore, is by no means
an end in itself but is a calculated component of the sales strategy adopted.

Die Aufgabe lautete: Positionierung von LOEWE Opta auf der Internationalen Funkausstellung in Berlin als Unternehmen mit technologischer Kompetenz und hohem Designanspruch.

Die Lösung: Trennung der 1.200 qm umfassenden Grundfläche in zwei Hauptbereiche, einen doppelstöckigen Händlerbereich mit 40 Arbeitsplätzen für Fachgespräche und einen Präsentationsbereich. Blickfang aus der Ferne und zentraler Verbindungspunkt ist der stoffumspannte „Leuchtturm". Als zweiter Blickfang im Nahbereich drehen sich drei große Zahnräder – Zitate aus Charlie Chaplins „Moderne Zeiten" – und präsentieren die TV-Geräte. In Filmstimmungen versetzen dann schließlich fünf monochrome Räume. Dabei symbolisieren die unterschiedlichen Farben der einzelnen Produktlinien jeweils ein bestimmtes Filmgenre.

The aim in this case was to introduce LOEWE Opta at the international broadcasting exhibition as a company with technological expertise and a high level of quality in design.

The solution was to divide the 1200 sq metres floor area into two main sections: a double-level commercial section with 40 workstations for specialist discussions and a presentation section. The "lighthouse" surrounded by fabric acts as a central meeting point and allows the visitor a view into the distance. As a second eye-catcher close by, three large cogwheels rotate – reminiscent of Charlie Chaplin's "Modern Times" – and present the TV sets. Five monochrome rooms then put the visitor into a "film" mood with the different colours of the individual product lines symbolising a specific film genre.

Film und Raum

Aussteller
LOEWE Opta GmbH, Kronach
Messe
IFA – Internationale Funkausstellung
Jahr
1995
Ort
Berlin

Größe
1.200 qm
Entwurf/Konzeption
Claus Neuleib, Peter Haberlander
Projektleitung
Mirka Nassiri, Robert Gamohn
Farbräume-Styling
Gaby Krauss
Licht
Müller Music
Ausführung
Arno Design GmbH, München
Illustration
Margit Pawle
Fotos
Frank Kotzerke

Film and Room

Exhibitor
LOEWE Opta GmbH, Kronach
Trade fair
IFA – international broadcasting exhibition
Year
1995
Location
Berlin
Size
1200 sq. metres
Design/conception
Claus Neuleib, Peter Haberlander
Project management
Mirka Nassiri, Robert Gamohn
Coloured rooms – styling
Gaby Krauss
Lighting
Müller Music
Implementation
Arno Design GmbH, Munich
Illustration
Margit Pawle
Photos
Frank Kotzerke

Dynamik, Tempo, Graffiti

Dynamics, Speed and Graffiti

Der Marktführer unter den Inlineskate-Herstellern wünschte einen Messeauftritt, der glaubwürdig die Aspekte vergegenständlicht, die mit der jungen, dynamischen Trendsportart in Verbindung gebracht werden. Inlineskate-laufen bedeutet, die scheinbar alltägliche Umgebung, die Nachbarschaft, die City im Rausch der Geschwindigkeit neu zu erleben.

The market leader among inline-skate manufacturers wanted a trade-fair stand which convincingly represented the characteristics associated with this young and dynamic new trend in sport. Inline skating means re-experiencing everyday surroundings such as the neighbourhood and the city in an ecstasy of speed.

This definition is implicit in the stand. When the visitor encounters the theme of graffiti – a typical feature of city life – it is not on a wall but on the floor. The stand architecture is constructed of modular and flowing skate-presentation elements which are arranged to give the impression of skating speed and a dynamic, "swooping" feeling of space. The presentation modules made of steel, stainless steel and plexiglass place the product at the centre of attention and, with the help of stretched fabric, create a quiet background to the presentation.

Above the stand architecture, a high-tech intersection is stretched which provides a visionary stage-setting for the theme by means of light and silhouettes.

Dieser Definition verpflichtet, begegnet der Messebesucher dem Thema Graffiti, als Zitat aus dem modernen Stadtbild, nicht wie gewohnt in der Vertikalen, sondern als Fußbodenbelag. Weiterhin baut sich die Standarchitektur aus modularen, geschwungenen Skate Präsentationselementen auf, die, im „Schlittschuh-Schritt" angeordnet, ein dynamisches, steilkurvenähnliches Raumgefühl vermitteln. Die Präsentationsmodule aus Stahl, Edelstahl und Plexiglas rücken das Produkt in den Mittelpunkt des Stands und schaffen mittels einer Stoffverspannung einen ruhigen Präsentationshintergrund.

Die Standarchitektur wurde mit einem „High-Tech-Kreuzgang" überspannt, der mittels Licht und Silhouetten für eine visionäre Inszenierung des skurrilen Themas sorgte.

Dynamik, Tempo, Graffiti

Aussteller
K2 Inlineskate
Messe
ISPO – Internationale Fachmesse für
Sportartikel und Sportmode
Jahr
1995 und 1996
Ort
München
Größe
110 qm (1995) und 200 qm (1996)

Dynamics, Speed and Graffiti

Exhibitor
K2 Inlineskate
Trade fair
ISPO – international trade fair for
sport articles and fashion
Year
1995 and 1996
Location
Munich
Size
110 sq. metres (1995)
and 200 sq. metres (1996)

Entwurf
Steiner Design, München
Thomas Bauer, Frank Schaffrath
(Neu: messebauer GmbH)
Realisation
H.Steiner, Berg / Starnberger See
Fotos
Susie Knoll

Design
Steiner Design, Munich
Thomas Bauer, Frank Schaffrath
(New: messebauer GmbH)
Implementation
H. Steiner, Berg / Starnberger See
Photos
Susie Knoll

Dauerhaft nur in der Erinnerung

Wolfgang Körber

„Was ein Mensch lernen sollte, ist, zu vergessen alles, was nutzlos in der Erinnerung ist, um zurückzuhalten mit Liebe alles, was nützen und erfreuen kann."
Petrarca

Ausstellungsbauten, entworfen für einen kurzen Zeitraum von oft nur wenigen Tagen, von unterschiedlicher Größe, einfach bis aufwendig realisiert und meistens für eine einmalige Verwendung gedacht, erfüllen eine Vermittlungsaufgabe. Sie müssen Produkte, Leistungen, Informationen mit ausstellungsspezifischen Mitteln im dreidimensionalen Raum erinnerungsfähig darbieten. Ausstellungsbauten stehen selten für sich allein, fast auschließlich dicht bei dicht, müssen sich nicht zuletzt deswegen gegeneinander behaupten, wenn möglich übertreffen. Man erwartet von diesen Bauten das Außergewöhnliche, Faszinierende, Einmalige; ja, das Dargebotene möge Freude und Begeisterung beim Betrachten auslösen. Wenn es also gelänge, das für den Augenblick Erdachte und Erbaute, alsbald unwiederbringlich Verschwundene, in der Erinnerung auf Dauer zu erhalten, dann hätten diese Bauwerke nicht nur ihren Sinn erfüllt, sondern auch den großen ideellen wie materiellen Aufwand gerechtfertigt.

Was bleibt erinnerbar? Wir wissen: All jenes bleibt erinnerbar, was über den Weg der emotionalen Wahrnehmung ins Langzeitgedächtnis gelangt. Es ist nie Gewißheit, sondern lediglich Hoffnung, daß die Wahl der emotionalisierenden Gestaltgebung richtig ist, um jenen individuellen Erwartungs- und Verständnispunkt der Mehrheit der Kommunikationspartner zu treffen, der das Erinnern bewirkt, damit auch Jahre später das unwiederbringlich Erlebte spontan wiedererlebbar wird.

Lasting Only in Memory

„What a person should learn is to forget everything in the memory that is useless in order to retain with love everything of benefit and pleasure."
Petrarca

Exhibition constructions perform a communicative function and are designed for a short period of time often lasting just a few days. They have different sizes, are simple or complicated and mostly intended for one-off use as well.
Their task is to display products, services and information with materials specific to exhibitions in three-dimensional space and they must do this in a memorable fashion. Exhibition structures are practically never isolated from others. They are nearly always erected very close together and have to compete with and even try to surpass each other. People expect these structures to be unusual, fascinating and unique; what is shown should even engender pleasure and enthusiasm. If the memory subsequently retains what has been created and built for the moment, what immediately and irrevocably disappears, then these constructions not only fulfil their purpose, they also justify the great mental effort and material expenditure entailed by them.

What remains in the memory? We know that everything which is perceived emotionally can be remembered and remains in the long-term memory. There can never be certainty, only hope, that the choice of an emotionalising design is the correct one, satisfying individual expectations and finding the understanding of a majority of the people addressed as well as stimulating the memory so that years later an irretrievable experience can be spontaneously relived.

Wer sich auf die Suche begibt nach den Maßstäben für eine emotionalisierende Gestaltgebung, die geeignet ist, eine bestimmte Vermittlungsabsicht zu transportieren, die den Abstand sucht zu den Gestalt-Banalitäten des gewohnten Umfeldes, wird die Arbeiten renommierter Designer studieren. Besser noch, er sollte unmittelbar den Schritt ins Freie wagen, dorthin, wo die Gestaltungsgrenzen unter Beteiligung von allen und allem permanent neu definiert werden. Dieses Aktions- und Definitionsfeld ist die Kunst. Im Freiraum der Kunst wird die Transformation der – unsere Lebensumstände bestimmenden – Faktoren unserer Zeit in Fragestellungen und Gegenentwürfen vollzogen. Ohne die Kunst als experimentelle Werkstatt und Forschung treibendes Ideenlabor würde das Spiel mit Assoziationen, Durchdringungen, Übertreibungen, Sensibilisierungen, Schockierungen, Enttabuisierungen die Entwicklung neuer Sichten und Empfindungen in Fülle nie entstehen können. Die Diskussion in der Öffentlichkeit über die vielfältigen Erscheinungen der Kunst dient der Sichtung, dem Verriß, der Aneignung. Gegenstände und Denkweisen unserer Umgebung werden über den Filter unseres Wissens von den künstlerischen Reflektionen wahrgenommen und neu ver- und bearbeitet.

If you want to find examples of 'emotionalising' design which are capable of conveying a particular communicative intention and which try to distance themselves from the banalities of our usual surroundings, the work of well-known designers should be studied. Even better would be a step into the unknown, to where the limits of design are being permanently redefined, with everyone and everything participating in the process. This field of action and definition is art. In the licence enjoyed by art, those aspects of our time which define our lives are questioned, re-designed and therefore transformed. Without art as an experimental workshop and a research laboratory of ideas, the whole game with its abundance of associations, penetrations, exaggerations, sensitisation, shocks, the removal of taboos, the development of new points of view and feelings would never be possible. The public discussion on the varied phenomena of art serves the purposes of inspection, attack and, finally, appropriation. The objects and ways of thinking in our surroundings are perceived, processed and re-processed by artistic reflection through the filter of our knowledge.

Hommage an die Kunst

Luxarama III

Seit 1972 existiert Luxarama, ein künstlerisches Lichtprojekt von Wolfgang
Körber. Bis jetzt sind drei Projekte – unterschiedlich in Aufwand und Größe – in
Partnerschaft mit der Industrie realisiert

Homage to Art

worden, mit dem Ziel, Licht, befreit vom
Alltagszwang, als Beleuchtung zu zeigen.
Luxarama III präsentiert das CO-AX
Niedervolt Stromschienen System der Fir-
ma LFF GmbH, bis zu einer Höhe von
ca. 2,20 m als Produktprogramm, darüber
bis in 6 m Höhe als programmgesteuerte
Licht-Inszenierung. Dies alles auf einer
Grundfläche von 33 qm.

Die tragenden Elemente der Standkon-
struktion sowie der Fußboden sind
aus unbehandeltem Stahl, die Wandflächen aus Stoffbahnen. Durch die Verwendung von Zug- und Druckelementen
wird eine hohe Steifigkeit der Konstruktion bei geringem Gewicht erreicht, trotz
Zugang übers Eck. Der Tresenblock ist
fast vollständig mit Elektrotechnik ausge-
füllt. Alles ist demontabel in leicht zu
transportierende Längen, platzsparend
zu lagern, in kurzer Zeit auch in anderen
Höhen wieder aufbaubar.

Luxarama III

Luxarama, an artistic project by Wolfgang
Körber, has been in existence since 1972.
Up to now, three projects of different
complexity and size have been created in
a partnership with industry, with the
aim of showing light freed from its everyday role as a provider of illumination.
Luxarama presents the low-voltage supp-
ly-track system of the company LFF GmbH.
Up to a height of approximately 2.20 m,
the stand consists of the product range
of the company and above this, to a
height of 6 m, a program-controlled light
setting is provided. This is all done on a
floor area of 33 sq. meters.

The load bearing elements of the stand
construction and the floor are made
of the untreated steel; the wall surfaces
are lengths of material. Due to the use
of tension and pressure elements, the
construction is very rigid while having
a low weight in spite of the fact that the
access is at a corner. The counter block
is almost completely filled with electronics.
Everything can be dismantled into easy-
to-transport lengths, stored in a small
space and reassembled in a short time,
even at different heights.

Hommage an die Kunst

Aussteller
Licht Form Funktion (LFF) GmbH, Solingen
Messe
EuroShop
Jahr
1996
Ort
Düsseldorf
Größe
33,18 qm
Raum
185,79 cbm
Konzept / Gestaltung
Wolfgang Körber, Solingen
Fotos
Herbert Jungbluth

Homage to Art

Exhibitor
Licht Form Funktion (LFF) GmbH, Solingen
Trade fair
EuroShop
Year
1996

Location
Düsseldorf
Size
33.18 sq. metres
Volume
185.79 cbm
Layout and design
Wolfgang Körber, Solingen
Photos
Herbert Jungbluth

Denken
Planen
Bauen

Dietrich Display GmbH

"Schon ein Geruch,
kann mancherlei entkräften"
Gottfried Benn
Erfahrungen, Gemeinsames,
Erinnerungen:
Wünsche, Verlangen,
Vergangenheit.

Die Sinneswände

Walls of the Senses

Dietrich Concept & Design und Dietrich Services sollten als neue Dienstleistungen – zusätzlich zu den herkömmlichen Leistungen eines Messebauunternehmens – angeboten werden.

Die Aufgabe: Wie kann man erreichen, daß möglichst viele unserer Besucher mit uns zusammenarbeiten wollen?

Das Kommunikationsziel: Dietrich konzipiert, plant und baut Kommunikationsplattformen auf Messen und Austellungen.

Die Vorgaben: Der Stand muß aus dem neuen „System T" gebaut werden. Das Budget für 1996 ist noch mal um 25% geringer als 1993.

In Teamsitzungen wurde ein Konzept mit folgendem Inhalt erarbeitet:
· Der Stand strahlt, er kommuniziert selbst, er regt zu eigenen Vorstellungen an. Die Sinne können an einer „Sinneswand" geprüft und geschärft werden.
· Über diese Erfahrungen beginnt die Kommunikation über die Kommunikation.
· Als Zugabe sollen Experten über Wahrnehmung referieren.

Dietrich Concept & Design and Dietrich Services were to be presented as new services in addition to the usual work done by the trade-fair construction company.

The problem was how to get as many as possible of the visitors to want to work with us.

The message: Dietrich designs, plans and builds communications platforms for trade fairs and exhibitions.

The specifications: The stand had to be built using the new "System-T". The budget for 1996 was again 25 % lower than 1993.

In team meetings, the following concept was worked out:
· The stand was to have a life of its own; it should communicate itself and stimulate people's imagination. A "wall of the senses" was to be provided so that people could test and sharpen their physical senses.
· This is how communication about communication was to begin.
· In addition to all this, talks were to be given by various experts on sensory perception.

Die Lösung: Ein aus „System T" errichtetes Gerüst trug in der äußeren Halbschale Drahtglas. Außen waren das Logo, die Firmenbezeichnung und der Slogan „Denken, Planen, Bauen" in spiegelndem Material aufgebracht. Auf der Innenseite der Glaswände waren in Form einer Art Wandzeitung die Firmenhistorie, die Dienstleistungen der neuen Dietrich-Firmen und die Konzepte der vorherigen EuroShop-Stände gedruckt. In einer inneren Halbschale wurden die „Sinneswände" eingerichtet, an denen Sehen, Riechen, Fühlen und Hören spielerisch geprüft werden konnten. Im Kern der Halbschale konnten Gespräche stattfinden und als weitere Wahrnehmung das Schmecken getestet werden. Das Publikum war überrascht. Über die Sinne fiel es leicht, ins Gespräch über die Kommunikation zu kommen.

The solution: A framework, erected using "System-T", bore wire-reinforced glass in an outer shell. On the outside, the logo, the name of the company and the slogan "Think, Plan, Build" were applied using a reflective material. The company history in the form of a kind of newspaper, the services of the new Dietrich companies and the concepts of the previous EuroShop stands were printed on the inside of the glass walls. Inside an interior shell, "walls of the senses" were set up for testing the senses of seeing, smelling, feeling and hearing in an entertaining manner.

At the core of the shell, it was possible for people to talk and test their sense of taste, the fifth sense. The public was surprised. By talking about the senses, it was all the more easy to move to the topic of communication.

Die Sinneswände

Aussteller
Dietrich Display GmbH, Friolzheim
Messe
EuroShop
Jahr
1996
Ort
Düsseldorf
Größe
144 qm
Gestaltung
Dietrich Team, 3-5 Mitarbeiter
Bauten
Dietrich Display GmbH
Fotos
Frank Kleinbach

Walls of the Senses

Exhibitor
Dietrich Display GmbH, Friolzheim
Trade fair
Euroshop
Year
1996
Location
Düsseldorf
Size
144 sq. metres
Design
Dietrich Team, 3 to 5 collaborators
Construction work
Dietrich Display GmbH
Photos
Frank Kleinbach

Gestaltungsanspruch der Messearchitektur und betriebswirtschaftliches Messekalkül im Wettstreit

The Design Demands of Trade-Fair Architecture versus Commercial Calculation

Gestaltungsanspruch der Messearchitektur und betriebswirtschaftliches Messekalkül im Wettstreit

Jörg Beier, Prof. Dr.
Professor at the Staat-
liche Studienakademie
in Ravensburg.
As head of department,
he is responsible for
the subjects of commerce
and trade-fair manage-
ment. In 1986, with
the support of AUMA
and other German
associations, he inaugu-
rated a special course
of studies for trade-fair
management, the only
one of its kind up to now.

Messearchitektur und betriebswirtschaftliches Diktat

Betrachter geraten ins Schwärmen: „Ein Exot der Messelandschaft, dieser Stand spiegelt die Vorstellung des Designers von Messen wider: Theater, Show, Einzigartigkeit".

Budgetvorgaben werden überschritten. Die Beteiligungskontrolle zeigt auf, daß hohe Kosten verursacht wurden, aber nur verhältnismäßig wenige Kundenkontakte geknüpft wurden. Hohe Entsorgungskosten des Standmaterials sind entstanden. Zusatzkosten beim Veranstalter werden berechnet. Die Logistik stellt sich als Engpaß heraus. Der organisatorische Ablauf auf dem Stand wird bemängelt.

Die Konsequenzen hieraus: Ein Messeauftritt unterliegt betriebswirtschaftlichen Zwängen. Zwänge sind natürliche Feinde kreativer Standbauarchitekten. Andererseits haben Designer und Architekten einen Gestaltungsanspruch, der sich aus ihrem schöpferischen und künstlerischen Selbstverständnis und architektonischen Notwendigkeiten ableitet. Der für beide Teile geeignete Weg kann nur ein Kompromiß sein.

Im folgenden soll aufgezeigt werden, wie der Messebau im betriebswirtschaftlichen Konzept der Beteiligungsplanung angesiedelt ist, welche Aufgaben abgeleitet aus den übergeordneten Zielen wahrzunehmen sind, welche Gestaltungsinstrumente dem Designer und Architekten zur Messestandgestaltung zur Verfügung stehen und welche Zielkonflikte existieren.

Trade-fair architecture and the dictates of business-management

Observers fall into raptures: "An exotic landmark in the trade-fair landscape, this stand reflects the imagination of the trade-fair designer: theatre, show and uniqueness."

And then come the problems: the budget has been exceeded. A check on the level of participation shows that high costs have been incurred but only relatively few customer contacts have been made. High disposal costs of the stand materials have resulted and extra fees are being charged by the organiser. The logistics turns out to be a bottleneck and the organisational procedure on the stand is found fault with.

The consequence of this is that a trade-fair appearance is subject to the constraints of business-management. Constraints are the natural enemies of creative stand-construction architects. In contrast, designers and architects present design demands which are derived from their creative and artistic nature and the architectonic necessities. The only suitable approach for both parties is to find a compromise.

The following is intended to show what place trade-fair construction occupies in the business strategy adopted for participating in a fair, what tasks derived from the superordinate goals have to be considered, what design tools are available to the designer and architect for designing the trade-fair stand and what conflicts of goals exist.

Stand construction as a part of trade-fair planning

A conception of participation

The trade-fair and exhibition policy of a company is a component of its overall marketing approach. Partly defined as an independent marketing tool, partly subsumed as an instrument of communication, the purpose of participation in trade fairs and exhibitions is to intentionally design the information directed at a sales market with the aim of controlling the behaviour of already-existing customers and potential ones as well.

Standbau als Teil der Beteiligungsplanung

Beteiligungskonzeption

Die Messe- und Ausstellungspolitik eines Unternehmens ist Bestandteil des Marketing-Mix eines Unternehmens. Teils als eigenständiges Marketing-Instrument definiert, teils als Kommunikationsinstrument subsumiert, dient die Beteiligung an Messen und Ausstellungen der bewußten Gestaltung der auf den Absatzmarkt gerichteten Informationen einer Unternehmung mit der Absicht, das Verhalten aktueller und potentieller Kunden zu steuern. Damit erhält die Messe- und Ausstellungspolitik Instrumentalcharakter und ist vorgelagerten betriebswirtschaftlichen Unternehmenszielen untergeordnet.

Voraussetzung für den optimalen Einsatz des Marketinginstruments „Messe- und Ausstellungsbeteiligung" ist die Erstellung einer Messekonzeption, in der alle wesentlichen Planungsinhalte systematisch erfaßt und beschrieben sind. Die Messekonzeption ist Leitfaden der Messepolitik, d.h. für das gesamte Messeprogramm, aber auch für die einzelne Beteiligungsplanung des Unternehmens.

Marketingstrategische Grundraster

Die Beteiligungskonzeption leitet sich aus der Marketingkonzeption und Marketingstrategie des Unternehmens ab. Eine effiziente Messepolitik ist nur möglich, wenn sich das Unternehmen dezidiert über folgende Fragen Klarheit verschafft hat:

• Welche Produkte und Märkte sollen zukünftig bearbeitet werden? Sollen die Märkte abgebaut werden oder bearbeitet das Unternehmen vornehmlich neue oder gegenwärtige Märkte. Tritt das Unternehmen mit neuen Produkten auf dem Markt auf oder sind es bereits etablierte Produkte, die angeboten werden (Marktfeldstrategie)? Damit wird messepolitisch die Art der Produktpräsentation fixiert und die Marktansprache vorgegeben: Marktdurchdringung, Produkt- oder Marktentwicklung, Diversifikation.

• Auf welche Art und Weise soll der Markt stimuliert werden? Ist eine Preis-Mengenstrategie geeignet oder wird eine Qualitätsstrategie präferiert (Marktstimulierungsstrategie)? Hieraus lassen sich klare Vorgaben für die Argumentationslinie eines Messeauftrittes gewinnen: Preis oder Qualität als Leitlinie.

The trade-fair and exhibition policy is therefore a kind of tool and is subordinate to higher-ranking business goals.

A precondition for making optimum use of the trade fair or exhibition as a marketing tool is the preparation of an overall conception in which all the essential plans are systematically included and described. The trade-fair conception is the central guideline for the policy to be adopted at the trade fair, i.e. for the whole trade-fair programme but also for the individual plans of the company.

The basic pattern of marketing strategy

The conception for trade-fair participation is derived from the marketing conception and strategy of a company. An efficient trade-fair policy is possible only if the company has definitively obtained clarity concerning the following questions:

• Which products and markets are to be concentrated on in future? Should the markets be reduced or does the company prefer to concentrate on new or existing markets? Does the company want to launch new products on the market or are established products to be offered (sales field strategy)? In this way, trade-fair policy defines the type of product presentation and how the market is to be addressed: penetration of the market, development of the product or market, or diversification.

• How is the market to be stimulated? Is a price strategy suitable or is a quality strategy preferable (market-stimulation strategy)? From these considerations, a clear basis for presenting the company's caseat the trade-fair can be obtained whereby price or quality is selected as the guideline.

• A mass market or a market split up into sectors? Which market segments and target groups are customers of mine? Does the product or the service provided only satisfy the needs of specific groups of customers or are a range of products to be offered which interest all potential buyers (market-splitting strategy)? The answers obtained can be of help in making decisions on which trade fair to choose, on the one hand, and which communications tools to select, on the other.

Jörg Beier, Prof. Dr.
lehrt an der Staatlichen Studienakademie Ravensburg und ist Leiter der Fachrichtung Handel/Messewirtschaft. 1986 begründete er mit Unterstützung des AUMA und anderer deutscher Verbände des Messewesens den bisher einzigen speziellen Studiengang für Messewirtschaft.

• Massenmarkt versus Marktparzellierung. Welche Marktsegmente und Zielgruppen gehören zu meinen Kunden? Erfüllt das angebotene Produkt oder die Dienstleistung lediglich die Bedürfnisse bestimmter Kundengruppen oder wird ein Sortiment offeriert, das alle anspricht (Marktparzellierungsstrategie)? Aus den Vorgaben können einerseits Entscheidungshilfen für die Messeauswahl gewonnen werden, andererseits wird die Auswahl der Kommunikationsinstrumente vorselektiert.

• Auf welchen lokalen, regionalen, nationalen oder internationalen Märkten findet das Unternehmen seine Käufer? In welchen Regionen wird das Produkt hauptsächlich angeboten? Welche Zukunftsmärkte werden avisiert (Marktarealstrategie)? Der unternehmenspolitische Grundsatz, kundenorientiert anzubieten, umfaßt auch die Notwendigkeit geographisch die Leistungen dort anzubieten, wo die Absatzmärkte liegen. Damit erhält der Aussteller eine klare Vorinformation, welche Veranstaltungen zu präferieren sind.

Elemente einer Marketingkonzeption

Die Festlegung jeder einzelnen Strategie, ihre sinnvolle Kombination und die Zusammenstellung der geeigneten Marketinginstrumente sind Teile der Marketingkonzeption und stellen die Vorgaben für die Messebeteiligung dar, ein bestmöglicher Messeauftritt kann nur dann verwirklicht werden, wenn sich diese weitgehend in der Beteiligungsplanung und -umsetzung wiederfinden und im Bewußtsein der Messemacher gegenwärtig sind.

Die Konzeption einer Messebeteiligung läßt sich folgendermaßen unterteilen:

- Strategische Integration der Messepolitik in die betriebliche Marketingstrategie
• Messebeteiligungen als eigenständiges Marketinginstrument und als Teil der Marketingkonzeption des Unternehmens
• Festlegung des gesamten Messeprogramms der Unternehmung und Ableitung der Vorgaben für die Messebeteiligung
• Messeauswahl unter strategischen Gesichtspunkten

• In which local, regional, national or international markets does the company find buyers for its products? In which regions is the product mainly on sale? Which future markets are aimed at (market-area strategy)? The basic principle of company policy, namely to offer products which are oriented to specific customers, also involves the necessity of selling goods and services where the sales markets are located. In this way, the exhibitor obtains a clear advance view of which events are to be preferred.

Elements of a marketing conception

The specification of all the individual strategic approaches, their rational combination and the incorporation of suitable marketing instruments are parts of the marketing conception and serve as the foundations for participation in a trade fair. The best possible trade-fair performance is only possible if these are incorporated in planning and implementation and are borne in mind by those responsible for the exhibition.

The conception for participation in the market can be divided up as follows:

- Strategic integration of trade-fair policy in the company marketing strategy
• Trade-fair participation as an independent marketing instrument and as part of the marketing conception of the company
• Specification of the whole trade-fair programme of the company and derivation of the foundations for participation in the trade fair
• Selection of the trade fair from strategic points of view

- Operational trade-fair planning
• External and internal analysis of boundary conditions: supply and demand, obligations within co-operative ventures with other companies, preparation of a list showing the strengths and weaknesses of the company
• Definition of the trade-fair goals
• Preparation of a briefing as the basis for operational trade-fair planning
• Trade-fair positioning
• Stand design and stand construction
• Face-to-face communication; selection and training of stand personnel
• Use of accompanying communications tools (public relations, advertising, sales promotion)
• Use of alternative presentation media
• Accompanying events (symposiums, presentations, talk shows)

- Operative Messeplanung
- Externe und interne Analyse der Rahmenbedingungen: Angebot und Nachfrage, Verpflichtungen innerhalb von Kooperationen, Erstellung eines Stärke-Schwächen-Profils des Unternehmens
- Festlegung der Messeziele
- Erstellung eines Briefing als Basis für die operative Messeplanung
- Messestandplazierung
- Standgestaltung und Standbau
- Face to face-Kommunikation, Auswahl und Schulung des Standpersonals
- Einsatz begleitender Kommunikationsinstrumente (Public Relations, Werbung, Verkaufsförderung)
- Einsatz von alternativen Präsentationsmedien
- Begleitende Event-Veranstaltungen (Symposien, Präsentationen, Talkshows)

- Planung der Messedurchführung
- Standübergabe
- Standorganisation (Fachbesucherorientierte Ablaufplanung, Motivation, Besuchererfassung)
- Interaktive Kommunikation mit dem Stammhaus
- Eigene Marktforschung auf der Messe
- Tageskontrolle

- Messenachbereitung und Messeerfolgskontrolle
- Nachmessegeschäft (Pflege und Fortentwicklung der Kundenkontakte)
- Messeerfolgskontrolle: Soll-Ist-Vergleich der Messeziele und des Messeerfolgs, Abweichungsanalyse
- Briefing für folgende Messebeteiligungen

- Messe-Controlling
- Überprüfung der Messebeteiligung vor dem Hintergrund der strategischen Unternehmensplanung und der Marketingziele des Unternehmens
- Revision und/oder Modifikation des Marketinginstruments „Messebeteiligung"

- Planning of how the trade-fair is to be conducted
- Handing over of the stand
- Stand organisation (procedural planning oriented to specialist visitors, motivation, visitor recording)
- Interactive communication with head office
- Market research at the fair
- Daily check

- Trade-fair follow-up and check on success
- Post-trade-fair business (nurturing and developing customer contacts)
- A check on the success of the trade fair: a comparison of set goals and goals achieved and of the success of the fair, analysis of deviations from goals
- Briefing for subsequent trade-fair participations

- Trade-fair controlling
- Investigation of trade-fair participation against the background of strategic company planning and the marketing goals of the company
- Examination and/or modification of the trade-fair as a marketing instrument

A conceptional understanding of participation in a trade fair clarifies the dependence of the trade-fair appearance on commercial constraints. Strategic marketing stipulations have to be taken into account, on the one hand, and, on the other, the trade-fair appearance is subject to a strict check on success. The exhibitors-and-trade-fair committee of the Deutsche Messewirtschaft e.V. (AUMA) discovered in 1993 that, on average, each company's expenditure for one square metre of stand area amounted to DM 1150. Just over 40% of the total costs were for stand construction, fittings and design. These data clearly indicate that the costs of participating in a trade fair are not to be neglected. The aim is, therefore, to plan, design and implement trade-fair participation in such a way that the cost-benefit ratio is improved.

Trade-fair goals as a prerequisite for optimum trade-fair participation

Efficient participation in a trade fair is only possible on the basis of sound goals. It is only with the operational formulation of trade-fair goals that operational planning for participation and a check on the success of the fair can be usefully carried out. Both economic and psychographic goals can be pursued at trade fairs and exhibitions.

Die konzeptionelle Darstellung einer Messebeteiligung verdeutlicht die Abhängigkeit des Messeauftritts von betriebswirtschaftlichen Zwängen. Einerseits sind strategische Marketingvorgaben zu berücksichtigen und andererseits unterliegt der Messeauftritt strenger Erfolgskontrolle. Der Aussteller- und Messeausschuß der Deutschen Messewirtschaft e.V. (AUMA) hat im Jahr 1993 ermittelt, daß im Durchschnitt jeder Unternehmer für eine Beteiligung DM 1150 pro qm-Standfläche aufwenden muß. Knapp 40% der Gesamtkosten entfallen auf den Standbau, -ausstattung und -gestaltung. Diese Daten zeigten deutlich auf, daß die Kosten einer Messebeteiligung nicht zu vernachlässigen sind. Ziel ist es daher, die Messebeteiligung derart zu planen, zu gestalten und umzusetzen, daß die Kosten-Nutzen-Relation optimiert wird.

Messeziele als Voraussetzung für eine optimale Messebeteiligung

Eine effiziente Messebeteiligung läßt sich nur auf der Basis von fundierten Messezielen durchführen. Erst mit der operationalen Formulierung von Messezielen werden auch die operative Beteiligungsplanung und die Messeerfolgskontrolle sinnvoll durchführbar. Auf Messen und Ausstellungen lassen sich sowohl ökonomische als auch psychographische Zielsetzungen verfolgen.

Ökonomische Ziele – Messe- und Nachmessegeschäft

Messeziele	Erfolgskriterien
Umsatz ankurbeln Umsatzausweitung	Zahl der Aufträge Auftragssumme verkaufte Stück • mit neuen Kunden • mit alten Kunden
Distributionsgrad erhöhen Neue Marktsegmente/ Käuferschichten hinzugewinnen	Zahl der Fach- und Privatbesucher Zahl der neuen Kundenkontakte (z.B. nach Region, Branche, Vertriebsschiene, Käuferschicht) Struktur der Besucher
Ausgeglichener/ positiver Deckungsbeitrag	Messeumsatz ./. Messekosten ./. Selbstkosten der verkauften Erzeugnisse >=0 (Messeertrag)
Marktanteil halten/ erweitern	Messeumsatz im Vergleich zur vorherigen Messe konstant/ größer
Kosten senken	Pro-Kopf-Quote: Messekosten/Zahl der Besucher

Economic goals – trade-fair business and post-trade-fair business

Trade-fair goals	Criteria of success
To boost sales To expand sales	Number of orders Total orders for goods sold • with new customers • with old customers
To increase the degree of distribution To acquire new market segments/ customer groupings	Number of specialist and private visitors Number of new customer contacts (e.g. according to regions, sectors of industry, sales routes, customer groupings) Structural classification of the visitors
To achieve a balanced/positive contribution margin	Trade-fair sales ./. trade-fair costs ./. prime costs of the sold products >=0 (trade-fair profit)
To expand or retain the share in the market	Trade-fair sales compared to previous trade fair are constant or greater
To reduce costs	Per-capita rate: trade-fair costs/number of visitors

Psychographische Ziele

Messeziele	Erfolgskriterien
Bekanntmachung des Sortiments	Zahl der Besucher Zahl der alten/neuen Kundenkontakte Zahl und Qualität der initiierten Presseveröffentlichungen Zahl der ausgeteilten Prospekte und Proben
Schaffung/Verbesserung von Markentreue, Produktbekanntheit	Gezielte Besucherbefragung • Bekanntheitsgrad • Erinnerung • Markenkenntnis • Produkteigenschaften • Produktmerkmale
Demonstration von Verbrauchernutzen	Anzahl der Vorführungen, Prospekte, Proben
Verbesserung der Firmenbekanntheit, des Firmenimage	Gezielte Besucherbefragung • Kenntnis von Art und Zahl von Firmeneigenschaften
Profilierung gegenüber Wettbewerbern	Gezielte Besucherbefragung • Kenntnisse Bekanntheitsgrad • Urteile über Firmen und Produkte
Aktivierung von Produktbewußtsein	Gezielte Besucherbefragung • Zufriedenheit mit den Produkten • Ermittlung von Kundenwünschen
Positive Beeinflussung der Meinungsbildner	Quantität und Qualität der Presseresonanz

Die letztlich individuell zu formulierenden Messeziele sind vielfältig. Sie sind operational zu gestalten, indem Inhalt und Ausmaß der Ziele quantitativ und qualitativ bestimmt werden. Hierzu zählt die Definition der Zielgruppen ebenso wie die Festlegung des Zeitraums, in dem die Ziele verwirklicht werden sollen. Neben den aktiven verkaufsorientierten Zielen, bietet sich auf Messen und Ausstellungen auch die Möglichkeit, Marktforschungsziele zu verfolgen und Personalakquisition zu betreiben.

Das marketingpolitische Grundraster, die Messekonzeption und insbesondere die messepolitischen Zielsetzungen bilden den Rahmen für den Messestandbau.

The individual trade-fair goals which finally have to be formulated are manifold. They have to be operationally organised by quantitatively and qualitatively determining their contents and dimensions. This includes definition of the target groups and determination of the time in which the goals are to be realised. In addition to the active sales-oriented goals, it is also possible to carry out market research at trade-fairs and exhibitions and to acquire personnel.

The basic pattern of marketing policy, the trade-fair conception and especially the goals relating to trade-fair policy form the framework for constructing the trade-fair stand.

Psychographic goals

Trade-fair goals	Criteria of success
To acquaint visitors with the range of products	Number of visitors Number of old / new customer contacts Number and quality of initiated press publications Number of brochures and samples distributed
To create/improve brand loyalty, product awareness	Specific questioning of visitors • How well known • Memorability • Knowledge of the brand • Qualities of the product • Characteristics of the product
To demonstrate the benefits to the consumer	Number of demonstrations, brochures, samples
To make the company more well known, to improve the company image	Specific questioning of visitors • Knowledge of the type and number of company qualities
To distinguish the company from competitors	Specific questioning of visitors • Knowledge of how well-known the company is • Judgements of companies and products
To activate product awareness	Specific questioning of visitors • Satisfaction with the products • Discovering the wishes of the customers
To exert a positive influence on opinion leaders	Quantity and quality of the press response

Planung des Standbaus

Integration des Standbaus in die Messekonzeption

Der Standbau verursacht die anteilig höchsten Kosten der gesamten Messebeteiligung. Seine konzeptionelle und planerische Einbindung erfolgt an mehreren Stellen der Beteiligungskonzeption. Die Formulierung der Messeziele bedeuten klare planerische Vorgaben für den Messebau. Diese Ziele sind Bestandteil des Messe-Briefing, in dem Strategie, Philosophie, Rahmendaten, Zielgruppen, Aktivitäten und insbesondere das Messebudget detailliert definiert und beschrieben sind. Aus diesen Vorgaben wird im Rahmen der operativen Planung die Standkonzeption entwickelt. Ihr Inhalt umfaßt beispielsweise Aussagen zur Umsetzung der Messekonzeption im Corporate Design des Standbaus, der Standgestaltung, der Bauweise, der Ausstattung, der verwendeten Materialien und der Exponate. Der Messestand ist die Plattform, auf dem sich das Unternehmen präsentiert. Insofern spielen die Vorgaben über die Standorganisation für die Messebauplanung eine wesentliche Rolle wie auch umgekehrt der Messestand mit seinen Vorgaben die konkrete Ablauforganisation beeinflußt. Auch der Messestand unterliegt einer betriebswirtschaftlichen ex post-Kontrolle. Neben Kosten und Funktionsfähigkeit wird ebenso überprüft, in welchem Umfang der Messestand dazu beigetragen hat, die messepolitischen Ziele zu unterstützen.

Briefing als Leitfaden der Planung

Eine wichtige Vorgabe für den Messestandbauer ist das Messe-Briefing des Ausstellers. In ihm werden das Grundverständnis der Beteiligung schriftlich formuliert und wesentliche Detailangaben für den Standbau vorgegeben:

- Bedeutung der Messe
- Stellenwert der Messe für das Unternehmen, die Branche und den Wettbewerb
- Aussteller- und Besucherstruktur
- Veranstalterinformationen

- Messeziele und Zielgruppen
- Übergeordnete Marketingziele
- Messestrategie
- Messeziele, insbesondere Corporate Identity-Ziele
- Besucherzielgruppen
- Unternehmensinterne Ziele

Planning of stand construction

Integration of the stand in the trade-fair conception

The construction of the stand incurs the highest proportion of the total costs involved in trade-fair participation. Its design and planning are integrated at several points within the overall conception. Formulation of the trade-fair goals means clear planning stipulations for construction of the stand. These goals are a component of the trade-fair briefing in which strategy, philosophy, peripheral data, target groups, activities and especially the budget are detailed, defined and described. Given these stipulations, the conception of the stand is developed within the framework of operational planning. The contents of this conception include, for example, statements on how to put the trade-fair conception into practice in the corporate design of the stand, the design of the stand itself, the method of construction, the fittings, the materials used and the exhibits. The trade-fair stand is the platform on which the company presents itself. To this extent, the stipulations for planning construction of the stand play an important role, just as the trade-fair stand itself – once completed – influences how procedures are concretely organised. The trade-fair stand is also subject to an ex post facto check on its commercial aspects. In addition to costs and feasibility, a check is also made to find out how much the stand has contributed towards fostering the goals specified in the trade-fair policy.

Briefing as a guideline to planning

The stipulations included in the trade-fair briefing are important for the builder of the stand. In this briefing, the basic idea of the company's participation in the fair is formulated in writing and important detailed information is specified for the construction of the stand.

- The significance of the trade-fair
- The importance of the fair to the company, the branch of industry and the competition
- The structure of exhibitors and visitors
- Exhibitor information

- Exponate auf der Messe
• Produkte nach Art und Anzahl
• Demonstrationshilfen als Ersatz oder als Unterstützung (z.B. Video, Modelle, EDV-Unterstützung)

- Event-Veranstaltungen
• Art der Veranstaltung (z.B. Talkshow, Symposium, Verlosung)
• Flächenbedarf

- Standpersonal
• Anzahl und Funktionsbereiche
• Ausstattung

- Budgetaufstellung
• Struktur des Budgets
• Budgetrahmen für den Standbau

- Rahmendaten
• Termine
• Erfahrungen der letzten Veranstaltung

Je genauer und ausführlicher die oben genannten Angaben vorliegen, desto besser läßt sich die Beteiligungsidee umsetzen. Allerdings müssen die Vorgaben des Messe-Briefing und die gestalterischen und technischen Möglichkeiten des Standbaus aufeinander abgestimmt werden.

Gestaltungselemente des Standbaus

Messestände sind Bauten, die auf Zeit errichtet werden, und in einer besonderen Umgebung kurzfristig ihre kommunikativen Wirkungen entfalten. Darüber hinaus werden aufbau- und abbautechnische Anforderungen an die Messekonstruktionen gestellt, die in neuerer Zeit um die Forderung nach Verwendung umweltverträglicher Messestände ergänzt wurde. Zur Umsetzung der Messezielsetzungen und zur Erfüllung der verschiedenen Anforderungen lassen sich eine Vielzahl unterschiedlicher Standbauelemente einsetzen; einerseits frei disponibel, andererseits eher restriktiv:

• Messestandplazierung in der Halle oder auf dem Gelände. Diese Entscheidung ist einerseits abhängig vom Platzbedarf des Messestandes und wird andererseits durch die Planungen des Veranstalters beeinflußt.

• Standarchitektur als Gesamtwahrnehmung des Messestandes (Einflußfaktoren des Raums: Größe, Form, Proportionen, Richtung, Grenzen, Erschließung, Ausstattung, Anbindung, Raumzusammensetzung, Raumkoppelung). Verantwortlich für den Gesamteindruck eines Messestandes ist das Zusammenwirken der verschiedenen Gestaltungselemente.

- Trade-fair goals and target groups
• Superordinate marketing goals
• Trade-fair strategy
• Trade-fair goals, especially corporate-identity goals
• Visitor target groups
• Goals internal to the company

- The exhibits at the fair
• Products according to type and number
• Demonstration aids as substitute or support (e.g. videos, models, EDP support)

- The events
• Type of event (e.g. talk show, symposium, lottery)
• Space requirement

- The stand personnel
• Number and areas of responsibility
• Equipment

- The budget
• Structure of the budget
• The framework of the budget for construction of the stand

- Peripheral data
• Times and deadlines
• Experience gained during the last event.

The more accurate and more detailed the above information is, the easier it is to put the plans into practice. The stipulations given in the briefing, and the design-related and technical possibilities involved in construction of the stand, however, have to be matched to each other.

Design elements of the stand

Trade-fair stands are constructions which are erected temporarily and unfold their communicative effect in a short period of time within a special environment. Requirements regarding construction and dismantling are also placed on trade-fair constructions and, lately, demands have been added for the use of environment-friendly trade-fair stands. In order to achieve trade-fair goals and satisfy the various requirements, a great variety of different factors relating to construction of the stand can be made use of, some of which can be employed as one wishes, others being more restrictive:

• Stand location in the hall or on the site. This decision is dependent on the space requirements of the stand, on the one hand, and, on the other, is influenced by the plans of the exhibitor.

• Standgrundriß
Je offener der Standtyp ist – z.B. Kopf-,
Reihen-, Eck- oder Blockstand – , um so
besser lassen sich kommunikative Messe-
konzeptionen umsetzen.

• Standbauweise
(System, konventionell, Mischbauweise)
Zu den wesentlichen Entscheidungs-
tatbeständen zählen die Höhe der Kosten,
die kreativen Gestaltungsmöglichkeiten
und die Häufigkeit des Messeeinsatzes.

• Standsyntax
(Proportionen, menschliche Körpermaße,
Kumulation und Gruppierung von Ge-
staltungselementen, konstruktive Ästhetik, gleichartige oder unterschiedliche
Elemente, verwendete Kontraste und Formen, Struktur und Textur des Messestandes, Ganzheitlichkeit der Darstellung).
Die Kreativität des Messearchitekten
findet in der Anwendung der Standsyntax
ihren Niederschlag. Sie trägt maßgeblich
dazu bei, ob der Besucher den Stand
positiv oder eher negativ empfindet und
bewertet.

• Art und Weise der Präsentation
der Exponate
Bei den meisten Messebeteiligungen
steht das Produkt im Mittelpunkt. Informationen, Inaugenscheinnahme und
Funktionsfähigkeit lassen sich mit einer
geeigneten Exponatpräsentation in idea-
ler Weise an den Fachbesucher weiter-
geben.

• Standbaumaterialien
Hierzu zählen unter dem Aspekt der
Standgestaltung alle Materialien, aus denen der Stand besteht; darüber hinaus
ebenso jene zu Dekorationszwecken.
Die Verwendung von verschiedenen Materialien ist nicht Selbstzweck, sondern
kann dazu beitragen, das Selbstverständnis, die Corporate Identity oder den
Tätigkeitsbereich des Unternehmens transparent werden zu lassen. Besondere
Bedeutung gewinnt dieses Thema unter
dem Aspekt des Umweltschutzes.

• Farbe und Licht
Beides sind kreative Gestaltungselemente,
die einerseits funktionsorientiert eingesetzt (Funktionslicht, CI-Farben) und
anderseits zur Emotionalisierung des
Messestandes oder Teile davon genutzt
werden können (Akzentlicht, Farben
schaffen Atmosphäre).

• Decken- und Bodengestaltung
Neben den Wänden dienen Decken und
Böden der Raumgestaltung und sind
wichtige Elemente zur Gestaltung des
Erlebnisraumes „Messestand".

• Stand architecture as an overall perception of the stand (influencing factors
of the stand area: size, shape, proportions,
direction, limits, access, fittings, links,
room composition, room interfaces).
The interplay of the different design elements is responsible for the overall impression of the trade-fair stand.

• Ground plan of the stand
The more open the type of stand is – e.g.
one of a row, at the head of a row, in a
corner, or part of a block –, the better
communicative trade-fair conceptions can
be put into practice.

• Method of construction of the stand
(system, conventional, mixed method)
Among the most important factors
in reaching a decision are the level of
costs, the possibilities for creative design
and the frequency with which the
stand is used.

• Stand syntax
(proportions, human physical dimensions,
accumulation and grouping of design
elements, constructional aesthetics,
the same or different elements, the contrasts and shapes used, the structure
and texture of the stand, the extent to
which the stand presents a coherent
appearance). The creativity of the trade-
fair architect finds expression in the
application of the stand syntax. It makes
a decisive contribution to whether the
visitor has a positive or negative response
to the stand.

• Method of presentation of the exhibits
At most trade fairs, the product is at
the centre of attention. A suitable presentation of the product is an ideal way of
providing the specialist visitor with information on the product, allowing him to
inspect it and having its performance
demonstrated.

• Stand construction materials
From the point of view of stand design,
these include all materials of which
the stand is made plus those which are
used for decorative purposes. The use
of different materials is not an end in
itself but can help to unveil the corporate
identity or the area of activity of the
company. This topic becomes especially
important from the point of view of
environmental protection.

• Colour and light
Both of these are creative design elements which are used functionally, on
the one hand, (functional lighting,
CI colours) and, on the other, can be used
to emotionalise the stand or parts of
it (accentuating light, colours creating
atmosphere).

· Ceiling and floor design
In addition to the walls, ceilings and floors
are used as part of the room design
and are important elements for designing
the stand as a place where visitors can
feel they have experienced something
important.

· Stand furnishings
The furniture rounds off the presentation,
performing functional tasks (seating)
and fulfilling design-related, communicative purposes (showcase for decorative
presentation of the product).

· Stand graphics
The transfer of various kinds of information to the visitor is one of the central
tasks of a trade-fair stand. In order to be
able to achieve these goals, graphical
elements such as texts, pictograms and
photos must be prepared and attached
to the stand but the visitor should not
be flooded with more information than
he can absorb.

· Audio-visual and interactive media
A group of design tools which are continuously being developed technically and
in relation to their application (e.g. the
Internet, interactive displays) and can
serve to support the transfer of information and persuasive argumentation.

· Corporate design and corporate behaviour of the stand personnel.
The success of a trade-fair stand and how
the visitor remembers the exhibitor
are mainly determined by the appearance
and behaviour of the stand personnel.
To this extent, this design component is
of strategic importance.

The use of these stand design elements
should be attuned to the goals of the
trade-fair. The way in which the stand is
designed should also ensure an optimum
of procedural organisation during the
trade-fair. This includes the division of the
stand into presentation, discussion and
service areas.

Trade-fair goals and their attainment
through design

An attempt at combination

The demand for a stand design oriented
to the company's trade-fair goals generates two questions. Is knowledge available as to which methods and measures
have to be used to achieve certain effects
on visitors? Which design elements in
stand construction promote these effects
and contribute towards achievement
of the goals?

· Standausstattung
Das Mobiliar rundet die Präsentation
ab und hat ebenso funktionelle Aufgaben
(Sitzgelegenheit) wie zusätzlich ge-
staltende, kommunikative Zwecke (Vitrine
zur dekorativen Produktpräsentation)
zu erfüllen.

· Standgrafik
Die Übermittlung von unterschiedlichen
Informationen an die Besucher zählt
zu den zentralen Aufgaben einer Messebeteiligung. Um dieses Ziel erreichen
zu können, müssen grafische Elemente
wie Texte, Piktogramme und Fotos der
Auffassungsfähigkeit der Besucher gemäß
erstellt und angebracht werden.

· Audiovisuelle und interaktive Medien
Ein Gruppe von Gestaltungsinstrumenten,
die sich ständig technisch und anwen-
dungsbezogen weiterentwickelt (z.B. Internet, interaktive Displays) und zur
Unterstützung der Informationsübermitt-
lung und Argumentation dienen kann.

· Corporate Design und Corporate
Behaviour des Standpersonals
Der Erfolg der Messebeteiligung, aber
auch die Erinnerung des Besuchers an den
Aussteller werden maßgeblich durch
das Auftreten und Verhalten des Standpersonals bestimmt. Insofern kommt
dieser Gestaltungskomponente strategische Bedeutung zu.

Der Einsatz dieser Standgestaltungselemente geschieht einmal in Abstimmung
auf die Messeziele. Zum anderen soll
mit der Art und Weise der Standgestaltung sichergestellt werden, daß eine optimale Ablauforganisation während der
Messe gewährleistet ist. Hierzu zählt unter
anderem die sinnvolle Aufteilung des
Messestandes in Präsentations-, Bespre-
chungs- und Dienstleistungsbereiche.

Messeziele und ihre gestalterische Realisierbarkeit

Versuch einer Verknüpfung

Die Forderung nach messezielorientierter
Gestaltung der Messestände wirft
zwei Fragen auf. Zum einen: Gibt es Erkenntnisse darüber, welche Instrumente
und Maßnahmen eingesetzt werden
müssen, um bestimmte Wirkungen bei
Fachbesuchern zu erzielen? Zum zweiten:
Welche Gestaltungselemente des Messestandbaus unterstützen diese Wirkungen
und tragen zur Zielerreichung bei?

Durchforstet man die Literatur zur Marketingforschung, dann wird deutlich, daß bisher zu beiden Fragen keine auch nur annähernd abschließenden Antworten gegeben worden sind und, wenn überhaupt, nur mit notwendiger kritischer Distanz Lösungen angeboten werden können. Die Vorkehrungen, die – neben der Standgestaltung – insgesamt vom Aussteller ergriffen werden, um bei den Fachbesuchern, auf Produkt und Unternehmen bezogen, Bekanntheit, Akzeptanz und Positionierung zu erreichen, sind äußerst vielfältig. Zu den Marketingmaßnahmen zählen Public Relations, Werbung, Verkaufsförderung und die persönliche Kommunikation. Daneben werden auch Maßnahmen der Produkt-, Distributions- und Preispolitik eingesetzt (vgl. Abbildung 1). Jedes Instrument und jede einzelne Aktivität erzeugt beeinflussende Wirkungen, die weder in ihrer jeweiligen Stärke noch als komplexes Ganzes vorhersehbar sind.

Darüber hinaus wirkt erschwerend, daß selbst das zu beeinflussende Objekt, der Besucher, nicht eindeutig definierbar ist und die Gruppen der Fachbesucher und des Publikums selbst heterogen und in ihren Reaktionen nicht voraussagbar sind.

If a look is taken at the literature on marketing research, it becomes clear that, up to now, nothing even approaching a clear answer to these questions has been given and, if the problem is mentioned at all, only with the necessary critical distance. The measures – besides stand design – adopted by the exhibitor to make the product and company known to the visitor, to gain his acceptance and to acquire a certain status are extremely varied in nature. Among the marketing tools, there are public relations, advertising, sales promotions and personal communication. In parallel to these, measures relating to the company's policy on products, distribution and prices are used (compare Fig. 1). Each tool and each individual activity generates influencing effects which are foreseeable neither as regards their power nor as a complex whole.

What also makes things difficult is that even the person to be influenced, namely the visitor, cannot be defined unambiguously and the groups of specialist visitors and the public are themselves heterogeneous with unforeseeable reactions.

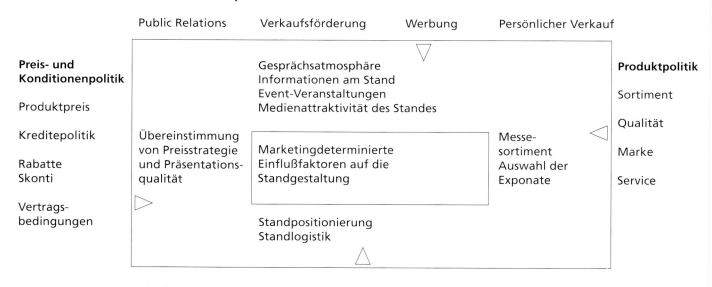

Abbildung 1
Marketingdeterminierte
Einflußfaktoren auf
die Standgestaltung

Communications policy

Public relations   Sales promotions   Advertising   Personal sales

Policy relating   Product policy
to prices
and conditions   Discussion atmosphere   Range of products
                              Information at the stand
Product price   Events   Quality
                              Media-attractiveness of the stand
Credit policy   Agreement of   Trade-fair   Brand
                         price strategy   Marketing-determined   selection
Discounts   and presentation influencing factors   of products   Service
                         quality   on stand design   Selection of
Terms of sale   exhibits

                              Stand positioning
                              Stand logistics

Distribution policy

Sales channels   Logistics

Fig. 1
Marketing-determined
factors which influence
stand design

Beide Problemkomplexe führen zentral in die Diskussion um die Relevanz unterschiedlicher Werbewirkungsmodelle. Im Grundsatz steht hinter den verschiedenen modelltheoretischen Ansätzen die Auseinandersetzung darüber, ob das Verhalten des Menschen fremdbestimmt oder aber vom freien Willen abhängig ist, d.h. selbstbestimmt. Man spricht entweder von emotionalen oder aber kognitiven Modellen.

Kognitive Theorien gehen davon aus, daß das Handeln des Menschen auf einer gedanklich bewußten, also selbstbestimmten Verarbeitung von Informationen beruht. Eine Auffassung, die von Praktikern, aber auch einem guten Teil der Forschung präferiert wird. Auf der anderen Seite wird in den emotionalen Theorien unterstellt, daß affektive Faktoren – ob bewußt oder unbewußt – das Denken selbst noch in vermeintlich rein kognitiven Denkprozessen beeinflussen.

Mit Hilfe des Messestandes werden einerseits die Voraussetzungen geschaffen, die Messebeteiligung organisatorisch und funktionell abzuwickeln, andererseits werden kommunikative Wirkungen erzielt. Danach spiegelt sich im Messestand das Marketing des Ausstellers im allgemeinen und die Messepolitik im besonderen wider. Messestände lassen sich als spezielle Werbeträger definieren, die übergreifend Elemente der Werbung, des persönlichen Verkaufs aber auch der Produkt- und Distributionspolitik enthalten.

Both problem areas lead to a central discussion on the relevance of different models of advertising effectiveness. Fundamental to this, behind the different theoretical approaches, there is the debate as to whether the behaviour of people is determined by others or whether it is dependent on free will, i.e. self-determined. These two approaches are described as the emotional theory and the cognitive theory.

Cognitive theories assume that the behaviour of people is based on the conscious, namely self-determined, processing of information – an approach which many practitioners and many researchers prefer. In emotional theories, in contrast, it is maintained that affective factors – whether conscious or unconscious – influence our processes of thinking, even those supposedly cognitive processes of thought.

With the help of the trade-fair stand, the preconditions are created for organising the company's participation in the fair and for the stand to perform the required functions but communicative effects are also aimed at. Accordingly, the marketing approach of the exhibitor and especially the trade-fair policy of the company is generally reflected in the trade-fair stand. Trade-fair stands can be defined as special vehicles of advertising which combine elements of advertising, personal selling and product and distribution policy as well.

Umfassende Experimente, die Hinweise auf die Werbewirkungen von Messe-ständen geben können, sind bisher noch nicht durchgeführt worden. Bisher lassen sich lediglich einige Studien belegen, in denen über Erfahrungen mit Blickauf-zeichnungsgeräten berichtet wird, die bei der Begehung von Messeständen ver-wendet wurden.

Die Erkenntnisse aus der Werbewir-kungsforschung können daher nur einge-schränkt auf die messezielorientierte Gestaltung von Messeständen übertragen werden. Es existiert keine optimale Rezeptur, sondern es lassen sich lediglich Verhaltensmaßregeln allgemeiner Art geben, die zudem im Einzelfall zu hinter-fragen sind. Untersucht man die ver-schiedenen Modelle zur Werbewirkung dahingehend, ob sie geeignet sind, Anregungen für die Messestandgestal-tung zu geben, dann scheint das sog. „Impactmodell" Ansätze für einen Trans-fer in den Messebau aufzuzeigen. Danach trifft der Verbraucher seine Kaufent-scheidung nach dem Grad der Bekannt-heit einer Marke oder eines Produktes.

Kennen ist zwar noch nicht kaufen, aber ein Impuls in die richtige Richtung. Beim Impactmodell steht die kognitive Theorie im Vordergrund. Messestände sind entsprechend so zu gestalten, daß der Besucher den Messestand, die Firma und die zentrale Werbebotschaft wieder-erkennen und sich letztlich auch daran erinnern kann.

Recognition (Wiedererkennung) und Recall (Erinnerung) werden als Art „Weg-bereiter" von Kaufprozessen gesehen. Obwohl ungeklärt ist, welche werbepsy-chologischen Vorgänge beim Verbraucher stattfinden, ob und welche anderen Faktoren zusätzlich auf die Kaufentschei-dung einwirken, scheinen Recognition und Recall grundsätzlich verkaufsfördernd zu sein. Nicht bestritten wird, daß das Gefallen der Werbung, ihre Glaubwürdig-keit und ihr allgemeiner Eindruck wichtige Parameter sind, das Kaufverhalten positiv zu beeinflussen. Insofern erzeugen affektive Erlebnisse beim Kontakt mit der Werbung einerseits und kognitive Erfahrungen bei der Bewertung der Wer-beaussage andererseits positive Einstel-lungen zur Werbung, zum Unternehmen und zum Produkt.

Comprehensive experiments which could give an indication of the advertising effectiveness of trade-fair stands have not yet been carried out. Up to now, only a few studies have been made in which reports of experience have been made with view recorders which were used during visits to a stand.

The knowledge gained from research into advertising effectiveness therefore can only be applied to a limited extent to trade-fair designs which are oriented to trade-fair goals. A perfect recipe does not exist; there are merely general rules of behaviour which have to be analysed in each individual case. If a close exa-mination is made of the different models of advertising effectiveness to see if they can stimulate ideas for designing trade-fair stands, the so-called "impact mo-del" seems to display features which are applicable to trade-fair construction. According to this model, the consumer makes his decision to buy according to the degree to which a brand or product is known.

Knowing is not buying, of course, but it can give a push in the right direction. In the impact model, the cognitive theory holds most sway. Trade-fair stands should be designed so that the visitor recognises the stand, the company and the cen-tral advertising message and then recalls the details as well.

Recognition and recall are seen as a kind of "forerunner" to the buying process. Although it is unclear what is happening in the mind of the consumer, whether and what other factors are also influen-cing the decision to buy, recognition and recall basically appear to encourage a decision to buy. It is undisputed that the pleasure given by advertising, its credibility and its general impression are important parameters for positively influencing buying behaviour. Affective experiences during contact with advertising, on the one hand, and cognitive experiences during the evaluation of advertising state-ments, on the other, generate a posi-tive attitude to the advertising, the com-pany and the product.

Für die Kreation eines Messestandes lassen sich Anregungen aus der Gestaltpsychologie entwickeln, mit deren Hilfe sich sog. „Gesetzmäßigkeiten" zur optimalen Gestaltung von Anzeigen oder im übertragenen Sinne für Messestände formulieren lassen.

Versteht man den Messestand – wie weiter oben dargelegt – als Werbeträger, dann läßt sich folgende Checkliste zur Überprüfung der Gestaltung von Messeständen aufstellen:

- Deuten Außenwirkung und Aussage des Messestandes auf einen Produktvorteil oder auf etwas Neues hin? Hat der Aussagegehalt des Messestandes informatorischen Wert?
- Vermittelt der Messestand eine Schlüsselbotschaft?
- Ist die Headline des Messestandes konkret, klar und direkt?
- Stehen die verwendeten Bilder, Plakate und anderen Medien in unmittelbarer Verbindung zur Headline?
- Wenn unterschiedliche Marketinginstrumente und Medien auf dem Messestand eingesetzt werden, was wurde zur Integration aller Medien und Maßnahmen unternommen?
- Wird der Produkt- oder Firmenname hervorgehoben? Kommt das Corporate Identity Profil des Unternehmens voll zur Geltung?
- Enthält der Messestand Gestaltungselemente, die ablenken oder zu viele geistige Voraussetzungen beim Betrachter verlangen?
- Ist der Messestand summa summarum einfach, direkt, aussagekräftig und anschaulich genug?

Die zentrale Botschaft, die hinter diesen Fragen steht, lautet: Erfolgreich sind diejenigen Messebeteiligungen, bei denen der Messeauftritt einfach und anschaulich ist, der Besucher direkt angesprochen wird und die ganzheitlich geplant und umgesetzt werden.

For the creation of a trade-fair stand, ideas can also be derived from Gestaltpsychology. These can be used to formulate "laws" for the optimum design of adverts or, adapted accordingly , for trade-fair stands.

If the trade-fair stand is regarded as an advertising vehicle – as discussed above –, the following check list can be drawn up to test the design of trade-fair stands:

- Do the external appearance and the "message" of the stand suggest a benefit of the product or something new? Is the "message" of the stand informative?
- Does the stand pass on a hidden message?
- Is the headline of the stand concrete, clear and direct?
- Are the images, posters and other media directly connected to the headline?
- When different marketing tools and media are being used on a stand, what has been done to integrate them all?
- Is the product emphasised or the name of the company? Is the corporate identity of the company shown to advantage?
- Does the stand contain design elements which distract or require too much mental effort on the part of the observer?
- Is the stand simple, direct, expressive and attractive enough on the whole?

The central message behind these questions is this: those trade-fair stands are successful where the stand is simple and attractive, where the visitors are addressed directly and which are planned and implemented as a whole.

Exhibition styles

In addition to these basic considerations, so-called exhibition styles were developed in the past which were derived from Ansoff's field strategies for the market. According to Ansoff, four options are open to a company in regard to marketing strategy:

If these market strategies are applied to trade-fair participation, the following implications can be drawn:

• Market penetration means that the exhibitor tries to increase sales with established products. To this end, old buyers have to be motivated to buy more and new buyers encouraged to buy for the first time. As the applications and possibilities of using the product are already know to a large extent, attention should be paid to nurturing customers and binding them to the product. In this case, an exhibition style strongly oriented to the customer is appropriate. If, however, the main focus of the trade-fair strategy is on the gaining of new customers, a style strongly oriented to the making of new customer contacts is recommended.

• With the strategy of product development, an attempt is made to offer a new product to groups of customers who are already known. The new product has to be introduced and all its applications demonstrated. This entails a product-oriented exhibition style.

• If new markets have to be opened up, the exhibitor is faced with the task of winning over previously unknown customers. At the same time, the product, the company and the brand have to be made known. This means that the exhibitor has to make sure that his performance at the trade fair has a comprehensive and memorable external effect. New customer contacts and open communication are of prime importance so that a contact-oriented exhibition style is preferred.

Ausstellungsstile

Über diese grundsätzlichen Feststellungen hinaus wurden in der Vergangenheit sog. „Ausstellungsstile" entwickelt, die aus den Marktfeldstrategien von Ansoff abgeleitet wurden. Nach Ansoff stehen einem Unternehmer vier Optionen für seine Marketingstrategie offen:

	Alte Produkte	Neue Produkte
Alte Märkte	Markt-durchdringung Kundenorientierter Ausstellungsstil	Produkt-entwicklung Produktorientierter Ausstellungsstil
Neue Märkte	Markt-entwicklung Kontaktorientierter Ausstellungsstil	Diversifikation Beratungsorientierter Ausstellungsstil

Abbildung 2
Marktfeldstrategien und Ausstellungsstile

Überträgt man diese Marktstrategien auf eine Messebeteiligung, dann lassen sich folgende Erkenntnisse für die Standgestaltung gewinnen:

• Marktdurchdringung bedeutet, daß der Aussteller versucht, mit den bereits etablierten Produkten vermehrt Umsätze zu erzielen. Zu diesem Zweck müssen alte Verwender zur höheren Umsätzen motiviert und neue Verwender zum Erstkauf angeregt werden. Da die Verwendungs- und Einsatzmöglichkeiten des Produktes bereits weitgehend bekannt sind, sollte das Augenmerk der Beteiligung auf Kundenpflege und Kundenbindung gelegt werden. In diesem Fall bietet sich ein stark kundenorientierter Ausstellungsstil an. Liegt der Schwerpunkt der Messestrategie jedoch bei der Neukundengewinnung, so ist auch ein stärker kontaktorientierter Stil empfehlenswert.

• Bei der Strategie der Produktentwicklung wird versucht, den bereits bekannten Kundengruppen ein neues Produkt anzubieten. Das neue Produkt muß vorgestellt und in seinen Anwendungsmöglichkeiten dargestellt werden. Daraus leitet sich ein produktorientierter Ausstellungsstil ab.

• Sollen neue Märkte erschlossen werden, dann steht der Aussteller vor der Aufgabe, bisher unbekannte Kunden für sich zu gewinnen. Zugleich müssen Produkt, Firma und Marke bekanntgemacht werden. Das bedeutet, daß der Aussteller bei seinem Messeauftritt auf umfassende und eingängige Außenwirkung achten muß. Neue Kontakte und offene Kommunikation stehen im Vordergrund, so daß ein kontaktorientierter Ausstellungsstil präferiert werden sollte.

	Old products	New products
Old markets	Market penetration Customer-oriented exhibition style	Product development Product-oriented exhibition style
New markets	Market development Contact-oriented exhibition style	Diversification Advice-oriented exhibition style

Fig. 2
Field strategies for the market and exhibition styles

• Die Aufgabenstellung für einen Aussteller ist dann sehr schwierig, wenn er seine Absatzaktivitäten diversifiziert. In diesen Fällen kann er auf Erfahrungen weder mit bekannten Märkten noch mit einem etablierten Produkt zurückgreifen. Darüber hinaus ist er auf der Suche nach neuen Kunden. Es gilt, die Anwendungsmöglichkeiten, den Nutzen des Produktes darzustellen und Problembewußtsein zu schaffen. Hierzu sind intensive Kontakte und Gespräche mit den Fachbesuchern notwendig, so daß ein beratungsorientierter Ausstellungsstil verwendet werden sollte.

Hinter der Definition von Ausstellungsstilen verbirgt sich die Erkenntnis, daß sich einzelne Messeziele – aufgrund der Komplexität eines Messestandes – nur bedingt unmittelbar in der Standgestaltung wiederfinden lassen; daß jedoch eine Leitlinie, wie sie der Ausstellungsstil darstellt, die strategische Marketingzielsetzung unterstützen kann. Die Gestaltungelemente sind entsprechend dieser Leitlinie zu überprüfen und einzusetzen.

Wird dieser Gedankengang beispielsweise auf eine kundenorientierte Messebeteiligung übertragen, so kann dies folgendes bedeuten:

• Im Vordergrund steht die Kontaktpflege, Gespräche mit bereits bekannten Kunden und Schaffung einer Umgebung und eines Umfeldes, in der Beziehungen zu den Kunden aufgebaut und vertieft werden können und der Kunde – über die geschäftlichen Absprachen hinaus – positive Erinnerungen an seinen Standbesuch mitnimmt. In diesem Grundverständnis sind die Gestaltungselemente des Messestandbaus entsprechend einzusetzen.

• Daher ist in diesem Fall eher eine geschlossene Standbauweise vorzusehen, die ausreichend Räumlichkeiten für Besprechungen und Bewirtung enthält. Räume, Formen und Proportionen sind so zu wählen, daß eine konzentrierte face-to-face Kommunikation ohne Störungen unterstützt wird. Ebenso sollten die Materialien für Wände, Decken und Böden derart aufeinander abgestimmt werden, daß sie in die gleiche kommunikative Richtung wirken. Unter derselben Maxime gilt es Farben und Lichteffekte auszusuchen, damit eine positive Gesprächsatmosphäre geschaffen werden kann. Auch die Auswahl der Standausstattung erfolgt mit dem Ziel, den Kunden und den Kundenkontakt in den Mittelpunkt des Messeauftritts zu stellen. Entsprechend sind informative Medien, wie Videofilme, Plakate oder PC- und Internetanwendungen eher begleitend im Hintergrund vorzuhalten, um den Kundenkontakt nicht zu überlagern.

• When an exhibitor wishes to diversify his sales activities, the tasks he is confronted with are very difficult ones. He is unable to refer to previous experience with known markets or with established products. Moreover, he is on the lookout of the product and to create the awareness of a problem wich the product can solve. Intensive contacts and talks with specialist visitors are necessary for this so an advice-oriented exhibition style should be used.

The definition of exhibition styles conceals the realisation that individual trade-fair goals – due to the complexity of a trade-fair stand – are reflected directly in the stand design only to a limited extent but that a guideline, such as represented by an exhibition style, can help to achieve the strategic marketing goals. The design elements have to be examined and employed in accordance with this guideline.

If these considerations are applied to a customer-oriented trade-fair appearance, this can mean the following:

• The most important aspects are the fostering of new customer contacts, talks with customers who are already known and the creation of an environment in which the relationship with customers can be developed and consolidated. The customer should also go away with positive memories of his visit to the stand. The design elements of the stand are to be employed accordingly, with this basic understanding in mind.

• In this case, therefore, a closed stand construction should be provided which has enough rooms for discussions and a catering service. Rooms, shapes and proportions should be selected so that concentrated face-to-face communication without interference is possible. The materials for the walls, ceiling and floor should therefore be matching so that they have a similar effect on communication and the same applies to colours and lighting effects which should be selected so that they can create a positive atmosphere for talks. The stand fittings should also be selected with the aim of placing the customer and customer-contact at the centre of things. Accordingly, informative media such as video films, posters or PC and Internet applications should be kept more in the background so as not to blot out customer contact.

• Bei aller Detailbetrachtung steht jedoch die ganzheitliche Konzeption des Messeauftritts im Vordergrund. Hierunter ist einmal die – wie oben beschrieben – architektonische Einheitlichkeit zu verstehen, wie aber auch andererseits die Ganzheitlichkeit der Beteiligung im Besonderen, die alle Marketingmaßnahmen im Vorfeld, während und nach der Messe umfaßt. Erst dann, wenn dieser Grundsatz beherzigt wird, steigt auch der betriebswirtschaftlich gewollte Nutzen.

Zielkonflikte

Bei aller Akribie der Planung und Durchführung der Messebeteiligung hat der Aussteller und als Dienstleister der Messebauer eine Vielzahl von Restriktionen zu beachten. Als erstes sind die Budgetvorgaben des Unternehmens zu beachten. Eine Messebeteiligung verursacht Gesamtkosten, die je nach Art und Bedeutung der Messe, Größe des Betriebes und je nach Aufwand, der von Seiten des Austellers betrieben wird, zwischen DM 600 und DM 1800 pro qm liegen kann. Da ein Marketingbudget von der Natur der Sache her begrenzt ist und zudem der Messeauftritt nur einen Ausschnitt aus dem Gesamtmarketingkonzept des Ausstellers darstellt, können – aus Sicht der Marketingeffizienz – nicht alle für sinnvoll erachteten Maßnahmen ergriffen werden. So werden Messestände beispielsweise mehrfach eingesetzt, ohne sie gemäß einer jeweils anderen Zielsetzung entsprechend zu verändern. Auch werden gerade in rezessiven Konjunktursituationen die Ausstellungsflächen begrenzt oder reduziert.

Dieses Abweichen von einer als angemessen bewerteten Standgröße kann jedoch auch durch den Veranstalter veranlaßt werden, wenn, wie es insbesondere bei internationalen Leitmessen der Fall ist, sich mehr Aussteller mit mehr Ausstellungsfläche beworben haben als an qm-Fläche zur Verfügung steht. Darüber hinaus werden vom Veranstalter einerseits und Genehmigungsbehörden andererseits Auflagen gemacht, welche die Gestaltungsmöglichkeiten des Ausstellers einschränken können. Hierzu zählen beispielsweise: Grenzwerte für die Bodenbelastung und Aufbauhöhe, Genehmigung für eine ein-oder zweigeschossige Bauweise, Verwendung von Lichteffekten, Einsatz akustischer Werbemittel, Vorschriften zur Verwendung von feuergefährlichen Standbaumaterialien, Vorgabe von Fluchtwegen und Einschränkungen bei der Vorführung von Maschinen.

• Although all these details have to be considered, the holistic conception of the stand has to be kept in the foreground. This means – as described above – architectonic unity and, in particular, a holistic approach to participation which includes all the marketing measures in the foreground before and after the trade-fair. Only if this basic principle is taken to heart can the commercially desired benefit increase as well.

Goal conflicts

However meticulously the trade-fair appearance is planned and conducted, the exhibitor and the trade-fair constructor have to take into account a multitude of restrictions. First of all, the budget stipulations of the company have to be considered. Trade-fair participation incurs total costs which can be between DM 600 and DM 1800 per square metre, depending on the type and importance of the trade-fair, the size of the company and the trouble to which the exhibitor wants to go. As a marketing budget is always limited and an appearance at a trade fair is only a small part of the exhibitor's overall marketing approach, not all the measures considered useful can be implemented from the point of view of marketing efficiency. Trade-fair stands, therefore, are used several times for example without being altered to fit in with a different set of goals. In addition, especially in times of recession, exhibition areas have to be limited or reduced.

This deviation from a stand size which is taken to be appropriate, however, can also result from a decision by the fair organiser if more exhibitors with more exhibition space have applied to take part than the space available allows. This is especially the case with large international trade fairs. The fair organiser and public authorities also lay down conditions which can limit the possibilities of design open to the exhibitor. Among these are: limit values for floor stress and building height, approval for one- or two-level constructions, the use of lighting effects, the employment of acoustic advertising materials, regulations regarding the use of inflammable construction materials, stipulation of escape routes and limitations on the presentation of machinery.

Die Diskussion um die Verwendung umweltverträglicher Messestände hat sich in den vergangenen Jahren verstärkt. Hierbei geht es einmal darum, welche der Materialien problemlos, d.h. ohne die Umwelt zu schädigen, entsorgt werden können. Zum anderen ist man bestrebt, den Materialverbrauch zu senken. Dies verlangt Materialien, die ohne Qualitätsverlust mehrmals eingesetzt werden können.

Jedoch kann dies auch zu Zielkonflikten führen. Die bewußte Beteiligungsplanung unter Umweltgesichtspunkten hilft Kosten bei der Entsorgung einzusparen, andererseits erhöhen sich Auf- und Abbaukosten. Teppichböden oder Wände in Plattenbauweise nutzen sich durch Auf- und Abbau sowie Einlagerung ab. Bestimmte optische Effekte auf Wänden und Plakaten lassen sich nur mit chemischen Farbzusätzen erreichen. Werbebroschüren in Hochglanzausführung wirken eingängiger und nachhaltiger als Prospekte auf Umweltpapier. Kommunikative Werbeziele können demnach in Konflikt zu Umweltzielen stehen.

Kosten-Nutzenanalyse – Kundenorientierung als oberstes Ziel – Schlußfolgerungen für den Standbau

Die bisherigen Ausführungen haben gezeigt, daß die betriebswirtschaftlichen Zwänge bei der Messebeteiligung allgegenwärtig sind. Ob restriktive Budgetvorgaben die Beteiligung einengen oder bestimmte Marketingzielsetzungen die Richtung vorgeben, in allen Fällen wird der Gestaltungsspielraum der Designer, Architekten und Messebauer eingeengt. Oberstes Gebot der Messebeteiligung ist, die vorgegebenen Messeziele zu erreichen. Die Kundenorientierung des Messeauftritts und die Kosten-Nutzenanalyse in Form der Gegenüberstellung von Kosten und von Kundenkontakten, Messeumsätzen, nachgelagerten Verkaufszahlen oder Imagewirkungen stehen hierbei im Vordergrund.

The discussion on the use of environmentally compatible trade-fair stands has increased in recent years. On the one hand, this concerns which materials can be disposed off without problems, i.e. without damaging the environment and, on the other hand, an effort is being made to lower the consumption of materials. Materials which can be used several times without a loss of quality are therefore required.

This can lead, however, to conflicts of goals. The conscious planning of participation from environmental points of view helps to save costs involved in disposal but construction and dismantling costs are increased. Carpets or walls made of panels become worn during construction, dismantling and storage. Certain optical effects on walls and posters can only be achieved with chemical colour additives. Glossy advertising brochures are more attractive and durable than brochures made of recycled paper. Communicative advertising goals can accordingly be in conflict with environmental goals.

Cost-benefit analysis – Customer orientation as the foremost aim – Consequences for stand construction

The above considerations have shown that the commercial constraints on trade-fair participation are ubiquitous. Whether restrictive budget stipulations curb participation or particular marketing goals specify the direction to be taken, the design leeway of designers, architects and builders is always constricted. The foremost aim of trade-fair participation is to achieve the stipulated trade-fair goals. Customer orientation during the fair and cost-benefit analysis in the form of a comparison of costs and new customer contacts, sales during the fair, subsequent sales figures or image effects are the most important.

However, it also became clear that these goals can only be attained if creative trade-fair builders and architects are integrated in the process of trade-fair planning. The "do-it-yourself" trade-fair builder will only be successful in exceptional cases.

Allerdings, und dies wurde auch deutlich, lassen sich diese Zielvorgaben nur realisieren, wenn kreative Messebauer und Architekten in die Beteiligungsplanung integriert werden. Der „do it yourself Messebauer" wird nur in Ausnahmefällen Erfolg haben.

Aus diesen Erkenntnissen lassen sich einige Grundsätze für die Partnerschaft zwischen Ausstellern und Dienstleistern des Standbaus ableiten:

• Designer, Architekten und Messebauer müssen frühzeitig in die Planung des Messeauftritts einbezogen werden, damit avisierte Messeziele und realisierbare Standgestaltung rechtzeitig aufeinander abgestimmt werden können.

• Wenn die dargebotenen Produkte und Dienstleistungen und die avisierte Zielgruppe nicht deckungsgleich sind, hilft auch die beste Standgestaltung nicht.

• Messezielsetzungen lassen sich nicht im Verhältnis eins zu eins in der Standgestaltung wiedergeben. Allerdings kann der Messebauer Stilrichtungen der Messestände, die vom Marketing des Ausstellers vorgegeben werden, in seinen Entwürfen berücksichtigen.

• Die Bedeutung der Messe und die Bedeutung des Ausstellers müssen sich in der Art und Weise der Präsentation niederschlagen.

• Das Gefallen (Likability) des Messestandes, die Glaubwürdigkeit der Werbeaussagen und ein vorteilhafter allgemeiner Eindruck des Messeauftritts fördern die Wiedererkennung (Recognition) und die Erinnerung (Recall) der Fachbesucher und des Publikums. Dies trägt dazu bei, daß positive Einstellungen beim Besucher entstehen, die grundsätzlich das Kauf- und Entscheidungsverhalten günstig beeinflussen.

• Aussteller und Messebauer haben darauf zu achten, daß Beteiligungen an Messen und Ausstellungen ganzheitlich geplant und umgesetzt werden. Das bedeutet, daß einerseits die Standgestaltungselemente aufeinander abgestimmt und integriert verwendet werden und andererseits die übrigen Marketinginstrumente, Werbung, Verkaufsförderung, Public Relations und der persönliche Kundenkontakt, zielgerichtet und als Einheit eingesetzt werden.

Given the above, several principles can be deduced which apply to the partnership between exhibitors and those providing their services:

• Designers architects and trade-fair builders must be integrated in the planning at an early stage so that the goals being aimed at and the stand design can be harmonised in good time.

• If the products and services being shown and the target group aimed do not match each other, even the best stand design is of no help whatsoever.

• Trade-fair goals cannot be reflected on a one-to-one basis in the stand design. In his plans for the stand, however, the trade-fair builder can take into account the stylistic directions stipulated by the marketing approach of the exhibitor.

• The significance of the trade fair and the significance of the exhibitor must find expression in the nature of the presentation.

• The likeability of the trade-fair stand, the credibility of the advertising message and an advantageous general impression of the trade-fair appearance increase the likelihood of recognition and recall by the specialist visitor. This contributes to the formation of a positive attitude on the part of the visitor which, in turn, has a basic influence on buying behaviour and decision making.

• Exhibitors and trade-fair builders have to ensure that participation in trade-fairs and exhibitions is planned and conducted holistically. This means that the stand design elements have to be matched to and integrated with each other. It also means that the other marketing tools such as advertising, sales promotion, public relations and personal contact with customers, have to be used coherently and with the specified goals in mind.

• Messen und Ausstellungen sind keine Bühnenbilder, die von einem festen Standpunkt betrachtet werden, sondern gestaltete Räume, in denen der Besucher und Betrachter eigenständiger Bestandteil ist.

• Jede Beteiligung an einer Messe oder Ausstellung mündet in der Messeerfolgskontrolle, die von den Verantwortlichen sowohl des Marketings als auch des Messebaus Rechenschaft verlangt, ob und in welchem Umfang die betriebswirtschaftlichen, marketingorientierten und gestalterischen Zielsetzungen erreicht wurden. Die Ergebnisse sind Vorgaben für die zukünftige Beteiligungsplanung des Ausstellers.

• Der Standbau kann nur den Rahmen für die Kommunikation der Menschen (Standpersonal und Fachbesucher) darstellen. Der Mensch ist das Maß aller Dinge.

Literatur

Becker, Jochen: Marketing-Konzeption – Grundlagen des strategischen Marketing-Managements, München 1993.

Beier, Jörg: Marketing auf Messen und Ausstellungen; in: Marketing; hrsg. v. Hans-Georg Geisbüsch, Richard Geml, Hermann Lauer, Landsberg/Lech 1991.

Müller, Otto (Hrsg.): Medium Messe, Frankfurt 1983.

Selinkski, Hannelore; Sperling Ute A.: Marketinginstrument Messe, Köln 1995.

Wilkens, Rainer: Werbewirkung in der Praxis, Essen 1994.

• Trade fairs and exhibitions are not stage sets which are viewed from a fixed standpoint but are designed areas where the visitor and observer comprise an independent component.

• Every participation in a trade fair or exhibition ends in a check on the success of the fair whereby both those responsible for marketing and construction are required to give reasons as to whether and to what extent the commercial, marketing-oriented and design-related goals have been reached. The results then act as a basis for the exhibitor's future participation in trade fairs.

• The stand construction can only provide the framework for communication between people (stand personnel and visitors). The person is the measure of all things.

References

Becker, Jochen: Marketing-Konzeption – Grundlagen des strategischen Marketing-Managements, Munich 1993.

Beier, Jörg: Marketing auf Messen und Ausstellungen; in: Marketing; edited by Hans-Georg Geisbüsch, Richard Geml, Hermann Lauer, Landsberg/Lech 1991.

Müller, Otto (editor): Medium Messe, Frankfurt 1983.

Selinkski, Hannelore; Sperling Ute A.: Marketinginstrument Messen, Cologne 1995.

Wilkens, Rainer: Werbewirkung in der Praxis, Essen 1994.

Bildnachweise
Picture References

S. 20: Indianer-Tipi
Kronenburg, Robert; Houses in Motion;
S. 12.

**S. 20: Hausboote auf einem Wasserlauf
in Shanghai**
Rudofsky, Bernard; Architektur ohne
Architekten; Bild 42.

**S. 20: Comedia dell'Arte in der Arena
di Verona**
Kronenburg, Robert; Houses in Motion;
S. 35.

S. 20: Zirkuszelt
Eames, Ray / Neuhart , John / Neuhart,
Marilyn; Eames Design; S.91.

S. 21: Crystal Palace, Westeingang
Friebe, Wolfgang; Architektur der
Weltausstellungen; S.25.

**S. 21: Crystal Palace, Mittelalterlicher
Hof**
Frampton, Kenneth; Grundlagen der
Architektur; S. 50.

S. 22: Maschinenhalle
Friebe, Wolfgang; Architektur der
Weltausstellungen; S. 104.

S. 22: Monument des Eisens
Die Deutsche Werkbund-Ausstellung
Cöln 1914; S.136.

S. 23: Glashaus
Die Deutsche Werkbund-Ausstellung
Cöln 1914; S. 135-137.

S. 24: Wolkenbügel
Thomsen, Christian W.; Architekturphantasien; S. 63.

**S. 24: Gedenkturm der III. Internationale
Vladimir Tatlin**
Tatlin; Ausstellungskatalog; S. 57.

S. 24: Café Kugelhaus
db 8 / 1996; S. 34.

S. 24: Pavillon der U.S.S.R.
Lohse, Richard P.; Neue Ausstellungsgestaltung; S. 17.

S. 26: Pavillon de l'Esprit Nouveau
Boesiger, W. / Girsberger, Hans;
Le Corbusier 1910-1965; S. 29.

S. 26: Österrr. Theaterausstellung
Lohse, Richard P.; Neue Ausstellungsgestaltung; S. 17.

S. 26: Stahlhaus Dessau, 1926
Design Report 1 / 1994; S. 14.

S. 27: Café Samt und Seide
Lilly Reich; MOMA; S. 24.

S. 27: Spiegelglashalle
Lilly Reich; MOMA; S. 24.

S. 27: Raum der DLW
Lilly Reich; MOMA; S. 23.

S. 28: GAGFAH / AHAG-Ausstellung
Walter Gropius, Werkverzeichnis Teil 2;
S. 148 f.

S. 29: Stand für eine Propagandafirma
Brüder Rasch; S. 97.

S. 29: Barcelona-Pavillon, 1929
Blaser, Werner; Mies van der Rohe,
Möbel und Interieurs; S. 56 ff.

S. 30: Hackerbräu-Bier-Ausstellung
Lilly Reich; MOMA; S. 28.

S. 30: Ausstellung des Dt. Werkbund
Walter Gropius, Werkverzeichnis Teil 2;
S. 152.

S. 30: Ausstellung des Dt. Werkbund
Bauhaus-Utopien; S. 192 f.

S. 30: Lesegalerie
Walter Gropius; Werkverzeichnis Teil 2;
S. 154.

S. 31: Die Wohnung unserer Zeit
Lilly Reich; MOMA; S. 9.

**S. 31: 10. Jahrestag der Faschistischen
Revolution**
Garofalo, Francesco / Veresani, Luca;
Adalberto Libera; S. 55.

S. 31: Italienischer Pavillon
Garofalo, Francesco/ Veresani, Luca;
Adalberto Libera; S. 84 f.

S. 32: Schweizer Ausstellung
Roth, Alfred; Die neue Architektur;
S. 175 ff.

S. 33: Finnischer Pavillon
Lohse, Richard P.; Neue Ausstellungsgestaltung; S. 43 f.

**S. 33 und 34: Le Pavillon des Temps
Nouveaux**
Lohse, Richard P.; Neue Ausstellungs-
gestaltung; S. 159-161.

S. 34: Finnischer Pavillon
Giedion, Sigfried; Raum, Zeit,
Architektur; S. 386.

S. 34: Weblee Portable Hut
Kronenburg, Richard; Houses in Motion;
S. 53.

S. 35: Wie Wohnen
Herbert Hirche; Architektur, Innenraum,
Design. 1945-1978; S. 5.

S. 35: Abteilung Bauen + Wohnen
Herbert Hirche; Architektur, Innenraum,
Design. 1945-1978; S. 18.

**S. 35: Stand der Stuttgarter Gardinen-
fabrik GmbH**
Herbert Hirche; Architektur, Innenraum,
Design.1945 – 1978; S. 42.

S. 36: Breda-Pavillon
Conrads, Ulrich; Phantastische
Architektur; S. 71.

S. 36: Philips-Pavillon
Le Corbusier; Le poème électronique;
S. 118 ff.

S. 37: Walking-Cities
Klotz, Heinrich; Vision der Moderne.

**S. 38: Mondhaus der NASA für längere
Aufenthalte**
Klotz, Heinrich; Vision der Moderne

S. 38: Living Pod / Cushicle
Chalk, Warrren / Cook, Peter / Crompton,
Dennis / Greene, David / Herron, Ron /
Webb, Mike; Archigram; S. 53 f

S. 39: Pneumatische Konstruktionen
Bodo Rasch; Zirkel 9; S. 55.

S. 39: Gelbes Herz
Haus-Rucker-Co 1967-83; S. 81.

S. 39: Die Wolke 1970
Coop Himmelblau.

S. 40: Amerikan. Pavillon
Pehnt, Wolfgang; Das Ende der
Zuversicht; S. 252.

S. 40: Dt. Pavillon
Architektur des 20. Jhd.; S. 320.

S. 41: Takara Beautilion
Drew, Philip; Die dritte Generation;
S. 72.

S. 41: Landmark-Turm
Detail 5 / 1970; S. 1034.

S. 41: Schweizer Pavillon
Detail 5 / 1970; S. 1030.

**S. 41: Telekommunikations Pavillon der
Nippon Telegraf & Telefon Corp.**
Detail 5 / 1970; S. 1032.

S. 42: Pavillon der Fuji-Gruppe
Detail 5 / 1970; S. 1027.

S. 42: Projekt Nr. 124, Peanut
Future Systems; S. 74.

**S. 42: Hyperraum-Truppentransporter
16.5. 2526**
Thomsen, Christian W.; Architekturphantasien; S.155.

**S. 42: Szene aus: 2001 – Odyssee im
Weltraum**
Sixties Design; S. 101.

S. 43: Micromegas
Daniel Libeskind; End Space; S. 21.

S. 43: The Peak
Zaha Hadid; GA Architect 5; S. 73.

S. 43: Folly
Thomsen, Christian W.; Architekturphantasien; S.139.

S. 43: Folly 9
du 11 / 1994.

S. 43: Folly 2
Osaka-Follies; S. 40.

S. 44: Videopavillon Groningen 1990
Daidalos August 1995; S. 104.

S. 44: Aerial Paris 1989
Thomsen, Christian W. ; Experimentelle
Architekten; S. 13.

S. 44: Momi -Zelt, Projekt 189
Future Systems; S. 130.

**S. 45: Buckingham-Palace-
Kartenhäuschen**
Baumeister 8 / 1995.

S. 45: Musical-Zelt „Neue Metropol"
Design Report 3 / 1995; S. 42.

S. 45: Festo-Ausstellungshalle
Design Report 1 / 1997; Foto: Joachim
Goetz.

S. 45: Info Box
Detail 8 / 1996; S. 1222; Foto: Jörg
Hempel.

S. 46: Laser Space
Feuerstein, Günther; Visionary
Architecture; S. 59.

S. 46: Aleph 2
ARCH+ 111; S. 38; Foto: Didier Boy de
la Tour.

S. 47: Niederländischer Pavillon
Foto: Tobias Hegemann.

S. 47: Demontage XV
Nomadologie; S. 265; Foto: Richie
Müller.

Die Bildnachweise zu den Messeständen (Seite 52 - 221) stehen bei den
jeweiligen Standlegenden.

Auswahlbibliographie
Selected Bibliography

750 Jahre Berlin 1987 – Berlin, Berlin – Journal 3; Berlin 1987.

AIT Themenhefte „Läden + Messestände" und „Bauten für Verkauf und Präsentation"; Leinfelden-Echterdingen; verschiedene Jahrgänge.

Akademie Schloß Solitude / Jean Baptiste Joly (Hrsg.); Fliegende Bauten, Konzeptionelle Entwürfe, Matthias Ludwig; Stuttgart 1993.

Alvar Aalto; Zürich 1974 (1963, 1971).

ARCH⁺ 1996 (131), InFormation – Faltung in der Architektur; Aachen 1996.

ARCH⁺ August 1988 (95), Das Verschwinden der Architektur; Aachen 1988.

ARCH⁺ Dezember 1993 (119 / 120); Aachen 1993.

ARCH⁺ März 1992 (111), Vilém Flusser; Aachen 1992.

Architectural Design 51, 1/2 1981, From Futurism to Rationalism; London 1981.

Architekturmuseum in Basel (Hrsg.); Zelte; Basel 1986.

archithese 1/ 89, Aus Versehen? Par mégarde?; Niederteufen (CH) 1989.

archithese 3/86, Kleine Architekturen / Petites architectures; Niederteufen (CH) 1986.

Badischer Kunstverein Karlsruhe, Vowinckel, Andreas / Kessler, Thomas (Hrsg.); Le Corbusier, Synthèse des Arts, Aspekte des Spätwerks 1945 – 1965; Berlin 1986.

Banham, Reyner; Die Revolution der Architektur, Theorie und Gestaltung im Ersten Maschinenzeitalter; Braunschweig 1990 (1960).

Bauen + Wohnen Jahrgang 1956; München 1956.

Bauwelt Nr. 39 / 1996, 18. Oktober 1996, „XS"; Gütersloh 1996.

Behne, Adolf: Ochs, Haila (Hrsg.); Architekturkritik in der Zeit und über die Zeit hinaus, Texte 1913 – 1946; Basel / Berlin / Boston 1994.

Berlage Institute Amsterdam, Postgraduate Laboratory of Architecture; The Berlage Papers 18; Amsterdam 1996.

Blaser, Werner; Mies van der Rohe – Möbel und Interieurs; Stuttgart 1981.

Blaser, Werner; Mies van der Rohe. Die Kunst der Struktur; Zürich / Stuttgart 1965.

Bodo Rasch, Ideen, Projekte, Bauten, Werkbericht 1924 bis 1984; Stuttgart 1984.

Boesiger, Willy (Hrsg.); Le Corbusier et son atelier rue de Sèvres 35, Vol. 7, Oeuvre complète 1957 – 1965; Zürich.

Boesiger, Willy (Hrsg.); Le Corbusier, Vol. 6, Oeuvre complète 1952 – 1957; Zürich 1985 (1957).

Boesiger, Willy (Hrsg.); Le Corbusier, Vol. 8, Oeuvre complète 1965 – 1968; Zürich 1986 (1970).

Bruno Taut 1880 – 1938; Akademie der Künste (Hrsg.); Berlin 1980.

Buck, Alex / Vogt, Matthias (Hrsg.); Rolf Heide, Designermonographien 6; Frankfurt am Main 1996.

Building, Machines, Pamphlet Architecture 12; New York 1987.

Cadwell, Mike; Small Buildings, Pamphlet Architecture 17; New York 1996.

Calvino, Italo; Die unsichtbaren Städte; München 1996 (1972).

Chalk, Warren / Cook, Peter / Crompton, Dennis / Greene, David / Herron, Ron / Webb, Mike; Archigram; Basel / Berlin / Boston 1991.

Ciré, Annette; Temporäre Ausstellungsbauten für Kunst, Gewerbe und Industrie in Deutschland 1896 – 1915; Frankfurt / Main.

Cliff, Stafford; The Best in Exhibition Stand Design: 2; London 1995.

Conrads, Ulrich / Sperlich, Hans G.; Phantastische Architektur; Stuttgart 1983 (1960).

Coop Himmelb(l)au (Prix, Wolf D. / Swiczinsky, Helmut); Coop Himmelb(l)au Austria, Biennale di Venzia 1996, Sechste Internationale Architekturausstellung; Klagenfurt 1996.

Coop Himmelblau; Architektur ist jetzt; Stuttgart 1983.

DAB 9 / 1996; Stuttgart 1996.

Daidalos Nr. 13, Zwischen innen und außen; Gütersloh 15. September 1984.

Daidalos Nr. 33, Transparenz und Verhüllung; Gütersloh 15. September 1989.

Daidalos Nr. 36, Innenwelten; Gütersloh 15. Juni 1990.

Daidalos Nr. 37, Balanceakte und Flugträume; Gütersloh 15. September 1990.

Daidalos Nr. 56, Magie der Werkstoffe II; Gütersloh August 1995.

Daniel Libeskind, End Space; London 1980.

db 5 / 1992; Stuttgart 1992.

db 6 / 1992; Stuttgart 1992.

db 9 / 1993, Haut und Knochen; Stuttgart 1993.

de Oliveira, Nicolas / Oxley, Nicola / Petry, Michael; installation art; London 1996.

Detail 5 / 1970; München 1970.

Detail 8 / 1996, Temporäre Bauten; München 1996.

domus Numero 512; Juli 1972.

domus Numero 519; Februar 1973.

Droste, Magdalena; Bauhaus; Köln 1990.

du – Die Zeitschrift für Kunst und Kultur No. 11 / 1994, Hochhaus und Pavillon. Die Stadt lebt nicht vom Block allein; Zürich 1994.

Eames Ray / Neuhart, John / Neuhart, Marilyn; Eames Design; New York 1989.

Eurodomus 4; 1972.

Expo 58, Album Souvenir; Bruxelles 1958.

Faegre, Torvald; Zelte, die Architektur der Nomaden; Hamburg 1980 (1979).

Falcke, Joachim; Gestaltung von Messeständen; München 1994.

Feuerstein, Günther; Visionäre Architektur Wien 1958 / 1988; Berlin 1988.

Feuerstein, Günther; Visionary Architecture in Austria in the Sixties and Seventies; Wien 1996.

Frampton, Kenneth; Grundlagen der Architektur, Studien zur Kultur des Tektonischen; Stuttgart / München 1993.

Friebe, Wolfgang; Architektur der Weltausstellungen 1851 – 1970; Stuttgart (Leipzig) 1983.

Garofalo, Francesco / Veresani, Luca; Adalberto Libera; New York 1992 (1989).

Gebrüder Rasch, Material Konstruktion Form 1926 – 1930; 1981.

Gibson, William; Biochips; München 1993 (1986).

Giedion, Sigfried; Bauen in Frankreich. Eisen, Eisenbeton; Leipzig / Berlin 1928.

Giedion, Sigfried; Raum, Zeit, Architektur; Basel / Boston / Berlin 1996 (1941).

Giedion, Sigfried; Walter Gropius Mensch und Werk; Stuttgart 1954.

Guidoni, Enrico; Architektur der primitiven Hochkulturen (Weltgeschichte der Architektur, Pier Luigi Nervi (Hrsg.)); Stuttgart / Mailand 1975 / 1976.

Günther, Sonja; Lilly Reich 1885 – 1947; Stuttgart 1988.

Haberl, Horst Gerhard / Strasser, Peter (Hrsg.); Nomadologie der 90er, steirischer herbst Graz 1990 bis 1995; Graz 1995.

Häberli, Alfredo W. / Lichtenstein, Claude (Hrsg.); Far vedere l'aria – Die Luft sichtbar machen; Zürich 1995.

Harten, Jürgen / Strigalev, Anatoli (Hrsg.); Vladimir Tatlin Retrospektive; Köln 1993.

Herbert Hirche; Architektur Innenraum Design 1945 – 1978; Stuttgart 1993 (1978).

Herzogenrath, Wulf (Hrsg.); Bauhaus-Utopien. Arbeiten auf Papier; Stuttgart 1988.

Herzogenrath, Wulf / Teuber, Dirk / Thiekötter, Angelika (Hrsg.); Die Deutsche Werkbund-Ausstellung Cöln 1914; Köln 1984.

Hiersig, Thilo C.; Die utopischen Architekturmodelle der 60er Jahre; Aachen 1980.

Ibsen, Henrik; Baumeister Solness; Stuttgart 1994 (1966 / 1892).

IL 5, Veröffentlichungen des Instituts für leichte Flächentragwerke (IL) Universität Stuttgart, Wandelbare Dächer; Stuttgart 1972.

IL 9, Veröffentlichungen des Instituts für leichte Flächentragwerke (IL) Universität Stuttgart, Pneus in Natur und Technik; Stuttgart 1977.

IL 29, Veröffentlichungen des Instituts für leichte Flächentragwerke (IL) Universität Stuttgart, Tent Cities / Zeltstädte; Stuttgart 1980.

Institut für Gebäudelehre und Entwerfen, TU Graz (Hrsg.); Coop Himmelblau. Architektur muß brennen; Graz 1980.

Jahresring, Jahrbuch für moderne Kunst 37, Präsentation und Re-Präsentation – Über das Ausstellbare und die Ausstellbarkeit; München 1990.

Jonak, Ulf; Sturz & Riß. Über den Anlaß zu architektonischer Subversion; Braunschweig / Wiesbaden 1989.

Kirsch, Karin; Die Weißenhof-Siedlung: Werkbund-Ausstellung „Die Wohnung" – Stuttgart 1927; Stuttgart 1987.

Klotz, Heinrich (Hrsg.); Haus-Rucker-Co 1967 bis 1983; Baunschweig 1984.

Kronenburg, Robert; Houses in motion. The genesis, history and development of the portable building; London 1995.

Kunsthaus Bregenz (Hrsg.); Hans Peter Wörndl. GucklHupf; Stuttgart 1995.

Kunst- und Ausstellungshalle der Bundesrepublik Deutschland GmbH (Hrsg.); Sehsucht. Das Panorama als Massenunterhaltung des 19. Jhd.; Frankfurt am Main und Basel 1993.

Landesbauordnung Nordrhein-Westfalen; Köln 1991 (1962).

Le Corbusier, Mein Werk; Stuttgart 1960.

Le Corbusier; 1922 – Ausblick auf eine Architektur; Braunschweig / Wiesbaden 1985, Nachdruck (1963).

Le Corbusier; 1929. Feststellungen zu Architektur und Städtebau; Braunschweig / Wiesbaden 1987 (1964).

Lehrstuhl für Baugeschichte, Universität Dortmund (Hrsg.); RISZ Heft 11, Zeitschrift für Architektur, Von der Vergänglichkeit des Bauens, 2. Dezember 1996; Dortmund 1996.

Lohse, Richard P.; Neue Ausstellungsgestaltung. 75 Beispiele neuer Ausstellungsform; Erlenbach-Zürich 1953.

Max Bill; Zürich 1983.

md; Leinfelden-Echterdingen; verschiedene Jahrgänge.

Mobili Italiani, 1961 – 1991, Le Varie Età dei linguaggi, Triennale di Milano, 12 Aprile – 12 Maggio 1991; Milano 1991.

Möller, Holger; Das deutsche Messe- und Ausstellungswesen. Standortstruktur und räumliche Entwicklung seit dem 19. Jahrhundert, (Forschungen zur deutschen Landeskunde Band 231); Trier 1989.

Müller, Alois Martin; MfG Zürich (Hrsg.); Daniel Libeskind. Radix – Matrix. Architekturen und Schriften; München 1994.

Müller, Sebastian; Kunst und Industrie: Ideologie und Organisation des Funktionalismus in der Architektur; München 1974.

Neue Gesellschaft für Bildende Kunst (Hrsg.); Inszenierung der Macht. Ästhetische Faszination im Faschismus; Berlin 1987.

Osaka Follies; London 1991.

Otto, Frei; Natürliche Konstruktionen. Formen und Konstruktionen in Natur und Technik und Prozesse ihrer Entstehung; Stuttgart 1982.

Pawley, Martin; Future Systems. Die Architektur von Jan Kaplicky und Amanda Levete; Basel / Berlin / Boston 1993.

Pehnt, Wolfgang; Das Ende der Zuversicht. Architektur in diesem Jahrhundert; Berlin 1983

Petit, Jean; Le Poème Èlectronique Le Corbusier; Paris 1958.

Philipp, Klaus Jan; Revolutionsarchitektur. Klassische Beiträge zu einer unklassischen Architektur; Braunschweig 1990.

Probst, Hartmut / Schädlich, Christian; Walter Gropius. Der Architekt und Pädagoge. Werkverzeichnis Teil 2; Berlin 1987.

Rat für Formgebung Frankfurt (Hrsg.); Design Report 3 / 1995; Hamburg 1995.

Rat für Formgebung Frankfurt (Hrsg.); Design Report 1 / 1997; Hamburg 1996.

Rat für Formgebung Frankfurt (Hrsg.); Design Report 3 / 1996; Hamburg 1996.

Rat für Formgebung Frankfurt (Hrsg.); Design Report 7,8 / 1995; Hamburg 1996.

Robbrecht, Paul / Daem, Hilde (Hrsg.); Aue Pavilions. Temporary Buildings for Documenta IX; Köln 1994.

Roth, Alfred (Hrsg.); Die Neue Architektur; Erlenbach-Zürich 1948.

Rowe, Colin / Slutzky, Robert; Transparenz; Basel / Boston / Berlin 1989 (1968).

Rudofsky, Bernard; Architektur ohne Architekten; Salzburg und Wien 1993 (1964).

Scheerbart, Paul; Das große Licht. Ein Münchhausen-Brevier; Leipzig 1912.

Scheerbart, Paul; Glasarchitektur; München 1971 (1914).

Schirmbeck, Egon / Schmutz, Eduard; Messestände. Temporäre Architektur für die Präsentation von Industrieprodukten und Dienstleistungen; Leinfelden-Echterdingen 1987.

Schmidt-Wulffen, Stephan (Hrsg.); Die Gruppe Geflecht. Antiobjekt 1965 – 1968; München 1991.

Schulz, Karin; Das Circuslexikon; Nördlingen 1988.

Simmen, Dr. Jeannot (Hrsg.); Schwerelos. Der Traum vom Fliegen in der Kunst der Moderne; Stuttgart 1991 / 1992.

Swift, Jonathan; Gullivers Reisen; Frankfurt am Main 1974.

Symposion Medium Ausstellung; Wien 1992.

The Architectural Review No. 1144; London 1992.

The Museum of Modern Art, New York (Hrsg.); Lilly Reich. Designer and Architect; New York 1996.

Thomsen, Christian W.; Architekturphantasien. Von Babylon bis zur virtuellen Architektur; München 1994.

Thomsen, Christian W.; Experimentelle Architekten der Gegenwart; Köln 1991.

von Moos, Stanislaus; Le Corbusier; Frauenfeld 1968.

Wachsmann, Konrad; Wendepunkt im Bauen; Dresden 1989 (1959).

Wenz-Gahler, Ingrid; Messestand-Design. Temporäres Marketing- und Architekturereignis; Leinfelden-Echterdingen 1995.

Werk, Bauen + Wohnen 1,2 / 92; Zürich 1992.

Werk, Bauen + Wohnen 3 / 96, Raum auf Zeit? / Au temps l'espace / Space for a time?; Zürich 1996.

Werk, Bauen + Wohnen 4 / 86; Zürich 1986.

Werk, Bauen + Wohnen 6 / 89; Zürich 1989.

Werk, Bauen + Wohnen 6 / 92, Provisorien / Constructions provisoires / Provisional Architecture; Zürich 1992.

Werkbund-Archiv (Hrsg.); Packeis und Pressglas. Von der Kunstgewerbe-Bewegung zum Deutschen Werkbund, Werkbund-Archiv Band 16; Gießen 1987.

Zaugg, Rémy; Herzog & De Meuron, une exposition; Paris 1995.

Adressen der Architekten und Designer

Addresses of Architects and Designers

Arno Design
Claus Neuleib
Herzogstr. 58
80803 München

Dietrich Display GmbH
Dietrich Concept & Design GmbH
Karlheinz Thurm
Steinäckerstr. 15
71292 Friolzheim

Alfred Hablützel
Beratung und Konzepte für Werbung,
Kommunikation, Design
Güterstr. 143
CH-4053 Basel

Rolf Heide
Heilwigstr. 39
20249 Hamburg

Dipl. Ing. Tim Heide
Kurfürstendamm 173
10707 Berlin

atelier holste
Innenarchitekten BDIA
Messestandgestaltung und
Innenarchitektur
Prof. Carl Holste
Hannoversche Str. 79
30916 Isernhagen

Kauffmann Theilig & Partner
Freie Architekten BDIA
Prof. Andreas Theilig
Zeppelinstr. 10
73760 Ostfildern

Prof. Wolfgang Körber
Eulerweg 4c
42659 Solingen

Prof. Dipl. Ing. Adolf Krischanitz
Getreidemarkt 1
A-1060 Wien

Burkhardt Leitner constructiv
Burkhardt Leitner
Am Bismarckturm 39
70192 Stuttgart

Richard Meier + Partner
Lisa Green (Public Relations)
475 10th Avenue, 5th Floor
New York City, N.Y.10018
USA

Sobek und Rieger
Ingenieurbüro im Bauwesen GmbH
Prof. Dr. Werner Sobek
Albstr. 14
70597 Stuttgart

Steiner Design
messebauer & partner
Thomas Bauer
Franz-Joseph-Str.10
80801 München

Dieter Thiel
Maiengasse 1
CH-4056 Basel

merz sauter zimmermann
Dipl. Ing. Sabine Sauter
Immenhoferstr. 22
70180 Stuttgart

Stefan Zwicky
Architekt BSA / SIA
Schulhausstr. 64
CH-8002 Zürich

Weitere Informationen und Unterstützung bei der Auswahl von Messestandgestaltern und Messebauunternehmen,
Hilfestellung bei der Vorbereitung einer
Messebeteiligung sowie die Broschüre
„Vom Messeziel zum Messestand" erhalten Sie beim:

Fachverband für Messe- und Ausstellungsbau e.V. (FAMAB)

Uta Straube
Berliner Str. 26
33378 Rheda-Wiedenbrück